THE WORLD OF ULYSSES S. GRANT

SERIES EDITORS

John F. Marszalek & Timothy B. Smith

AMERICA'S HARDSCRABBLE GENERAL

★★★★

ULYSSES S. GRANT, FROM FARM BOY TO SHILOH

JACK HURST

Southern Illinois University Press
Carbondale

Southern Illinois University Press
www.siupress.com

Printed in the United States of America

25 24 23 22 4 3 2 1

Cover illustration: Grant on horseback by Wyeth. Library of Congress, Prints & Photographs Division, LC-USZ62-71918

Library of Congress Cataloging-in-Publication Data

Names: Hurst, Jack, author.

Title: America's hardscrabble general : Ulysses S. Grant, from farm boy to Shiloh / Jack Hurst.

Other titles: Ulysses S. Grant, from farm boy to Shiloh

Description: Carbondale : Southern Illinois University Press, [2022] | Series: World of Ulysses S. Grant | Includes bibliographical references and index. | Summary: "A detailed analysis of the impact of Grant's civilian experience—both as a youth and later, farming and scrambling between the Mexican War and the Civil War—in helping mold a military method that is a model for excellent American generalship: always go forward, win or lose, so that even losses become essential elements of final victory"—Provided by publisher.

Identifiers: LCCN 2021059824 (print) | LCCN 2021059825 (ebook) | ISBN 9780809338856 (cloth) | ISBN 9780809338795 (paperback) | ISBN 9780809338801 (ebook)

Subjects: LCSH: Grant, Ulysses S. (Ulysses Simpson), 1822-1885. | Grant, Ulysses S. (Ulysses Simpson), 1822-1885—Military leadership. |Generals—United States—Biography. | United States. Army—Biography.

Classification: LCC E672 .H87 2022 (print) | LCC E672 (ebook) | DDC 973.8/2092—dc23/eng/20211208

LC record available at https://lccn.loc.gov/2021059824

LC ebook record available at https://lccn.loc.gov/2021059825

Printed on recycled paper ♻

SIU
Southern Illinois University System

To Sis—

Carol H. Carlson—

who, like Grant, has always

loved horses

CONTENTS

MAPS

✯✯✯✯

AMERICA'S HARDSCRABBLE GENERAL

INTRODUCTION: "GETTING" GENERAL GRANT

Ulysses S. Grant is to America's military generalship what Abraham Lincoln is to its presidency: a once-undervalued figure whose towering character, courage, and genius are of a homely cast, obscured by hardscrabble beginnings. And Grant, unlike Lincoln, accomplished all he did without even seeming to fix his eyes on a prize—other than victory. To that end, he focused single-mindedly on whatever job was before him, letting the future take care of itself. Thus, in American history's most extreme upheaval, the Civil War, Grant appears churned up from the bottom by destiny.

But he was not. The quiet, ever-pressing competence that propelled Ulysses S. Grant to the top of his nation's army was not external. Its energy emanated from within the man, asserting itself in ways unrecognizable to observers looking for a "man of the hour." Yet the evidence was there. The problem was, Grant was not where his era's observers were in the habit of looking. Why peer twice at a common sight in his day: another man on horseback?

In Grant's era and well past it, most men and many women had to be able equestrians, just as most people today have to know how to drive a car. So horsemanship was unlikely to be recognized as an indicator of an officer's military merit. Yet for most of the country's history, America's combat generals had to be more than passable horsemen. Indeed, until the early twentieth century, just to get around a battlefield an officer had to be able to control a mount while evading bullets, other riders' (or panicked rider-less) horses, and solid or exploding artillery shells—and brave the chaos loosed by all of them. So although such a detail might be deemed extraneous in a study of a historic officer's tactics and strategy, it perhaps should not be. Especially might that be so in the case of Grant, who was not only arguably America's best supreme modern combat leader—as well as its greatest general—but also very possibly his era's finest horseman. His equestrian mastery illustrated and embodied the element that formed the bedrock of his greatness: lack of fear.

The topic of horsemanship also indicates something about the nature of this book. It is not a conventional military biography. It is not an account of Grant's soldiering from his West Point cadetship in the 1840s to its triumphal denouement at Appomattox in 1865. Yet this volume does purport to be a military biography, however unconventional. What it attempts to do is chart the rise of a man's extraordinary personal powers, to profile the origin and development of his hard-eyed focus on victory.

It thus will be the biography of this man's military mindset more than of the man himself. To be such, it must begin in the farm roads and fields of Grant's youth and end at the threshold of his greatest triumphs: the masterpiece that was Vicksburg, the miracle that was Chattanooga, and the bloody and protracted Virginia brawl in which he hounded Robert E. Lee to the death of the Confederate States of America.

In Grant's time there had arisen two great military thinkers, each of whom learned his lessons on opposite sides during the European campaigns of Napoleon Bonaparte. One was a Swiss French baron, Antoine-Henri Jomini, who believed that battles and wars could be all but plotted out and won by mathematics and geometry, mostly avoiding such distractions as domestic politics and individual personalities. The other great thinker was a Prussian commoner, Carl von Clausewitz, who discerned that wars were impossible to dissociate from those things because they affected entire populations. He saw that wars themselves were quintessentially political, hugely influenced by societal forces that no prudent general could ignore.

Grant's fellow officers on both sides of America's bloodiest conflict generally labored to follow Jomini's precepts.[1] Grant ignored them and confessed he never read them. He never read Clausewitz, either, at least not until the late 1870s; the Prussian's work was not translated into English until then, and Grant could not read German. Nonetheless, as scholar Paul Schmelzer has shown, Grant's military story is principally Clausewitzian, because he was spiritual heir to the Prussian without knowing it.[2] By embodying the best of the character of the civilian Union heartland he defended, Grant embodied Clausewitzian war.

Unlike most of their upper-crust general officer peers, Clausewitz and Grant were born lower middle-class, the stratum that primarily peopled their armies. Whereas Grant started as a horse-obsessed farm boy, Clausewitz began as an eleven-year-old soldier in the Prussian army. Each saw combat up close and often in his wars, and each died writing books that remain classics. Signally, both rejected the nineteenth century's dominant military theory. That theory was Baron Jomini's chivalrous and gentlemanly one, under which war's violence was limited by small forces that touched few civilians. Its primary objectives tended to be geographic points rather than armies. Protection of lines of advance and retreat was deemed more important than speed of movement. Warring had an antiseptic, geometric design and, despite nods to the contrary, a fundamentally cautious character.

The Clausewitzian approach was less mechanical, academic, and dogmatic. The Prussian stressed war's inevitable unpredictability, savagery, and emotional effects on troops and private citizens. Having seen masses of civilians join Bonaparte's ranks under the allegiances and edicts of the French Revolution—of which the American Civil War would become, in scale of violence, the Western Hemisphere's rough equivalent—Clausewitz believed some of the primary keys to victory were superior numbers, societal commitment, and the waging of all-out war. Most important, perhaps, was his view, emphatically unlike Jomini's, that war was the ultimate extension of civilian politics and was continually influenced by them.

Both Clausewitz and Grant grasped that great generals' tactics and strategies are not, and cannot be, mere products of mathematics—at which, by the way, Grant was gifted. No, great generals' tactics and strategies tend to be produced by lessons the generals' individual backgrounds teach them and are shaped by the obstacles they encounter. Hence, they must be men of strong but open mind. Grant's formative years, like those of Clausewitz, were more apt to encourage such open-mindedness than those of American upper classes, who were accustomed to viewing themselves as masters of their worlds. Grant's beginnings were very different from the way the overwhelming majority of his fellow officers in the Civil War started out. His beginnings appeared as undistinguished as Grant himself, a fact that led many, perhaps most, of his foes and even his friends to presume him inferior. His close wartime friend William T. Sherman got near the heart of both the dismissal of Grant's talents by peers and the ultimate superiority of his methods in an admission in March 1864, by which time those methods had all but won the Civil War in the western theater: "My only points of doubt was in your knowledge of grand strategy and books of science and history," Sherman wrote him, "but I confess your common-sense seems to have supplied this."[3]

For all the belittlement and diminution of him that occurred before and during the Civil War—and by Southern-leaning historians through the late nineteenth and much of the twentieth centuries—Ulysses Grant turned out to understand a lot that few others did, and it was not confined to horses. Clausewitz, had he been around to be asked, would likely have opined that *everything* Grant understood molded the leader he became.

It also went a long way toward molding what the United States became. With the rise of Grant in the Civil War, Clausewitz's view of national conflict triumphed over Jomini's. The aggressive attacks so favored by Robert E. Lee, the paragon of Southern soldiery, were, as respected military author Russell Weigley has observed, more Napoleonic than strictly Jominian.[4] But Lee was more Jominian than Clausewitzian in that he never found a strategy that could take enough advantage of his attacks to win the war. It should be swiftly added, though, that Lee *did* have a strategy, and its thrust was not only more than a little Clausewitzian—that is to say, politically aimed—but also very nearly successful. His aggressive campaigns were, after all, specifically directed at the psyche of the North's civilian population. His attacks were meant to forestall a victory by the materially richer Union until its people wearied of war and rejected President Abraham Lincoln's steadfast policy of saving, at all costs, the original republic.

Lee's ploy would have succeeded had Lincoln not found, in the nick of time, an extraordinary little figure far more firmly rooted, as Lincoln himself was, in the middle of American society than the aristocratic Lee. The general whom Lincoln found was extraordinary not just despite his early lack of interest in militarism and war but to a considerable extent *because* of it. He differed so dramatically from his peers because he was as skeptical of their high-flown philosophies as they were dismissive of his humble roots and appearance. Most of them continued to be dismissive until well after he received the surrender of the second of the three major Confederate armies that he captured during the war. None of *them*, meanwhile, captured any.

His instinct for how to do it—his bent toward incessant war to the death of the enemy's armies and government—was there earlier than most historians indicate, earlier than even Grant himself indicates. He and they say he realized after the fury of Shiloh in April 1862 that the majority of white Southerners were committed to their rebellion and would not easily be induced to abandon it. Yet Grant's inherent drive to win was likely there much earlier, perhaps in Mexico if not before. Six months previous to Shiloh he exhibited the same tendency. After his raid on Belmont, Missouri, in November 1861, he rejected a Jomini-influenced staff officer's suggestion that they threaten the rear of Confederates at Columbus, Kentucky, to get them to withdraw from that bluff-crowning fortress. "Better to attack and capture the whole force where they are," Grant said. "Why allow them to withdraw and follow and fight them in the interior of Mississippi or Alabama under greater disadvantages?"[5] That answer was grounded in a yeoman's common sense, but with a crucial caveat: it was the common sense of a mind strong enough to face the hard fact that a fight would have to be made sometime and sooner was surely better than later, when the Confederates would be on ground certain to be friendlier.

It is little wonder that Grant went his own military way, and not just because he was roundly underestimated. He, unlike so many officer peers—but like so many men in his ranks—realized he was there for a single purpose. It was not to make a reputation or protect one already made that would enable him to move on to high political office, the goal of a number of officers who considered themselves better-born. It was, instead, the fervent hope of his men in ranks: to get the job done and go home. He was not a military genius (which has occasionally been suggested during the present era of his reputation's long-overdue reclamation)[6]—at least not in the term's usual sense. He did, though, have the intelligence to doubt tactics and strategy that his close-to-the-ground judgment told him were questionable at best.

What he was, was a resolutely quiet man of incongruous restlessness, one with a good though not brilliant mind and deep inner resolution. Like many other former yeomen, he acquired most of his "genius" from experience. It allowed him to puzzle out solutions to his problems with the common sense Sherman cited. Clausewitz gently suggested that there is more than one way to skin a battlefield cat when he wrote, "If a decision by fighting is the basis of all plans and operations, it follows that the enemy *can frustrate everything through a successful battle*."[7] In other words, a great general must develop a strategy and a persona that can survive defeat. Grant evolved that kind of strategy and combined it with an astonishing abundance of hardheaded perseverance. As Russell Weigley notes, "He showed himself free from the common fixation of his contemporaries upon the Napoleonic battle as the hinge upon which warfare must turn. Instead, he developed a highly uncommon ability to rise above the fortunes of a single battle and to master the flow of a long series of events, almost to the point of making any outcome of a single battle, victory, draw, or even defeat serve his eventual purpose equally well."[8]

That was Grant's genius.

1.

FARM BOY

✯✯✯✯

UNDERCLASS EQUESTRIAN

He was first a little boy who loved horses.

The most striking of the few stories of his youth dramatically underscores the depth of this obsession. A number of times neighbors in little Georgetown, Ohio, rushed to Mrs. Grant's door to inform her that her child was again playing among the horses at the hitch-rails of the family's tannery across the street, swinging on their tails and crawling under their bellies amid the hooves. The neighbors doubtless expected the boy's mother to shriek, throw aside whatever she was doing, and dash out to snatch up her son before the great beasts could step on his head or kick the life out of him. But Mrs. Grant did none of these things. She kept on at her work of the moment and, perhaps with a sigh, displayed the extraordinary aplomb that in more famous times would characterize her son. Her response to the worried townspeople was as unemotional as if they were discussing something as irrevocable and routine as the weather.

"Horses," she said, "seem to understand Ulysses."[1]

Ulysses Grant would soon prove that *he* understood *horses*, too. At age five he rode one at top speed standing on its back on one leg, holding only the reins.[2] A few years later, at the nation's military academy at West Point in an otherwise unremarkable cadetship, he rode a horse named York to a West Point jumping record that stood for a quarter century.[3] During the Mexican War shortly after that, he and a horse named Nelly out-galloped hails of musket fire during urban fighting at Monterrey to summon a resupply of ammunition for embattled troops. Also in Mexico, he became famed within the ranks for breaking, riding, and taming wild Mexican horses, including one so unruly that other Americans feared even to approach it.[4]

He often gave credit to the horses for their exploits, rather than claiming it for his own uncanny ability with them. He preferred his mounts spirited, deliberately choosing ones that were the most difficult, perhaps to test his horsemanship or to unbridle certain energies surging invisibly within him. In 1863 in New Orleans during the Civil War, likely under a liquid influence that made *him* more spirited, he chose a steed so violent that it bashed him against a streetcar. The injuries confined him more than a week to a bed where he required help just to turn over. He then graduated to crutches, and with them strapped to his saddle he hastened to a defeated, besieged, and hungry Union army at Chattanooga. He arrived at the Tennessee town only after having to be lifted onto and off his mounts through two chilly, rain-drenched days on a wretched road across the Cumberland Mountains. And under his command, after he inaugurated a plan to break the siege and bring in rations, Federal soldiers swarmed—of their own volition—up the surrounding mountains and routed the thunderstruck Confederates.

So what *about* that small boy who swung from the horses' tails? Was he extraordinarily brave, incredibly naive, or just stupid—or all three? At various times over the following years the man he grew into would be thought to be each.

Great generals enter the world like everybody else: as babies. Grant, his parents' firstborn, was the product of opposites. Jesse Root Grant was a self-educated, hard-driving, politically interested small businessman who began as a tanner and branched out. He was garrulous, overbearing, and very opinionated—but not cruel; his son could not remember ever being punished by him. Jesse seems to have had a salesman's gift of gab but a politics too rough-edged for wide popularity. Apprenticed in youth to the father of abolition activist John Brown and early acquainted with the son, Jesse became first a supporter of Democrat Andrew Jackson, then a Henry Clay Whig, and finally and ever after an abolitionist Republican. His opposition to slavery was fierce and vocal, although maybe as outraged by the commercial advantage its free labor gave slaveholders as by the utter disadvantage it imposed on enslaved people themselves. Jesse participated in local debating societies, managed once to get elected mayor of Georgetown, and inveterately perused, and submitted his insights to, newspapers. Grant's portrait of Jesse in his *Personal Memoirs* seems written by a man surprised to recall all that his early-deprived father had achieved.[5] Except for a fair talent for one-to-one conversation with people he knew, the son was about as unlike the father as possible.

Jesse's wife, the former Hannah Simpson, was plainly the source of much of the younger Grant's persona. In sharp contrast to her husband and far outdoing her apolitical eldest son, she was such a diehard Democrat that in old age she refused to visit the son's Republican White House.[6] But she was very quiet. She and Grant were not close, her intense and pious Methodist introversion seeming to preclude such intimacy. But her influence on him was immense. He inherited her imperturbability, her infrequency and rectitude of speech, and, apparently, the deep determination to keep his feelings private. These are all excellent traits for a military commander, and they were all overtly operative. The title of Grant's *Personal Memoirs* could perhaps more accurately be titled simply *Memoirs.* Although wonderfully and succinctly descriptive of the world through which he passed, they offer hardly more than superficial hints of his personal reactions to it.

A recent military biographer has written that seekers of keys to Grant's later greatness are hard put to find any in his early years.[7] If that is so, the seekers must not have known where to look or how to recognize what they saw. The foundational and all-important key is in plain sight on page 12 of the *Personal Memoirs*:

> In my early days, every one labored more or less, in the region where my youth was spent. . . . While my father carried on the manufacture of leather and worked at the trade himself, he owned and tilled considerable land. I detested the [leather] trade, preferring almost any other labor; but I was fond of agriculture, and of all employment in which horses were used. We had, among other lands, fifty acres of forest within a mile of the village. In the fall of the year choppers were employed to cut enough wood to last a twelve-month. When I was seven or eight years of age, I began hauling all the wood used in the house and shops. I could not load it on the wagons, of course, at that time, but I could drive, and the choppers would load, and some one at the house unload. When about eleven years old, I was strong enough to hold a plough. From that age until seventeen I did all the work done with horses, such as breaking up the land, furrowing, ploughing corn and potatoes, bringing in the crops when harvested, hauling all the wood, besides

> tending two or three horses, a cow or two, and sawing wood for stoves, etc., while still attending school.

The problem here for the unsuccessful seekers is obvious: there is no mention of cannon, swords, or pistols or daydreams of bayonet charges and shot-riddled flags, just of timbering and leather-making, wood and wagons, plows and potatoes and horses, the stuff by which sweat and yeomen—and maybe men in ranks, but certainly not generals—was made. So the unsuccessful seekers make the same error made by most of Grant's contemporaries. They mistake his beginnings for nothing and move on.

But—except for the equally crucial matter of character—Grant's formative background is everything. He shared it with millions who served in his armies, because at least three-quarters of Americans in the early 1800s were farmers. Having participated so fully in his early world, continually staring between plow handles and over wagon tongues at the hindquarters of horses, he became mentally anchored in and mindful of that milieu forever, attuned to the prevalent moods yet strangely unfettered to most of the prejudices found in it. He understood and identified with the men who filled his ranks and well knew the dominant attitudes of their parents, wives, and sweethearts. Few if any of his officer peers were so attuned. They had anchored themselves to, if anything, the tastes, views, and biases of their society's upper classes.

But to leave it there is to miss the significance of Grant's background by miles. A yeoman-style farm was night-and-day different from the plantations of so many of the Civil War's Southern generals, as well as from the wealthy rural estates of many Northern ones—to say nothing of the urban comforts of those such as prominent Philadelphia physician's son George B. McClellan. Such individuals had the physical labor on their properties performed for them by either enslaved people or hired servants. The yeoman farmer, by contrast, rarely had the luxury or financial means of calling anybody besides perhaps a friendly neighbor to help if a machine or tool broke. He mostly had to come up with a way to repair or replace it himself, even if he had to improvise a substitute. If he needed another shed or barn or even a house, he usually had to *build it* himself. Such an existence instilled second-nature self-reliance, the habit of working very hard, a perpetual sense of urgency, and a drive to get things done with whatever resources were at hand, rather than wait and hope for eventual assistance. This life also provided a handy store of knowledge of how a number of manual jobs *were* done and how long it took to do them and recognition of the need to get them done in time to harvest crops.

Such knowledge, work habits, and mindset of driven-ness are godsends to a commander, and Ulysses Grant was one of very few top Civil War generals who possessed them.

ACQUAINTED WITH HUMILIATION

Early on, probably as he rode or drove horses farther and farther from home, Grant acquired a quirk of mind central to the strategy of the commander he became.

He loved driving to places he had not seen before. He recalled that when he found he had inadvertently passed an intended destination, he would not turn around. Instead, in apparent interest in new sights, he would keep going until he found another road "in the right direction, take that," and come into his destination from a different side. The specific particulars seem lost to history, but this tendency hardened into a habit and then a superstition—a "strange dread," biographer Lloyd Lewis put it.[8] Grant came to believe it was unlucky to return on a path he had traveled. This surely reinforced his relentless refusal to retreat during the Civil War.

No wonder he liked to travel. The environment of Grant's youth permanently stamped itself on his mind and persona, and the fact is hardly remarkable. That environment was vivid. Ohio was still transforming itself from wilderness when he was growing up in it. It had been a state for barely thirty years, and free public education had yet to arise there.

Georgetown, a hamlet only a few miles from the incessantly traveled Ohio River, was perhaps comparatively cosmopolitan by 1830s standards. The river, though, could be a source of tension as well as regional and national news. The area was regularly, if secretly, visited by freedom-seeking enslaved people desperate to get to Canada or anyplace else where they could live without the specter of chains—and of the traumatic reality of slave-catchers dogging their heels. Maysville, Kentucky, where Grant boarded with an uncle while attending an academy for a year, was a minor slave-trading center. In nearby Ripley, Ohio, he spent another year attending a Presbyterian academy run by the Reverend John Rankin, one of the most active Underground Railroad stationmasters in the nation. Thus, southwest Ohio was a good place for a boy to learn the advisability of keeping his eyes open and his mouth shut, also excellent habits for a military commander.

All of this doubtless contributed much toward making Grant what he became, but its rusticity evoked pause if not scorn among higher-placed later acquaintances. In private they called him everything from stupid to a sot, but more important was the way in which they said such things: *loftily*. Grant was beneath them. Robert E. Lee on the eve of Appomattox told subordinates he "would rather die a thousand deaths" than surrender to Grant. The remark is generally taken as reflecting a vaunted warrior's abhorrence of the idea of losing a long and epic struggle, but is it only that? The late great critic Edmund Wilson wrote in *Patriotic Gore* that Lee "would hardly have spoken thus of McClellan."[9] Oh? Why? Was it because the insufferably conceited Union major general trod Lee's same approximate plane of society, while Grant shambled well below? Would surrender to McClellan rather than to Grant, for Lee, have been much more . . . ahem . . . seemly?

McClellan, like Lee, knew Grant from the antebellum army, but the memory was plainly not fond. When Grant went to see him in 1861 seeking to reenter the swelling wartime army at appropriate rank after several years' absence, he was kept waiting outside McClellan's office for two days before he gave up and went home.[10] Grant had hoped McClellan would remember him from their mutual prior service, and his problem, likely, was that McClellan did. Back in 1853 at Fort Vancouver, leading a western expedition to find a railroad route through the Cascade Mountains, McClellan had got his party outfitted, and himself out*raged*, by the attentions of an inebriated Fort Vancouver quartermaster. Grant.[11]

Luckily for the Union, the governor of Illinois finally gave the ex-quartermaster a colonelcy and command of a rowdy volunteer regiment that a previous candidate had been unable to handle, and Grant rose rapidly to brigadier general. Still, however, he was generally regarded by McClellan and other higher-ups as a binge waiting to happen. A senior officer abortively chosen to replace him just before he captured Fort Donelson privately opined that Grant was "little more than a common gambler and drunkard."[12] Actually, Grant rarely had enough money to be much of a gambler, and many if not most of his superiors likely drank more than he did. Yet the difference between him and them was assumed to be vast. He had had dirt and calluses on his hands, for God's sake. *They* were "gentlemen."

So during the Civil War virtually all generals, friend or foe, were Grant's betters in their own eyes. Opposing him in gray were a host of plantation masters, owners of many acres and human beings. Nowhere was the difference more striking than at Appomattox, where the immaculately uniformed Lee surrendered to a mud-spattered, slovenly looking Grant, who, intent on victory, had outrun his base of supplies and thus had no other clothes when Lee's request to meet him arrived. The metaphorical upshot of their confrontation was resounding—both then and now: the impeccable Lee affecting to represent the dregs of a once-vaunted Army of Northern Virginia now barefoot and in rags, while Grant, who never cared for appearing in the splendor of high rank, looked pretty much like one of his troops. This symbolic man-of-the-masses air was one he shared with Abraham Lincoln, critic Wilson suggests, and "was perhaps something new in the world."[13]

Like McClellan from Fort Vancouver, Lee remembered Grant, too, but from Mexico. At Appomattox, Lee's appearance was so grand that it struck one Federal officer as "formal—a little too formal." He unbent enough to have moments of stiff affability, but his distraction, grief, wounded-to-the-hilt pride, and distaste for this whole process pervaded the encounter. He told one staff officer that he dressed to the nines because he expected Grant to arrest him[14] and, as one writer has inferred, wanted to look like a victor even if he could not be one.[15]

Grant was late arriving, which did not appear to make Lee any happier.[16] When Grant mentioned that they had met in Mexico, Lee replied that he had lately remembered that they indeed had met, but he had been unable to recall a thing about what Grant looked like.[17] Grant took no offense. Lee was, after all, sixteen years older and had considerably outranked him in Mexico. Grant in fact worried that his sullied clothes might offend Lee,[18] as they very likely did. But, as Grant generously noted in the *Personal Memoirs*, the pair's "conversation grew so pleasant that I almost forgot the object of our meeting."[19]

When they got down to business, Lee remained formidably formal, as if he shrank from demeaning himself by actually negotiating with this little commoner in the muddy uniform. Whenever Grant's conversation wandered to their "old-army" days or similar digressions, Lee soon pushed him back to the job at hand. To Grant's written provision allowing Confederate officers to retain their horses and sidearms, Lee said the provision "would have a happy effect upon his army." Instead of deigning to make a request on behalf of some of his enlisted men, though, he merely commented, as Grant remembered it, that the Confederate army "was organized a little differently from the army of the United States (still maintaining by implication that we were two countries)" and that Confederate non-officers in the cavalry and artillery owned their own horses. Did Grant's terms mean they could not keep them? Grant said Lee's understanding of the terms he had written out was correct—but he pledged on the spot to direct his troops to instead allow the enlisted Confederates to retain their horses.[20]

To Edmund Wilson, the source of Grant's magnanimity seems to have been his ability to put himself in the adversary's boots. Wilson notes that "it is plain from his handling of his subordinates that he disliked to humiliate people. He himself had known humiliation."[21] Carl von Clausewitz wrote that a great commander's successful prosecution of strategy involves taking account of political and social realities both inside and outside his army, and implicit in that is an ability to see from his adversary's point of view. Grant not only saw from there but empathized.

The nobility of Lee's bearing has often been remarked upon, but at Appomattox and throughout the war Grant and his cause were much the nobler of the two. There was nothing grand about Grant except the scope of his vision. It took in not just the foe but also the all-important pawns in the game, the Africa-rooted enslaved people. Clausewitz wrote that war is like a duel of physical strength between two wrestlers,[22] and many Southern partisans have been quick to point out that Grant enjoyed the war's preponderance of material resources. Fewer partisans of any stripe, though, have noted another difference, one that Clausewitz deemed all-important: that Grant and the cause in which he deeply believed were far stronger *morally*, too.[23] That cause was no less than the dual one of not just saving the Union but making it finally try to fulfill the grandiose Jeffersonian promise that within it "all men are created equal."

As Grant would have seen it, it was the only fair thing to do.

WEST POINT: COMPLICATING WAR

Grant never meant to become a soldier.

His ambition (if his low-momentum impulse toward a future could even be called that) was to be a farmer, where he could work with his beloved horses. Thus, he had no need for ambition, since in youth he already had done what he hoped to do for the rest of his life. As for soldiering, his father's stinking tanning shed had instilled in the son an intense aversion to blood. He went to West Point only because the thrifty Jesse insisted and wangled him an appointment to a slot from which another candidate had washed out. The son feared he could not pass even the entrance exam and worried about the shame he would bring on the family if he did not. The father of the failed cadet he replaced, who lived near the Grants in Georgetown, was so mortified he forbade his son from coming home. He instead enrolled the youth in another school.[24]

Grant's lack of confidence in his ability to survive at West Point was understandable. The kind of country schools and academies he had attended and what they taught were well behind the better institutions east of the Alleghenies. And some of the cadets had already taken college classes; the precociously brilliant McClellan had actually attended the University of Pennsylvania before arriving at West Point at the age of fifteen.[25] Grant had never been a zealous student, which was understandable, too. Much schooling in those days, particularly in what was then called the West, was by rote, and the *Personal Memoirs* indicate Grant had grown more than weary of having to repeat such mind-numbing definitions as "A noun is a name of a thing."[26] His shyness and his goal of earning his living outdoors around animals, rather than in an office or other place of human-centered activity, also factored into his aversion to school. He did not want to be at the academy and wished Congress would abolish it as an unnecessary national expense, as was being discussed in the newspapers at the time he attended.[27]

Arriving at West Point in 1839, he could hardly have made a less-imposing impression. Seventeen and still growing, he stood just five-foot-two and weighed 117 pounds. His stride was awkward, with his upper body pitching—slouched and droop-shouldered—slightly forward. Meeting him in later life, observer Charles Francis Adams would say he "toddled."[28] He remained shy in groups—worse around females—did not dance, and had trouble marching in unison with his fellow cadets. He had no sense of music, not even rhythmic drumbeats.[29]

Grant was in a tiny minority at West Point. Fully half of its cadets were from the plantation South, 45 percent from the Northeast, and just 5 percent from the so-called West.[30] Plus he was singular even for a western agricultural rube. He never cursed, and his general behavior displayed a rectitude likely spawned by his mother's quiet piety. Another cadet remembered him at that time as seeming almost "girlish" in his diffidence.[31] And he obviously, likely because of his tannery-induced abhorrence of blood, had had little use for spilling it with firearms. "I had never been a sportsman in my life; had scarcely ever gone in search of game, and rarely seen any when looking for it," he recalled wryly in his memoirs.[32]

Such a comparatively colorless youth, especially one with such lack of family distinction, could hardly be expected to make friends readily among the 250 or so cadets—the crème de la crème—at the academy. He did make some, however, or maybe the friends made him. He seems to have been lucky to quickly meet, and be befriended by, a comparatively gigantic second-year man from Georgia, six-foot-two future prominent Confederate general James Longstreet. Robust and mischievous as a cadet, Longstreet told the *New York Times* on the day of Grant's death that he and Grant "became friends at our first meeting."[33] Jesse Grant would not have been pleased. Longstreet had come from a Georgia plantation. He had spent the second half of his youth as the virtual adopted son of a Yale-educated uncle who was a zealous adherent and friend of U.S. senator John C. Calhoun of South Carolina, the foremost political mouthpiece of slaveholders. Longstreet's preferred activities were the opposite of Grant's. The larger man loved football and rigorous military training, whereas Grant disliked martial exercises and was too small for contact sports. A schoolmate back in Ohio remembered that when such rowdy games were played, Grant sat bashfully on a stump and watched.[34] But—and this was surely important to the advent of their friendship—neither was much interested in school and both were fond of the outdoors. This early comradeship with the well-connected Longstreet, which lasted past the Civil War until Grant's death, likely gave him a somewhat higher profile among other cadets.

Even so, besides a fair talent for mathematics, Grant does not seem to have stood out—except at horsemanship, a potentially perilous pursuit where he was hands-down the best at the academy. He was as impressive and daring in the saddle as he never appeared to be on foot. He would retain that air on horseback for the rest of his life, and its significance should not be overlooked. From boyhood on, it delivered to the world—as his modesty never otherwise allowed—the first and strongest evidence of the enormous courage that lay beneath his placid surface.

At the academy he had two different roommates, Rufus Ingalls of Maine for the first three years and Fred Dent of Missouri for his final year. Dent, who became his brother-in-law, remembered him at West Point as being "the clearest headed young man I ever saw. He always wanted to do what was right, and we all had great respect for him." Even Dent, though, added, "He was . . . a great deal better than he looked." Ingalls, although a lifelong friend, was not impressed with Grant's academic industriousness; he could not detect much. "In his studies," Ingalls recalled, "he was laggard and careless. Instead of studying a lesson, he would merely read it over once or twice; but he was so quick in his perceptions that he usually made very fair recitations even with so little preparation."[35]

Thus, at West Point Grant remained as indifferent a student as he had been before. As at the schools his father had packed him off to back in Ohio and Kentucky, he simply was not much interested. But anyone paying attention should have noticed that he had a good enough mind. He did well in math, which he later recalled came naturally to him. But in French he was at sea, his spelling was wretched, and he was mediocre at best in most of his other subjects. He hated tactics, strategy, drill, and other military courses, not that there were many at the academy. West Point was one of less than a handful of engineering colleges in the United States, and graduation from it was widely regarded as setting a man up for success in life. With little ongoing need for soldiers in America then, most cadets appear to have gone there for professional civilian training rather than to ready themselves for a military career.

For manufacturing great Civil War commanders, it was just as well. West Point was all but useless as preparation for effective strategizing in what, with hindsight's wisdom, became known as the "irrepressible conflict." The armies of the early 1860s would be vastly larger than West Point's professors and textbooks of 1840 could imagine, let alone plan for. In another respect, West Point instruction was *worse* than useless. It taught the strategy and tactics of Jomini.

It is hardly surprising that Grant—coming from a farm boy's do-it-yourself, figure-it-out-on-your-own background—would not be enthralled. As Clausewitz observed, "The means and forms that the strategist employs are so very simple . . . that it seems ridiculous in the light of common sense when critics discuss them, as they do so often, with ponderous solemnity.

Thus, such a commonplace maneuver as turning an opponent's flank may be hailed by critics as a stroke of genius, of deepest insight, or of all-inclusive knowledge. Can one imagine anything more absurd?" Then, in what certainly sounds like a full-throated swipe at Jomini, the Prussian war-scholar went on to add, "It is even more ridiculous when we consider that these very critics usually exclude all moral qualities from strategic theory, and only examine material factors. They reduce everything to a few mathematical formulas of equilibrium and superiority, of time and space, limited by a few angles and lines. If that were really all, it would hardly provide a scientific problem for a schoolboy."[36]

Yet virtually every Civil War general on either side would plot his campaigns and battle plans around the math-like principles of the Swiss baron. These theorems and diagrams postulated that any successful military operation must be one in which one's troops possess the advantage of "interior lines." This essentially meant that friendly forces, when separated, must take positions allowing them to unite faster than those of the enemy, whose "exterior" lines—basically denoting more widely separated positions—would leave those positions vulnerable to attack by superior numbers. Under Jomini's principles, the physical goals of combatants were points on a map. They tended to be railroad junctions, crossroads, and cities or towns whose locations gave them strategic value. Jomini's principles encouraged a heightened consciousness of defense rather than fostered offensives. The most envied result in Jominian war was for a commander to maneuver troops so ingeniously as to capture a strategic point without having to fight at all.[37]

Jominian philosophy, and its worse-than-worthlessness for the Civil War, was perhaps best exemplified during that war by an 1862 campaign led by Henry W. Halleck, Grant's commander at the time and a premier Jominian scholar.[38] Following the Confederate surprise attack on Grant's troops at Shiloh, Halleck came south to take personal command of the army and show the world what miracles military intellect could achieve. He then led a slow-motion saunter in which Halleck, with a 100,000-man army—which dwarfed that of his Confederate opponent—directed a monthlong move that covered just twenty miles between the Shiloh battlefield and the important railroad junction of Corinth, Mississippi. Toward the end of the trek Halleck had his men dig entrenchments each night to prevent Confederates from catching him unawares, drastically reducing marching time.

When he finally occupied Corinth virtually without firing a shot, he assumed he had won a great, bloodless victory and proclaimed it to be such.[39] It was bloodless, all right, but a far bigger boon to Confederates than to Halleck's Federals. It allowed his enemies to (1) abandon Corinth without him even knowing; (2) change their western commander; (3) take trains south from Corinth to Mobile, Alabama, and then north again all the way to Chattanooga, Tennessee; and (4) prepare an invasion of Kentucky from more than 200 miles east of Halleck's army.

So much for Jomini. Grant, who had no interest in West Point military precepts, let alone Jomini's, was better off knowing next to nothing about them. Unlike virtually all of his fellow future Civil War officers, friend or foe, he kept his mind free of such preconceptions that led some to their ruin.

This, though, should not be taken to mean that West Point taught Grant nothing. It did, for example, teach him to understand the parlance of American generalship—"by the right flank," "interior lines," and such—which he himself used sparingly. Most of its valuable lessons, however, seem to have been unintended. One was that of familiarizing him with many of his peers. The quiet and diffident youth from rustic Ohio was a keen observer of his fellow cadets, noting and remembering their quirks. He would employ these impressions as he fought alongside or against many of them in the American continent's bloodiest war.

William Tecumseh Sherman, a cadet whose energetically overt personality was the opposite of Grant's, and phlegmatic George Thomas, who displayed little of his drive, were mutual friends who were both in their final year at the academy when Grant arrived. In the terrible war nearly two decades in their future, Sherman would become Grant's closest friend among high Union officers; Thomas, on the other hand, he would view as slow. Beginning their third year when Grant came were fellow Ohioan William S. Rosecrans, for whom Grant would take over after the personally shaken Rosecrans suffered a near-rout at Chickamauga, and future Confederates Richard Ewell, who would fight under Robert E. Lee in the eastern theater, and Earl Van Dorn, a hotheaded Mississippi dandy who would capture and burn a Grant supply base during the Vicksburg campaign. In the class behind Grant at West Point would come Kentuckian and future Confederate general Simon Bolivar Buckner, who would surrender to Grant at Fort Donelson. When Grant was a senior, members of the entering class would include the precocious McClellan, whose superciliousness and lack of nerve Grant would have to endure in army politics in the early Civil War, and rough-hewn and zealously religious future Confederate warrior Thomas J. (Stonewall-to-be) Jackson, who would die of his own men's bullets at Chancellorsville in northern Virginia before Grant came east to take command.

While these and other fellow cadets were, to a greater or lesser degree, studying Jomini, Grant was studying *them*—and the rest of his environment. His watchfulness seemed to take in everything. The year he arrived at West Point, the academy curriculum added a class in drawing as a means of teaching the future officers how to map and otherwise represent on paper the features of terrain on which they might have to fight. Grant appears to have been apt enough, and more, in this course. He drew pictures that imply at least a passing talent for art, a sharp eye for subjects, and an emotional attachment to those he chose. A horse with its head half-buried in a feedbag exhibits the expected Grant affection for equines. In this only-good-Indian-is-a-dead-Indian era he also penned a sympathetic-looking representation of a Native American family negotiating with a trader.[40]

Such drawings, while connoting an artistic bent, are more valuable in illustrating Grant's eye for detail of all kinds. He studied not just people but animals and topography, seeing the land and its streams, hills, and valleys with the beguiled eye of the prospective agriculturist—and the keen interest of one who might have been deciding whether to purchase. His background taught him to really *see* and then to accurately remember what he saw.

He also listened. Being of so few words himself, his never drowned out those of others, even later on when his carried the most weight. At Fort Henry in 1862, Brigadier General Lew Wallace was struck by his commander's rapt, quiet attention at a meeting he called to discuss the impending advance on Fort Donelson. "From the first," Wallace wrote, "his silence was remarkable. . . . In battle, as in camp, he went about quietly, speaking in a conversational tone; yet he appeared to see everything that went on. . . . At the [Fort Henry] council . . . he smoked, but never said a word."[41]

He had arrived at West Point with one militarily helpful habit already developed: wide reading. As much as he merely endured assigned classroom material, he avidly perused other kinds of volumes for his own enjoyment. The bulk of his preferred reading was made up of novels. His favorites included the Britons Edward Bulwer-Lytton and Frederick Marryat and the Irishman Charles Lever as well as such Americans as James Fenimore

Cooper and Washington Irving. His literary enthusiasms were such that while at West Point he even ordered books from publishers. Additionally, in what seems a radical departure for a youth so shy (he was all but tongue-tied in groups of more than two or three people), he became president of what must have been a tiny West Point literary society, the Dialectic.[42] The books he liked were predominantly adventure tales, but they doubtless helped develop his eye for the way words best fit together on paper. It was a skill with which his pen served him and the nation for the rest of his life, at no time more crucially than on battlefields of the Civil War. In that great conflict, as his many genteel peers were manifesting the verbose and imprecise pretentions of their proud class, Grant's own dispatches to subordinates were straight to the point, crystal-clear, and, like Grant himself, devoid of affectation. "No matter how hurriedly he may write them on the field, no one ever had the slightest doubt as to their meaning, or ever had to read them over a second time to understand them," Major General George G. Meade's chief of staff recalled.[43]

They were unmistakable in what they ordered and what the writer expected the recipient to do upon receipt, set forth in sentences as spare and impactful, if not as mannered, as Hemingway's. The British poet and critic Matthew Arnold, who met Grant in England after the Civil War and found him dull, would nitpick the language of the *Personal Memoirs* as "without charm and . . . high breeding" but ultimately found that they possessed "in general the high merit of saying clearly in the fewest possible words what had to be said, and saying it, frequently, with shrewd and unexpected turns of expression." American critic Edmund Wilson wrote simply that the *Personal Memoirs* "may well rank . . . as the most remarkable work of its kind since *The Commentaries of Julius Caesar*."[44]

The style building in the brain behind Grant's pen would become perfected in the Civil War. In one of his postwar observations on the intended business of West Point, Grant enunciated what should have been the academy's salient lesson more succinctly and memorably than any instructor at that institution likely ever did. The description not only captures how to accomplish the desired end but also communicates an element that far too many gentleman generals neglected: the urgency involved. "The art of war is simple enough," Grant said. "Find out where your enemy is. Get at him as soon as you can. Strike him as hard as you can and as often as you can and keep moving on."[45]

In other words, do not just conduct reconnaissance and then fight a battle when you get around to it; give your foe no rest. *Hound him to the death. Grab, and never surrender, momentum.* That onetime farm boy's definition of how to fight a war enunciated its central problem as if it were just another hard job to be tackled and done, another crop to be sown and reaped. It sums up with classic Grant finality the guts of a study pondered ever since soldiers used bows and arrows.

To learn most of his conception of its mechanics, however, he had to leave West Point. Resolutely standing ready to discharge any obligation he had incurred (in one of the several lean times ahead, he would insist on repaying Longstreet's loan of five dollars made fifteen years earlier,[46] even though five dollars was likely all he had), Grant felt he had contracted a duty to repay the nation for his free education.

A lot of graduates—especially ones whose families had influence—fled the commitment as soon after graduation as they could. Leonidas Polk, son of a prominent North Carolina banker and eventually one of Grant's principal opponents in the Civil War's western theater, vanished into the vestments of the Episcopal clergy after four months in the army. Lloyd Tilghman, son of a Maryland congressman, left similarly early and would spend much of his life engineering the construction of railroads before becoming Grant's opponent at Fort Henry and again in the Vicksburg campaign. Tilghman would die during the latter at the Battle of Champion Hill.

Despite his determination to fulfill his promise, Grant did not look forward to soldiering. He apparently found that a ten-week furlough home from West Point after two years was like breaking out of jail. Ohio time passed quicker than West Point time, he said.[47] While he was still a cadet, a mathematics instructor suggested that after graduation he try to return to the academy as an assistant math professor, and Grant began to think of discharging his military obligation that way. He planned to then leave the army for a professorship at some small college.[48] He even procured more math textbooks and studied them toward that end.

He eventually wrote a letter of solicitation to the professor who had suggested the assistant math professorship, but with war clouds forming over Mexico, the appointment did not happen. He then requested assignment to the cavalry, to which his extraordinary horsemanship would seem to have entitled him, but the cavalry turned out to be a coveted assignment, and the army, in its customary "wisdom," could find no vacancies just then.

He was allowed to seek a second choice, but for some reason he did not request the artillery or the engineers, perhaps because those tended to be reserved for the academy's top graduates. Thus Grant, graduating around the middle of his class, chose and was given a slot in the humblest arm—and utter guts—of the service.

The infantry.

2.

MEXICO

✵✵✵✵

DESTINY MANIFESTING

Grant had to go to Mexico to begin learning what kind of officer he wanted to be. By the time he got there, he already was familiar with the kind he did *not* want to be, acquiring a fair idea of that at his first duty assignment after graduation—Jefferson Barracks, Missouri. "It . . . seem[ed] to me, in my early army days," he recalled in the *Personal Memoirs* with a touch of his wry humor, "that too many of the older officers, when they came to command posts, made it a study to think what orders they could publish to annoy their subordinates and render them uncomfortable. I noticed, however, a few years later, when the Mexican War broke out, that most of this class of officers discovered they were possessed of disabilities which entirely incapacitated them for active field service."[1]

This passage seems more than just an example of Grant's quiet irony. It is perhaps a subtle peek into the nature of many thoughts he left unsaid. It also belies the rube-like naïveté often attributed to him. Even though he would turn out to be a poor judge of financial matters and of civilians who declared themselves experts on them, his view of life in general was clear-eyed. The above example shows the little he thought of spit-and-polish officers who used rank as a personal entitlement to discomfit subordinates whose job was doing the real work of the army. These same commanders, when chips started falling, avoided the army's hardest and primary job—combat—and thus proved unworthy of the national trust placed in them. Grant obviously sided with the annoyed subordinates. He retained much of the same attitude after earning the right to become their tormentor. He instead became a combat infantryman's idea of a good officer: legendarily brave and ever mindful of how men in the bottom ranks—who *had* to be brave—saw things.

Jefferson Barracks had its share of the other kind of officer, but its troops also contained friends. Longstreet was there, and Fred Dent. The Dent family's plantation lay just five miles away, on the outskirts of St. Louis, and Fred invited Grant and Longstreet, a relative of the Dents, to enjoy its comforts. There, at age twenty-three, Grant met Fred's seventeen-year-old sister, Julia, and started thinking of taking a wife. His deep reserve, the seeming product of disgust at the boastful garrulousness of his father and a strong identification with the stoicism of his mother, was broken by Julia Dent.

How and why this came to be can only be conjectured. Julia had received instruction from Miss Mauro's Academy for Young Ladies in St. Louis[2] and, when Grant met her, had just finished a triumphal entry onto the St. Louis social scene. Dark-haired, trim-figured, and vivacious, she possessed confidence, intelligence, and two expressive brown eyes. One of the latter, however, was either crossed or lazy, depending on the account. She typically appears in pictures in profile because of it. Whatever the irregularity of her eye, she was rumored to have already collected several interested admirers. More striking than beautiful, she was her father's favorite and exactly what Grant wanted. When Colonel Dent eventually offered him her younger sister Ellen instead, Grant said no: "I want Julia."[3] He began to pour out his feelings to her in person, often as they rode horses together across the Dent plantation, and later in a flood of letters.

The courtship, though, was interrupted by Grant's new vocation. In May 1844, barely a year after his graduation from West Point, Grant and his unit, the Fourth Infantry, were ordered to Louisiana to join an "Army of Observation" watching Texas for the purpose of inciting the Mexican War.

The war with Mexico bore many similarities to the American Civil War a decade and a half down the road. One was that Dixie's slavery caused both. By the 1840s the so-called peculiar institution was already bitterly dividing the United States, and its proponents were seeking new fertile ground for it.

As the nation anxiously—with hope or dread—awaited a vote by Texans on whether to approve the idea of their territory's annexation by the United States, the presidential election of 1844 pitted the Whigs' venerable Senator Henry Clay of Kentucky against former Speaker of the House James K. Polk of Tennessee. Clay claimed to be in favor of annexation solely if it could be achieved "without war, and with the common consent of the Union"—which meant he opposed it, since Northern resistance ensured that there could be no "common consent." Polk, by contrast, was a full-throated annexationist.

To appease or mislead Northerners, or perhaps because he could see farther down the road than his fellow Southerners, he also stumped for "reoccupation" of the Oregon Territory, despite rival British claims there. But Texas was the election's overriding issue, and the victory narrowly went to Polk, 1,339,494 to 1,300,004.[4]

The new American president was hell-bent for a war, which he hoped would be short and sweet, over Texas. Like his predecessor, Virginian John Tyler, Polk lusted after the part of northern Mexico that lay in not just what is now Texas but also New Mexico and California. The reason for wanting Texas was all too obvious. A true acolyte of the lifelong conqueror President Andrew Jackson (and even dubbed "Young Hickory"), Polk was supported by Southerners wishing to annex Texas to expand territory congenial to slaveholding. He was smart, single-minded, and so partisan in behalf of his causes that he pledged to serve just one White House term so as, seemingly, to allow for one more possible presidential run by the aging intellectual leader of American slavocracy, South Carolina senator John C. Calhoun.

Calhoun, though, quickly became an opponent of Polk's aims. He feared that going after New Mexico and California, which were unlikely to be welcoming to slavery, would prove a hindrance to Southern planters' expansionist ambitions. Pursuit of these territories would be more apt to fuel the fire of rising abolition sentiment. Polk, in contrast, appeared to care more about stretching America's boundaries to the Pacific Ocean, thereby laying claim to dominion over the entire continent.[5] Polk had a point that remains historically critical. For the United States to become the colossus that visionaries like Polk foresaw, it could not long share borders within its continent with established European powers—like England in Oregon. If it did, America would become just one of a maze of nations segmented like Europe itself.

But restricting himself to one term left Polk little time to accomplish his grand design. To cloak their aim to take the republic coast to coast, Polk's Democrats needed a high-flown marketing slogan, and in the summer of 1845 they got one for the ages. An issue of the New York Jacksonian magazine *Democratic Review* declared that it was "time now" for Democrats' Whig opponents to shut their mouths about annexation, that bringing Texas into the United States would represent fulfillment of "our *manifest destiny* to overspread the continent . . . for the free development of our yearly multiplying millions."[6] It thus whitewashed American imperialism and the spread of slavery, an institution that made the opening lines of the Declaration of Independence a cruel joke.

America's Mexican adventure was made even less attractive by the discrepancy of strength in the prospective opponents. In Mexico, Polk could hardly have found a weaker foe. Mexico was home to perhaps 7 million residents, compared with close to 20 million in the United States;[7] its economy was in extreme debt and disarray; and its government very wisely wanted no part of war. Its leaders virtually begged to negotiate with Washington over the claims of Americans who had established farms and ranches in Mexico's northern territory and now contended these properties were theirs. Polk, a colorless and childless hard worker devoted solely to national party politics and what he deemed his duty, made a show of seeking negotiations while actually dodging them. Meanwhile, he conspired with a representative of deposed Mexican dictator Antonio López de Santa Anna to get Santa Anna back into Mexico from exile in Cuba, help him take power again, and conclude a peace treaty advantageous to the United States. Polk soon sent Zachary Taylor's Army of Occupation out of Louisiana into Texas to find an excuse to fight while readying another military force, soon to become the "Army of the West," to head for New Mexico from Kansas as soon as war was declared.

Grant, who knew nothing of the secret Santa Anna deal and apparently little of the Army of the West, was not in sympathy with the Polk position, and he became less so the older he got. In the *Personal Memoirs* he makes that plain: "The occupation [of Mexican territory], separation [of some of it from Mexico] and annexation [of the separated lands by Washington]," he writes, "were, from the inception of the movement until its final consummation, a conspiracy to acquire territory out of which slave states might be formed for the American Union. Even if the annexation itself could be justified, the manner in which the subsequent war was forced upon Mexico cannot."[8] This comment appears to be more one of disgust with politics and their potentially tragic effects than of a particular horror of slavery. The "peculiar institution," after all—its bestial nature notwithstanding—had been an all-too-real feature of the background of Grant's life to that point, both in the escapees whose presence had to have been continually whispered about in Georgetown and Ripley and in its full-on, shameful reality across the Ohio in Maysville, Kentucky. For another, Grant probably had endured enough abolition bluster from his overbearing father to disabuse him of much overt antipathy to slavery. He possibly preferred not to think about it. He seems to have felt more empathy for the Mexicans, both soldiers and civilians, whom Polk's war took cruel advantage of. He did, though, compare the lot of the majority of them to that of Southern enslaved people. "The people of Mexico are a very different race of people from ours," he wrote to a friend. "The better class are very proud and tyrannize over the lower and much more numerous class as much as a hard master does over his negroes, and they submit to it quite as humbly."[9]

Despite his disaffection with the political motives for the incipient conflict, Grant was a soldier and more than sufficiently conscious of that to do his duty. He also kept his eyes and mind open and learned much that would benefit him a decade and a half later in an unimaginably larger and bloodier struggle, which he would contend to the end of his life had been brought on by the Mexican one. In a sentence that could almost have been written by Carl von Clausewitz, Grant said, "Nations, like individuals, are punished for their transgressions." He added, "We got our punishment in the most sanguinary and expensive war of modern times."[10]

Thus, even before it began, the Mexican War belied one of Antoine-Henri Jomini's cardinal tenets and exemplified one of Clausewitz's. It not only was crammed full of the politics the Swiss baron had claimed war had, or should have, little to do with but also was precipitated by them. And they involved the same issue that started the greater war fifteen years later: the perpetuation of slavery.

There would be large lessons to be learned in Mexico by the few officers who had not crowded their minds too full of Jominian precepts at West Point. As the eminent historian Daniel Walker Howe has noted in his *What Hath God Wrought*,[11] Mexico in several ways resembled the future Confederate States of America. It was an overwhelmingly rural, agricultural, and sparsely populated country boasting far fewer resources than the United States, but its territory appeared too vast to be conquered. Also like the Confederacy, its government would try to gain intervention by foreign nations to insure it against defeat. The U.S. Navy would blockade its ports to rob it of supplies. And at bottom, its last best hope—again, like that of the later Confederacy—was that its very vastness would enable it to hold out until the foe wearied of invading.

In 1846, though, nobody saw the later war coming. So nobody knew that the lessons of Mexico were theirs to learn or that they needed to be learned at all. The outlines could only be pondered and committed to memory by an officer embracing new experiences and not laboring under the delusion that West Point had already taught him all he needed to know.

Such an officer was Second Lieutenant Ulysses S. Grant.

ROUGH AND READY

His first instruction offered by the Mexican War came months before he arrived in Mexico. It had to do with that most important question for any young officer: What kind of leader did he wish to become? The answer quickly became personified—in manner, at least—by the Army of Occupation's commander, Brigadier General Zachary Taylor.

Taylor was a charismatic and laconic longtime frontiersman, soldier, and farmer. Through a long military career fighting mostly Native Americans in the Midwest and Florida, he had acquired the nickname "Old Rough and Ready." He was, as implied by the second of his nickname's trio of adjectives, the antithesis of a West Pointer. Although a relative of founding father James Madison, he was born in 1784 not in Virginia's high-toned Tidewater but, rather, in that state's Orange County, in the eastern shadow of the Blue Ridge Mountains. What is more, his family moved in the year of his birth across the Blue Ridge to Kentucky, where his father, a former Revolutionary soldier, was appointed to a government position with the port of Louisville.

America's interior was threatened by Indians and Spaniards then, and the younger Taylor grew up amid incipient danger. Such minimal education as he acquired came from a New England tutor hired by his father. The son volunteered for military service at the age of twenty-two and in 1808 was commissioned a first lieutenant of infantry. Thirty-eight years later, on the brink of the Mexican War, he was a prominent colonel and a substantial property owner, with a home in Louisiana and a large plantation.[12] Such fame as he enjoyed had come mostly from an 1830s encounter with Native Americans in Florida, where he was luckier than seven other commanders. The Seminoles, previously quite successful with guerrilla tactics, became so confident in the strength of their defensive position that they rashly decided at the Battle of Okeechobee to stand and fight—and fell to a Taylor bayonet charge.[13]

Vigorous at sixty-one, Taylor impressed Grant, despite the old man's lack of great mastery of tactics or strategy.[14] He was nationally important, had spent his youth just down the Ohio River from where Grant did, and, like Grant, was not inclined to stand on ceremony. He customarily walked among his troops in farmer-style garb—blue-jean breeches, knee-length linen duster, and a hat woven from palmetto leaves.[15] Grant recalled in his memoirs that Taylor "never made any great show or parade, either of uniform or retinue. In dress he was possibly too plain, rarely wearing anything in the field to indicate his rank, or even that he was an officer." Grant added that he saw Taylor in uniform just once and only heard of him wearing it one other time.[16]

The general's lack of "show" was just the first of many traits that would impress itself on Grant, and if it did not elicit admiration among the majority of West Pointers, it helped make Old Zack beloved by the men in ranks.[17] He seems to have been as lax about discipline as he was about attire. One soldier wrote in his diary that Taylor was "a very pleasant old man and very sociable not only to officers but to buck privates also. He is not a proud man at all. When he came to see [our regiment] he rode a mule and looked like an old man a going to mill. He left us and bid goodbye as though he had always been acquainted with us and told us to be good boys and fight like men if needs be."[18]

Grant, at the time only a temporary second lieutenant, impressed Taylor, too. One day at the Gulf fishing village of Corpus Christi, before the army headed inland to its first battle, Taylor saw Grant, who was commanding a detail of men, jump into the water to show them how he wanted a channel cleared of oyster-bed snags. Other young officer-onlookers laughed until they were silenced by an observation from Old Zack. He wished, Taylor said, that he "had more officers like Grant who would stand ready to set a personal example when needed."[19]

Somebody soon put money where Old Zack's mouth was. Grant was promoted to full second lieutenant.[20]

FOOT SOLDIER, MOUNTED

The army is known among its own to be an institution of "hurry up and wait." For months Grant—tortured by dreams of marrying Julia—fidgeted through much more waiting than otherwise.

He had reported to the Fourth Infantry on June 3, 1844, near Natchitoches, Louisiana, about thirty miles from the Texas border. A year and a month later, on July 2, 1845, the regiment finally boarded riverboats for New

Orleans, then plied the Gulf from there to Corpus Christi, a small village at the mouth of the Nueces River. The Mexican government contended the Nueces was the southern boundary of Texas. There Taylor established a base and began to train and gather more men. By October, they numbered 4,000.

Small detachments from Corpus Christi twice had to trek to San Antonio and Austin to pay other small garrisons stationed there, and in November 1845 Grant, heeding Taylor's suggestion that officers accompany the 200-plus-mile expedition, volunteered. Grant's recollection in his *Personal Memoirs* reflects not just his sharp eye for detail but also the retentiveness of his memory forty years later.

> There was not at the time an individual living between Corpus Christi and San Antonio until within about thirty miles of the latter point, where there were a few scattering Mexican settlements along the San Antonio River. The people in at least one of these hamlets lived underground for protection against the Indians. The country abounded in game, such as deer and antelope, with abundance of wild turkeys along the streams and where there were nut-bearing woods. . . .
>
> From [San Antonio] to Austin there was not a single residence except at New Braunfels, on the Guadalupe River . . . a settlement of Germans who had only that year come into the State. At all events they were living in small huts, about such as soldiers would hastily construct for temporary occupation. From Austin [returning by a direct route] to Corpus Christi there was only a small settlement at Bastrop, with a few farms along the Colorado River; but after leaving that, there were no settlements except the home of one man, with one female slave, at the old town of Goliad. Some of the houses were still standing. Goliad had been quite a village . . . , but some years before there had been a Mexican massacre, in which every inhabitant had been killed or driven away. This, with the massacre of the prisoners in the Alamo [at] San Antonio, about the same time . . . furnished the strongest justification the Texans had for [fighting Mexico].[21]

President Polk, needing an incident to induce Congress to declare war, ordered Taylor to move 150 miles south to the Rio Grande. "We were sent to provoke a fight," Grant later recalled, "but it was essential that Mexico should commence it. . . . Mexico showing no willingness to come to the Nueces to drive the invaders from her soil, it became necessary for the 'invaders' to approach to within a convenient distance to be struck. Accordingly, preparations were begun for moving the Army to the Rio Grande, to a point near [the Mexican town of] Matamoros. It was desirable to occupy a position near the largest centre of population possible to reach, without absolutely invading territory to which we set up no claim whatever."[22]

On March 8, 1846, Taylor ordered the troops into motion. The Fourth Infantry moved out on March 11. In the run-up to the departure, Grant's horses had gotten loose from a camp servant and vanished onto the prairie, and the company commander, Captain McCall, asked Grant if he did not want to get another horse to ride. Grant said no, that he belonged to a company of foot soldiers and would share the lot of his men. McCall, who had gotten a horse for his servant, did not like the idea of one of his lieutenants walking while a servant rode, so he bought Grant a three-dollar Mexican mustang to ride on the journey. Grant accepted the animal because he "saw the captain's earnestness in the matter," but "I was sorry to take [the mustang], because I really felt that, belonging to a foot regiment, it was my duty to march with the men."[23] That anecdote conveys an idea of how close in class and responsibility Grant felt to the men under him.

His humorous accompanying account of his experience with his new horse, recently acquired from Mexicans who had just caught the animal in the wild, gives a similar hint. It is self-effacing evidence of Grant's equestrian talent, affection for horseflesh, and lack of professional ego over his status as an officer. "The day we started was the first day the horse had been under saddle," he recalled in his memoirs.

> I had, however, but little difficulty in breaking him, though for the first day there were frequent disagreements between us as to which way we should go, and sometimes whether we should go at all. At no time during the day could I choose exactly the part of the column I would march with; but after that I had as tractable a horse as any with the army, and there was none that stood the trip better. He never ate a mouthful of food on the journey except the grass he could pick within the length of his picket rope.[24]

On March 19, the advance reached a river called Arroyo Colorado thirty miles north of Matamoros. Running through timberland beneath banks thirty feet high, the stream was wide and deep enough to accommodate boats, and Taylor's men had no pontoons or specialists in bridge construction. Suddenly the Americans were threatened, too, with human obstacles. It was Grant's first brush with incipient combat. On the river's opposite bank, Mexican buglers began making calls as if marshaling troops. Taylor, though, was uncowed, and Grant characteristically has left little record as to his personal concern at that moment when seemingly faced with his first battle.[25]

The arroyo was a significant impediment to the supply wagons and artillery, and Taylor halted. On the twentieth, a Mexican cavalry officer sent a message that an American crossing of the river would mean war. On the twenty-first, the Mexican general at Matamoros sent Taylor a proclamation denouncing the American invasion and saying it would be met with overwhelming force. Taylor promptly informed the messenger that if any Mexicans were seen on the south side of the Colorado when his men entered the water, he would order his artillery to fire. Cavalry then splashed forward into the river and forded it, and whatever Mexicans were there quickly left. Not a shot was fired.

Taylor next ordered a road cut down the steep bank and up the other side. The American troops waded across and, using a long rope, pulled over the supply wagons, artillery, and Mexican mules.[26]

REVELATION IN BULLETS AND BLOOD

Part of how most generals get to be generals is enduring—and distinguishing themselves in—battle,[27] and Taylor's long career had seen much of it.

Grant continued studying him. On the south side of the Colorado, Taylor put his little army of fewer than 3,000 men into its most impressive formation—three brigades strung out side by side across the stark prairie—and headed it for the Rio Grande.[28] Then, after ordering the column to move slowly ahead, he rode east with an escort[29] to a coastal village twenty-seven miles north of Matamoros[30] to set up a supply depot and confer with naval officers bringing provisions from New Orleans. When the troops reached the village, Point Isabel, they found the residents gone and several of the principal buildings burned.

By March 28 Taylor was back in front of Matamoros with his troops.[31] He set them to building a primitive, cannon-studded fortress quickly dubbed

Fort Texas.[32] Almost immediately, two American cavalrymen were captured, but the next three weeks constituted a strange mixture of tension and frolics as some 3,000 Americans and 6,000 Mexicans[33] faced each other across the river.

Much of the daily scene was hardly martial. Mexican girls of the lower middle class, having no other place to bathe but the river, came out to do it nude.[34] Desertions began occurring—as many as fourteen in a night—as the girls and the Mexican generals proffered every temptation, from implied sexual comforts to overt offers of 320 acres of land apiece[35] to any American willing to switch sides and become a Mexican citizen. They also offered freedom to any enslaved person who would desert his or her master and join the Mexicans.[36]

But unfriendlier incidents happened, too, and proliferated. Mexican sentinels sometimes fired at lusty Americans trying to swim the river. On April 12, Matamoros commander Pedro de Ampudia warned Taylor that if he refused to withdraw within twenty-four hours, "arms, and arms alone, must decide the question." Taylor replied, with courtesy, that he was acting on his government's orders and had no authority to leave on his own. He added that he "wish[ed] it understood that I shall by no means avoid" a fight.[37] Five days later, one of Grant's fellow lieutenants in the Fourth Infantry, along with an enlisted man, was shot and killed while searching for another officer who had turned up missing. The lieutenant's body was found with a bullet hole in the skull, but there was no proof that it had been put there by Mexican troops rather than by guerrillas.[38]

Then came an incident that was unmistakably official. Two American captains—one of whom was the eventually prominent tactics author and Confederate general William J. Hardee—were captured while on a mission from Taylor to investigate rumors that a horde of Mexican cavalrymen had crossed the Rio Grande above their position. Even worse than the captures, the ambush in which they occurred saw Mexicans kill sixteen Americans and take captive forty-five other troops besides the captains.[39] But there was a bright side, at least from the Washington point of view. President Polk finally had what he had aimed for. Taylor sent the president a message that "hostilities may now be considered to be commenced."[40]

Through all this, Grant entertained hopes that there still would be no battle, that the Mexicans would simply submit. But clouds promising wider conflict continued darkening. Taylor prudently ordered some of the ships at Point Isabel to move southward and blockade the Rio Grande to prevent seaborne Mexican resupply missions. Soon he received reports that a large number of Mexican troops had crossed the Rio Grande downriver from Matamoros, apparently heading for the Point Isabel supply cache. Provisions at Fort Texas were running low, and Taylor on May 1 abruptly left 550 men at Fort Texas and marched hard for Point Isabel.[41] Grant heard that Taylor had vowed that if necessary he would "cut his way through" to his depot "no matter how superior their numbers."[42] Grant then endured the hardest march he had made up to then. Leaving Fort Texas at 3:00 P.M., Taylor drove his troops forward for twelve full hours, then gave them hardly more than a good nap before continuing to Point Isabel, which they reached without incident the next noon.[43] "Our march was mostly through grass up to the waist, with a wet and uneven bottom; yet we made thirty miles in much less than a day," Grant wrote home. "I consider my march on that occasion equal to a walk of sixty miles in one day on good roads and unencumbered with troops."[44]

For the few days it took Mexican laborers to load Taylor's 300 wagons[45] with food, clothing, ammunition, and cannon landed from the ships anchored offshore, the troops lay in their tents beside the Gulf. On the morning of May 3, Grant heard a low, thundering rumble from the southwest that old veterans said came from cannon, signifying that back at Matamoros the Mexicans had crossed the river and begun shelling Fort Texas. The results were unknown until the return of an officer Taylor immediately dispatched to find out. Grant wondered what Taylor was feeling "during this suspense."[46]

"A great many men, when they smell battle afar off, chafe to get into the fray," he noted in his memoirs, adding that this sort of bravado is generally for show. But most such men change "as they approach danger" and "become more subdued. This rule is not universal, for I have known a few men who were always aching for a fight when there was no enemy near, who were as good as their word when the battle did come. But the number of such men is small."[47] Grant himself was of neither species. He had never pretended that he looked forward to fighting. He said that as he headed for the cannon thunder, he "felt sorry that I had enlisted."[48]

On May 5, the officer sent to Fort Texas returned with word that its commander said he could hold out, and two days later Taylor, reinforced by some of the Point Isabel garrison, headed back toward Matamoros with his loaded, slow-moving wagons, including eighty drawn by oxen. At noon on May 8, eleven miles from Point Isabel, they met 7,000 Mexicans[49] in line of battle astride the road at a timber patch called Palo Alto. Grant later remembered that the enemy consisted "largely of cavalry armed with lances" and that their "bayonets and spearheads glistened in the sunlight."[50]

Taylor halted out of range of the Mexican cannon and threw out his own troops and artillery, along with a battalion to guard the rear. He then exhibited his consideration for his troops by ordering a platoon from each company to stack arms, collect all of each company's canteens, and fill them from a stream to their right. While they did this, Taylor sat on his horse—"Old Whitey"—with a leg thrown across his saddle horn onto the same side of the horse as the other leg while he chewed a jaw full of tobacco. When the platoons returned and distributed the canteens, Taylor did not regale the troops with a patriotic oration or any other kind. He simply, with no fanfare, ordered them forward. As they pushed toward the opening Mexican artillery fire, Grant looked around him and thought about the loneliness of leadership: "What a fearful responsibility General Taylor must feel, commanding such a host and so far away from friends."[51]

From birth, apparently, Grant had never feared gunfire. According to Jesse Grant, at age two his son had not even flinched as a pistol was put in his hands and the child was helped to pull its trigger.[52] But in Mexico on May 8, 1846, the situation differed. The adult Grant obviously thought of, and soon saw with his own eyes, what gunfire—and cannonballs—could do to men. As the Americans proceeded about 3:00 P.M. toward the Mexican line at Palo Alto, the twelve-pounder Mexican cannon fired balls of solid shot that at first were unable to reach the American lines. The balls bounced along the ground and rolled through the ranks as the men sidestepped.[53]

But when the Americans got within 500 yards, Taylor halted them and ordered his own guns to the front—eight six-pounder howitzers and two eighteen-pounder cannon, all firing exploding shot—and opened fire with grape and canister. The barrages cut a "perfect road" through the Mexican ranks, Grant wrote.[54] He saw the first meaningful deployment in the Western Hemisphere of Napoleonic horse-drawn field cannon[55] and watched them do "a great deal of execution."[56] He wrote Julia that Mexican officers urged their infantrymen forward into the American cannon fire to no avail, some of the captives saying their officers had "slashed among them with sabers at a dreadful rate" to try to push them into braving the U.S. ordnance.[57]

As the infantry stood at order arms and watched, Taylor's barrage continued until dusk, at which time the Mexicans were seen falling back. Old Zack ordered another advance, this time to the position the Mexicans had vacated. The withdrawing foe kept up "a brisk fire," Grant remembered, and the approaching Americans began to incur losses. Near Grant, a Mexican cannonball decapitated an enlisted man, and his "brains and bones," as well as "splinters from his musket," knocked other men to the ground. In passing, the same cannonball carried away the lower jaw of a captain, who died two months later, unable to eat or talk. The fighting closed with the fall of night.[58]

It had not been much, compared to almost any of Grant's later battles, but it was his first and stayed with him. He remembered looking "at the long line of battle, consisting of three thousand men," and wondering how Taylor "ever had the nerve to assume" that mental burden. "And when, after the fight, the casualties were reported, and the losses ascertained to be nearly sixty . . . the engagement assumed a magnitude in my eyes which was positively startling."[59] His memory—"of the first fight I ever saw"—would return to the forefront of Grant's mind eighteen years later, after his Civil War army of about 100,000 soldiers squared off against Robert E. Lee in the horrific Battle of the Wilderness. There Grant's army would lose 17,666 men. By then, he said, the comparatively meager losses incurred at Palo Alto "would scarcely be deemed important enough to report to headquarters."[60]

The Wilderness, unlike Taylor's victory at Palo Alto, would turn out to be at best a savage draw, the kind of traumatic encounter that had sent the Army of the Potomac under such generals as George B. McClellan, Ambrose Burnside, and Joseph Hooker reeling back toward Washington. But the Wilderness would portend no such movement. There, in 1864, Grant exhibited a mindset vastly different from that of his predecessors. During the battle he briefly abandoned his usual aplomb to rebuke a panicked Federal brigadier who galloped up in the middle of the fight wailing that all was lost. The stampeded officer seemed to anticipate a repeat of another battle that had raged in that same Wilderness the year before, when Lee had whipped Hooker to a literal fare-thee-well at the Battle of Chancellorsville. Grant would have none of such thinking. The erstwhile western farm boy had learned in Mexico, if not indeed at West Point, that rank and pedigree should not cow him. "I am heartily tired of hearing what Lee is going to do," Grant told the officer. "Some of you seem to think he is suddenly going to turn a double somersault and land on our rear and on both our flanks at the same time. Go back to your command and try to think what we are going to do ourselves, instead of what Lee is going to do."[61]

Grant thereupon instituted a new Federal response to a Lee masterstroke—and initiated the first eastern theater demonstration of his philosophy of letting no reverse divert him from his drive to ultimate victory. Instead of recoiling 'and retreating in the face of the battle's appalling casualty list, Grant stoically ordered his advance to continue farther into Virginia. And his men carrying rifles were overjoyed, ecstatic that they would not once again have to cede and reconquer ground they had so bloodily fought over.

Grant's post-Wilderness decision to go forward and maintain pressure on Lee seems in the spirit of his memory of Palo Alto and Old Zack. The great biographer Jean Edward Smith termed that decision pivotal. It was, Smith wrote, "the final turning point of the war."[62]

BULLETS "HAVE LESS HORROR WHEN AMONG THEM"

When Taylor sought to renew the battle of Palo Alto on the morning of May 9, 1846, the last Mexicans were vanishing to the south toward Matamoros. Shaken by the superior killing power of the American cannon, they had all but stampeded from Palo Alto.

Taylor ordered his army forward onto "ground . . . strewed with the bodies of dead men and horses," Grant wrote Julia. It was "terrible to . . . see the amount of life that had been destroyed." The Americans estimated the casualties at "from three hundred to five hundred" killed and thousands wounded, compared to their own loss of not many more than a dozen killed and "probably fifty wounded."[63] Taylor sent forward two 150-man scouting detachments to follow the Mexicans' trail, while the rest of his army guarded the heavily laden supply wagons. One of the two scout detachments was led by the captain of Grant's company, who left Grant in command of the unit. It was, Grant later recalled, "an honor and responsibility I thought very great."[64] Since the infantry had yet to do any fighting, it seems unlikely, though, that this "honor" bestowed on a second lieutenant was reflective of much. The captain may have taken the other officers with him on the reconnaissance.

The scouts found the Mexicans entrenched six miles farther on, at Resaca de la Palma. The enemy had taken position behind a onetime bed of the Rio Grande, which had long since changed course, leaving a dry ravine linking ponds that had once been pools in the river. On the ravine's south bank, the Mexican troops had thrown up primitive breastworks of fallen trees behind thick, thorny undergrowth they termed chaparral. Taylor sent the rest of his troops forward, except for 300 guarding the wagons. Grant's company was on the right, and he led the men through such openings in the chaparral as he could find. He described the vegetation as so thick that he could stand within five feet of another person and have no idea he was not alone.[65]

Musket balls started flying, and he ordered his men to lie down. They held that position until it became obvious that the Mexican fire was not directed at them. Then Grant got them up and sought another route toward the fighting, most of which was occurring to the left. They charged toward it and thought they captured some enemy soldiers. Actually, the U.S. Cavalry had already taken some artillery and infantry, including Grant's assumed captives. The rest of the Mexican army, even though reinforced from Matamoros overnight and outnumbering the Americans nearly four to one, fled headlong to the Rio Grande. Some 300 of them drowned trying to swim across in the spring torrents, and 2,000 were taken prisoner. A staggering 1,200 had been killed. Taylor reported his loss as 34 killed and 113 wounded.[66]

Grant reflected that the battle could have been won as easily without his presence. He wryly compared his "exploit" to that of "the soldier who boasted that he had cut off the leg of one of the enemy. When asked why he did not cut off his head, he replied: 'Someone had done that before.'"[67]

But over these two days Grant had learned important things about himself. On May 8, the two armies had not closed the interval between themselves sufficiently to contend hand to hand, but the shooting had kept up so fiercely that it started a fire that obscured the whole field with smoke for a while. Yet during the whole four hours he "did not feel a sensation of fear," he wrote Julia, until the decapitation by cannonball and the grisly wounding of the captain occurred nearby. "There is no great sport in having bullets flying about one in every direction," he told her, "but I find they have less horror when among them than when in anticipation."[68]

To a friend, he described the wounding of the captain more fully, along with its gruesome result: the officer's lower jaw was "gone to the windpipe and the tongue hanging down upon the throat." But Grant said that he "scarcely thought of the probability or possibility of being touched myself (although nine-pound shots were whistling all around)." To his friend's understandable curiosity as to how it felt, he responded, "I do not know that I felt any particular sensation. War seems much less horrible to persons engaged in it than to those who read of the battles." During the night, despite an expectation of renewed fighting in the morning, he told this friend, he believed "all slept as soundly on the ground at Palo Alto as if they had been in a palace. For my own part, I don't think I ever dreamed of battles."[69]

He likely was not exaggerating. During the Civil War, his battlefield aplomb, although characteristically understated by the general himself, became legendary and was an important aspect of his leadership. So was his personal aura, if such it can be termed. There was nothing showy about him. Whereas many other officers preened and under fire seemed to be acting, plainly hoping to excite admiration or inspirational effect (or newspaper notice), most of the time Grant—like Zachary Taylor back in Mexico—would appear to be just Grant being Grant. George G. Meade, who had been in Mexico and commanded the Union's principal eastern Civil War army when Grant arrived from the West, even said that seeing Grant again "put me in mind of Old Zack."[70]

Under Old Zack, Grant already had learned more about war than he had in his classes at West Point. He knew it, too. In his memoirs he observed that officer training "in actual war" is "far more efficient" than the kind received in military schools.[71] Taylor, who may well have never heard of Baron Jomini, had acquired his own strategy and tactics in the "efficient" manner Grant specified: by battlefield trial and error. Old Zack seemed oblivious to the far superior numbers of the Mexicans and the common West Point assumption that prudent attacking of a dug-in enemy required a numerical advantage of at least three to one. Taylor used his artillery to decimate large fractions of the Mexican numbers, thereby multiplying the importance of his own. He seemed to give no thought to retreating, thus personifying Clausewitz's ideal commander, a man of "a special type of mind . . . a strong, rather than a brilliant one."[72] It was a definition that would also come to well describe General Grant.

In addition to Taylor's understated toughness, there was the old general's obvious comfort in his own skin. His manner of dress was careless in the extreme. Grant would not go so far as to don Taylor's palmetto hat and farm clothes, but he would mostly wear the enlisted man's jacket with general's stars just pinned on its shoulders. This plainness would be part and parcel of his unostentatious lack of fear. It would say to the troops that General U. S. Grant was one of *them*, not some dandified, never-blistered, tender-gutted pseudo-Napoleon such as McClellan—or that supercilious general's host of officer admirers. Like the sergeants and corporals and privates, Ulysses Grant would be "just," if that is the term, another workman, another farm boy or mechanic or dockworker who had come there only to help land the cargo, repair the machine, or harvest the victory—in other words, to get the job done. In 1864 these hordes of other farm boys and mechanics and dockworkers would be immensely gratified to finally have a leader who was not ashamed to look like them—and appeared as bound and determined as they were to finish this job and go home.

They would begin to often see him amid the whistling bullets and exploding shells that they themselves had to endure, and there is a brotherhood that develops among men who brave such things. Grant would later write, from an unassailable position of experience, that "actual war . . . is a far more efficient training" for military officers than "school."[73] Instead of inhabiting a rear, safe desk in Civil War Washington, he would be an extension of the lieutenant who in Mexico felt that if his men were foot soldiers he needed to be one, too. As a general, he would be there with *them*, obliviously writing orders and directing aides to all parts of the field, half-smoking and half-chewing a cigar while speaking as unexcitedly as if he were asking to have potatoes passed at the dinner table.

After he went east to command all the Union armies—and to personally supervise operations against the fabled patrician Robert E. Lee and Lee's vaunted Army of Northern Virginia—he would be still "new" to eastern Federals, but this undersized, slouching figure who had been so forgettable on arriving among West Point's "higher"-born cadets a quarter century earlier now would make a searing impression on the men in ranks. At Spotsylvania, sitting on a fallen tree writing a dispatch and glancing absently up as a shell burst directly in front of him, he would be paid, in homely fashion, an infantryman's supreme compliment. The soldier, a wounded member of the Fifth Wisconsin being carried past his preoccupied commander, would note that the new eastern leader was of unprecedented stock in his new theater of action.

"Ulysses," the man would be overheard to tell comrades, "don't scare worth a damn."[74]

BATTLE OF MONTERREY

Having bloodily stampeded the Mexicans from the environs of Matamoros, Zachary Taylor readied his troops to conquer northern Mexico. But the preparations took a while. Gathering additional supplies and legions of new volunteer troops required from May until August and involved braving much Clausewitz-remindful political and journalistic criticism back home. Taylor, U.S. politicians and journalists claimed, was proceeding too slowly.

Some reasons for the delay were societal. The new volunteers—hailing from such predominantly rural states as Maryland, Texas, Kentucky, Georgia, and Tennessee—were wildly undisciplined, spawning charges of rape, murder, and lesser violence. They were troublesome in other ways, too. Volunteers were generally native-born and wanted no part of associating with the many immigrants who filled the ranks of Taylor's regular army forces. Cosmopolitan lieutenant George Meade, who would command the Army of the Potomac under Grant seventeen years later, was critical of Southern troops who, as former slaveholders, seemed to expect somebody else to carry their water and bring them firewood. Grant watched and remembered Taylor's forbearance in the face of unruly behavior from many of the new volunteers, a species with whom the general had likely dealt since his earliest army days.[75] It was the same species that would cram the hurriedly drafted or conscripted Union ranks of the Civil War.

Grant, too, would be tolerant of such troops in the latter struggle but, perhaps partly because of his West Point sojourn, would hold officers responsible for the behavior of their men. A prime example came after some units in the 109th Illinois Infantry, angry after preliminary announcement of the Emancipation Proclamation as well as enactment of a July 1862 law permitting recruitment of African Americans into military service , tried to get themselves captured. The incident occurred during a disastrous Confederate raid by Grant's old West Point schoolmate Earl Van Dorn on a Grant supply base at Holly Springs, Mississippi. Grant responded by instituting courts-martial against officers of the units—not against the men themselves.[76]

At Matamoros, Mexico, in 1846, Taylor had to reorganize his swelling ranks, which had grown to 12,000 men. With supply a major concern for a drive inland, he reduced his expeditionary force to 6,500, apparently because dysentery and other physical maladies had severely weakened some of his units. Possibly because of this attrition, Second Lieutenant Grant found himself in command of the Fourth Infantry's Company C as of July 22. Almost immediately, though, Taylor ordered each of the regiments to designate a quartermaster to take charge of the regimental pack trains that would have to carry their equipage on the trek. Grant's facility with math and his reputation for handling equine livestock apparently led the Fourth Infantry on August 14 to saddle him with the new designation, to his great chagrin. He protested formally and mightily against occupying any position "which removes me from sharing in the dangers and honors of serving with my company at the front," but his objection was fruitless. Brigade commander John Garland rejected his protest, saying Grant's contrary wishes "cannot be considered. . . . His observed ability, skill, and persistency in the line of duty" made his superiors "confident that Lieutenant Grant can best serve his country in the present emergencies under this assignment."[77]

Resisted though it was, the importance of this appointment in Grant's military maturation cannot be exaggerated—notwithstanding the probability that it was not an honor that would have been conferred on a scion of an influential family who hoped to wrap himself in battlefield glory. Nonetheless, unlike the army's refusal to find a spot for him in the cavalry, this assignment made sense. It was also, noncombat or not, a huge and essential job.

Lloyd Lewis in *Captain Sam Grant* notes that Grant, Jesse Grant's former teamster, "had known the business of transportation from infancy." Plus, as the "son of a successful businessman," Grant could be expected to be able to

> do the business of the regiment, pay out the money, keep the long accounts balanced, find . . . harness for the animals, and secure clothing for the men . . . buy fodder and grain for horses and mules, and see that the men had fruit, vegetables, and fresh meat to supplement the regular ration of hard bread, sugar, coffee, salt and "side meat or middlings." He must keep the men supplied with haversacks for food and knapsacks for clothes. If wood for the campfire ran short, he must get coal which arrived on ships from Ohio and Pennsylvania.[78]

As might be expected of such a multifaceted task, the headaches were endless. None was bigger for this extraordinary equestrian than that brought about by many of the animals that pulled his wagons—mules. Legendary for their balkiness, they sorely tried his patience and his equanimity. In the *Personal Memoirs* he said he was "not aware of ever having used a profane expletive in my life; but I would have the charity to excuse those who may have done so if they were in charge of a train of Mexican pack mules."[79]

Grant would turn out to be excellent at this assignment he so bitterly decried. Soon it would be observed by a fellow lieutenant that "there was no road . . . so constructed . . . but that Grant, in some mysterious way, would work his train through and have it in the camp of his brigade before the campfires were lighted."[80] During the Civil War, Grant's troops would rarely run short of whatever they needed to do their work. He would also adapt his supply trains to the needs at hand and even improvise and create new trains out of whole cloth—as when, during the climactic period of the Vicksburg campaign, he used requisitioned civilian vehicles to haul food appropriated from the countryside.[81]

In August 1846, Grant had to help get his regiment's supplies taken 100 miles inland up the Rio Grande as Zachary Taylor moved his little army to the village of Camargo, using a patchwork fleet of steamboats to haul most of its supplies. The troops themselves marched the riverbank under cover of darkness to escape the worst of the August heat. At Camargo they left the river and trekked 150 miles southwest to Monterrey, northern Mexico's provincial capital. The city straddled a pass through the Sierra Madre; every step toward it took the Americans deeper into enemy territory. Surely some of them mentally shivered, the stifling Mexican heat notwithstanding, as they remembered accounts of Napoleon's stumbling, frozen, starving retreat from deep inside snowy Russia thirty-four years earlier.

Taylor's force arrived at the outskirts of the heavily defended capital of northern Mexico on September 19, 1846. Again, that era's conventional wisdom held that attacking a dug-in enemy required a numerical advantage of at least three to one. Taylor, having been joined by two regiments of Texas cavalry, could field a total of only some 7,200 soldiers—and, although he could not know the specifics at the time, he faced a Mexican force approaching twice that many. Yet he remained undaunted. He had seen the Mexicans retreat, sometimes in disorder, from Palo Alto, Resaca de la Palma, and Matamoros, and he felt he had momentum.[82]

The problem was where to attack Monterrey. A hill-crowning and moat-encircled citadel, built on the foundation of an unfinished cathedral and girded by earthworks, protected the city of 15,000 people. Referred to by the American troops as the Black Fort, the immense structure's cannon frowned on Taylor's army across an intervening plain. The Santa Catarina River and the mountains protected Monterrey's south side. Two forts, Teneria and Diablo, guarded the east, and the cannon-bristling Bishop's Palace and Fort Soldado, the west. The latter pair of installations overlooked the road—and the Mexicans' supply route—leading southwest to Saltillo farther into the mountains.

Texas Rangers whom Taylor sent forward as scouts came back with word that sandbag-protected soldiers occupied the city's rooftops, while barricades blocked its streets.[83] Assaulting the forbidding Black Fort in Taylor's front would cost too many lives, and the river and the Sierra Madre gave the Americans no good means of getting at Monterrey from the south. Believing Mexican general Pedro de Ampudia would not abandon his fortifications to attack outside them, Taylor divided his force to threaten the Mexican general from the east and west at the same time. The main effort would be to the west, aiming to cut the Saltillo road. A secondary sally would threaten the city's eastern end and keep Mexicans on that side from aiding resistance to the western strike.

Taylor laid these plans on September 20. Grant and the Fourth Infantry took position northeast of the city in a depression that protected Taylor's heavy artillery. From there they watched Brigadier General William J. Worth's division pass through cornfields to the northwest to get to its assault site. Overnight it rained, and in the morning Grant and his regiment, serving with the other division, Brigadier General David Twiggs's, marched forward after Worth was heard attacking.[84]

One company was ordered to remain in the Fourth Infantry camp to guard it and its supplies. Since supply was Grant's special domain, the regimental quartermaster was designated temporary commander of this rear company. The appointment quickly became more temporary than intended. When firing from the Mexicans and the Americans got going with "great fury," Lieutenant Grant abandoned his post. "My curiosity got the better of my judgment, and I mounted a horse and rode to the front to see what was going on," he later remembered. "I had been there but a short time when an order to charge was given, and lacking the moral courage to return to camp—where I had been ordered to stay—I charged with the regiment."[85]

The decision might well have proved fatal. Grant later came to view the charge as "ill-conceived, or badly executed," and little wonder. Because the Fourth Infantry commander, Lieutenant Colonel Garland, led the regiment straight ahead, rather than to the left and out of range of the fire of the Black Fort, his men were subjected to a crossfire from both right and left. They saw nearly a third of their number killed or wounded in "a few minutes." The companion charge of the Third Infantry farther to the left lost virtually nobody.[86]

The Fourth's survivors retreated toward the Third, and Grant was likely lucky not to have been a casualty. As one of a very few mounted men in the charge, he surely made a conspicuous target. In fact, the lieutenant who was regimental adjutant got so winded and weary from running on foot in the charge and retreat that he requested and was given Grant's horse—and, once mounted on it, was quickly killed. Grant, who meanwhile found another horse, became the adjutant's temporary replacement.[87]

The fighting continued as the regulars, dramatically reinforced by volunteers from Tennessee and Mississippi, managed to take Fort Teneria and enter a couple of streets on Monterrey's eastern periphery. The cost of Taylor's operations that day was high: 394 casualties, including 44 officers, most of the loss coming on the city's east edge where Grant was. Taylor soon ordered his men out of the fire from the rooftops and barricades. During the night it rained again, and another soldier found Grant in the dripping gloom of the battlefield. He had come looking for the body of the erstwhile adjutant who had borrowed his horse. He had found the corpse and when discovered was holding the head of a wounded man, giving him a drink of water.[88] Characteristically, no mention of his battlefield search for the adjutant or his care for the wounded man appears in the *Personal Memoirs.*

The battle covered three days. On the second, the Mexicans on Grant's side of Monterrey kept up a steady fire that held Twiggs's men at bay, but to the west Worth captured Fort Soldado and then the Bishop's Palace. After that, the Americans had the city surrounded, and on the second night, September 22, the Mexicans in front of Twiggs withdrew to the center of the city, leaving in Mexican possession only the Black Fort, on its hill a thousand yards north, and the city blocks around the central plaza. On September 23, Worth's and Twiggs's men entered the city and began working toward each other. Worth's made faster progress because his Texans, presumably more familiar with Mexican dwellings, avoided fire from the roofs and the street barricades by battering down the earthen walls between the houses and moving that way, house to house, through their interiors.

On the other side of Monterrey, things were slower and hotter. New acting adjutant Grant was still at the front. When the attack stalled and ammunition ran low a short distance from the city's center, Lieutenant Colonel Garland asked for a volunteer to take a request for more ammunition back to Twiggs or Taylor. It was a tense moment. If the Mexicans had divined the American predicament, they could have attacked and overwhelmed that half of the American assault. Lieutenant Grant, on a mare named Nelly, volunteered to go.

"My ride back was an exposed one," he later remembered. "Before starting, I adjusted myself on the side of my horse furthest from the enemy, and with only one foot holding to the cantle of the saddle, and an arm over the neck of the horse exposed, I started at full run. It was only at street crossings that my horse was under fire, but these I crossed at such a flying rate that generally I was past and under cover of the next block of houses before the enemy fired. I got out without a scratch."[89]

His spectacular gallop, though, proved unnecessary. Before the ammunition he requested could be delivered, the Fourth's infantrymen for whom he had sought it pulled back out of Monterrey. On the west side, however, Worth's men, tunneling from building to building, got close to the plaza at the city's heart. General Ampudia, thinking a smaller perimeter would be easier to defend, had ordered his men to concentrate around the plaza. They complied with chagrin and flagging morale, feeling they had whipped the Americans on the east side of the city but then had to give up ground they had tenaciously held. Taylor had made a mistake by letting his intended diversion on the east side become a heavy, costly assault, but Ampudia made a worse one psychologically: giving up ground his men had defended with valor.

SURRENDER OF MONTERREY AND AFTERMATH

Ampudia was cut off from outside aid and facing ultimate starvation. Some of his ammunition was stored in a cathedral, which the Americans were preparing to shell.[90] He saw little alternative but surrender.

After two meetings with Taylor, he agreed to take his army out of Monterrey, retreat sixty miles southward, and not attempt to fight again for two months. Taylor, with no means of dealing with prisoners numbering in the thousands, allowed the Mexicans to march out under their own officers, retaining their weapons, horses, and six pieces of artillery.[91] Texans desiring revenge for the massacres at the Alamo and Goliad were incensed, as was President Polk, but Taylor's aim was plainly not lost on Grant. His terms to Confederates at Vicksburg in 1863 were not only similar but also inspired by some of the same considerations; the mechanics of imprisoning the large Vicksburg garrison would tie up men and boats needed elsewhere.[92]

The terms Grant gave Lee at Appomattox in 1865 likewise would be almost identical to Taylor's. The same sort of feeling he would show for the Confederate men in ranks at Appomattox was what he professed to feel for the Mexican troops at Monterrey. "My pity was aroused by the sight of the Mexican garrison . . . marching out of town as prisoners," he later remembered. "Many of the prisoners were cavalry, armed with lances, and mounted on miserable little half-starved horses that did not look as if they could carry their riders out of town. The men looked in but little better condition. I thought how little interest the men before me had in the results of the war, and how little knowledge they had of 'what it was all about.'"[93]

George G. Meade, who would be beside Grant at Appomattox and was a fellow member of Taylor's army in 1846, saw method in the magnanimity of the general's terms. He said Taylor had rejected considerations of "military necessity" in favor of "higher and nobler" motives—at least two of the three of which are discernibly Clausewitzian. Their purposes, according to Meade, were first "to grant an opportunity to the two governments to negotiate for peace. Second, to stop the unnecessary effusion of blood, not only of soldiers, but of women and children who were crowded in with the troops. Third, as a tribute of respect to the gallantry of the Mexicans."[94]

Clausewitz, discussing the difference in importance between the physical aspects of war and the moral ones, said "the physical seem little more than the wooden hilt, while the moral factors are the precious metal, the finely-honed blade."[95] General Taylor saw the future political—and moral—advantage in treating the enemy with humanity and respect. An enemy so treated might more easily come to surrender. President Polk the politician, who soon would be coveting a Mexican surrender, did not immediately see the connection.

Probably the next-to-last thing Polk wanted to see respected was Mexican gallantry. Unquestionably, though, the *last* thing he cared to see recognized was Zachary Taylor. The old general was not just a Whig in this deeply polarized era and thus anathema to such Democratic politicians as Polk but also a Whig with the kind of common touch that resonated resoundingly with potential American voters. Old Rough and Ready's victories south of the border were already reaping thick U.S. newspaper headlines, which apparently bothered not only Polk but Taylor himself. "I have a horror of being made a lion of," the general wrote to a friend,[96] voicing a modesty that would someday come to fit General Ulysses S. Grant.

Taylor's "horror" was as unavailing as it would come to be for Grant nearly two decades hence. In midterm elections that quickly followed the late-September capture of Monterrey, the Whigs won both houses of Congress and started ballyhooing Taylor for president. Polk, hoping to hobble the general's incipient candidacy as well as drive deep enough into Mexico to force an end to this increasingly unpopular war, soon sent south a new army commander. This was another Whig but one far stiffer, showier, and less politically attractive than Taylor: the U.S. army's gigantic, spit-and-polish, glory-craving general-in-chief, Winfield Scott. Scott too was known to have designs on the White House, but there was no other choice available to Polk. All the high-ranking generals who were Democrats were volunteers, not regular army.

Lieutenant Grant seems to have been quite conscious of the Washington political machinations, once he learned of them. As he put it in his memoirs, "It was no doubt supposed that Scott's ambition would lead him to slaughter Taylor or destroy his chances for the Presidency, and yet it was hoped that he would not make sufficient capital himself to secure the prize."[97]

But the switch in commanders was not yet known down in Monterrey, where Grant, the Fourth Infantry, and Taylor all marked time until early January. During the interim, Quartermaster Grant established a bakery whose proceeds subsidized a regimental fund for the recreation of the idled warriors. Then they got orders to go back to the mouth of the Rio Grande on the Gulf, which they all took to mean that the war was over and they were going home. President Polk fostered this misapprehension by purposely or unintentionally neglecting to inform General Taylor that Scott was taking over leadership of U.S. troops in Mexico.[98] By this time, Grant's division commander, Twiggs, had been transferred, and the Fourth Infantry at Monterrey was directed to join General Worth on that general's northward march from Saltillo. The trek with Worth to Camargo on the Rio Grande turned out to be a breakneck, frazzling affair that taught Grant, or at least reemphasized to him, another lesson in generalship. "I found General Worth a different man from any I had before served under," he wrote.

> He was nervous, impatient and restless on the march, or when important or responsible duty confronted him. There was not the least reason for haste on the march, for it was known that it would take weeks to assemble shipping enough at the point of our embarkation to carry the army, but General Worth moved his division with a rapidity that would have been commendable had he been going to the relief of a beleaguered garrison. . . . Some commanders can move troops so as to get the maximum distance out of them without fatigue, while others can wear them out in a few days without accomplishing so much. General Worth belonged to this latter class.[99]

At Camargo, troops boarded steamboats and headed back down the Rio Grande. They disembarked at the site of the battle of Palo Alto and soon learned jolting news. The war was not over. General Scott had arrived on the Mexican coast at Point Isabel on December 27, and Grant and his regiment were to join his expedition and sail farther south to Veracruz for a campaign against Mexico City.[100] This information was disquieting, and to no one more than Old Zack himself. It was also utterly illustrative of the truth of Clausewitz's view that wars are at least as shot through with politics as they are with bullets and cannonballs.

Grant was with Taylor when the general learned in a letter from Scott that not only would Taylor's army not be reinforced for further Mexican operations but also almost all of his regulars would be transferred to Scott. Grant later told some Civil War staff members that the morning Taylor learned this and that Scott had ordered him to fall back on the Rio Grande if necessary, the old general "sat down to breakfast in a brown study, poured out a cup of coffee, and instead of putting in the sugar he reached out and got hold of the mustard-pot and stirred half a dozen spoonfuls of its contents into the coffee. He didn't realize what he had done until he took a mouthful, and then he broke out in a towering rage."[101]

During the six weeks required to gather boats enough to carry the army and its supplies to Veracruz, Grant had time to reflect on what he had learned under Taylor. Some of it was new, while other parts doubtless reinforced inclinations he had had since his days staring between Ohio plow handles at the rear ends of horses.

These lessons were crucial. One was that being a great officer did not require a man to view himself as superior to the men he led; to the contrary, he might well benefit from the opposite view. He should trust in them and himself and exercise particular forbearance in leading volunteers, many of whom were half-trained at best. He did not have to try to impress them by making flowery speeches and wearing "every medal the law allowed," as he had seen Scott do in an awe-inspiring visit to the cadets at West Point.[102] Instead, he must be comfortable in his own skin and in whatever uniform he chose to wear. He did need to refuse to be cowed by the foe, numerical disparities notwithstanding. To be worthy of the men he led and the country for which they fought, he should shun retreat and, instead, try to find the best way forward using such means as he had on hand. He should skillfully use such resources as artillery and the psychology of perseverance to equalize his numbers with those of a stronger foe. And he must convey his ideas as simply and plainly as possible to avoid tragic misconstruction in crises.

"Taylor was not a conversationalist," the student would reflect with obvious admiration in the *Personal Memoirs*, "but on paper he could put his meaning so plainly that there could be no mistaking it. He knew how to express what he wanted to say in the fewest well-chosen words, but would not sacrifice meaning to the construction of high-sounding sentences."[103]

Finally, to have a chance at greatness a general must be ever mindful of—but not slavish to—the wishes and moods of his nation's political leadership and its people. There could hardly have been a sterner warning about the dangers of doing otherwise than President Polk's shabby repayment of Old Zack for Mexican victories.

Clausewitz might well have nodded an "I told you so."

"I WILL ACCOMPANY MY REGIMENT IN BATTLE"

Despite Grant's fervent hopes, the war was hardly over. Emphatic proof came in February 1847, when Winfield Scott marched Grant and 13,000 other troops aboard ships and steamed them toward Veracruz 200 miles to the south.

Grant's new commander was the definitive picture of gentlemanly generalship. He was a prosperously born, cultivated, and well-connected Virginian who had attended William & Mary, after which he studied law in his hometown, Petersburg. President Jefferson in 1812 appointed him an army officer, and he rose fast.[104] A comparative giant for his time at six-foot-five, he was brevetted a brigadier general by the time of his wounding in the 1814 battle of Lundy's Lane on the Niagara frontier, which put him on the level of fame that Andrew Jackson attained at New Orleans months later. Jominian before knowing there was a Jomini (just as Grant would become Clausewitzian before knowing—if he ever did—that there was a Clausewitz), Scott "clearly felt most at home with a small professional army," writes military historian Russell F. Weigley. "In strategy he was at his best," Weigley adds, "in a war of limited objectives which could be pursued by maneuver and occupation of territory rather than by ruthless destruction."

> The pre-Napoleonic, eighteenth century style [of war was] most congenial to him. He [would] conduct . . . the [Mexican] campaign with strict regard for the rights of the citizens of the invaded territories, with every effort to confine bloodshed and suffering to the enemy's armed forces and to avoid inflicting them on civilians. He [would] impose . . . stringent regulations to compel orderly conduct from his soldiers in their dealings with the Mexican populace and to confine the opportunities for friction to the minimum necessary for the sustenance of his army and the morale of his troops. . . . Throughout his campaign he [would] avoid . . . all-out battle whenever it was possible to do so and husband . . . lives by substituting maneuver for combat with all the frugality of a general of the *ancien regime*.[105]

He exhibited these penchants, as well as a profound talent for planning, almost immediately. Scott's Veracruz-bound armada gathered for its final rendezvous in a harbor seventeen miles beyond the target. There, in early March, Grant and other officers heard that Scott somehow had acquired a Santa Anna battle report claiming the Mexicans had whipped Taylor's motley collection of mostly rookie volunteers on February 22–23 at Buena Vista, near Saltillo southwest of Monterrey. Americans greeted this adverse news with skepticism. Not only was it well known that Santa Anna's word was all but worthless, but the report itself admitted that the Mexicans had retired from the battlefield.[106]

On March 9 Scott meticulously launched the largest amphibious assault in American military history up to that time, only to have it be dwarfed sixteen years later by Grant's crossing of the Mississippi River to open the climactic phase of the Vicksburg campaign. Now Scott sent Worth's 4,500-man division splashing out of specially built landing craft onto a beach three miles from Veracruz—and found the Mexicans did not attempt to defend the shore because their commander was saving his 5,000-man garrison for defense of the city.[107] Scott, too, was frugal with his numbers. Unwilling to assault the heavily defended place and lose precious troops needed for his impending drive on Mexico City, he initiated a siege and was heartened on March 15 by new details of the Buena Vista battle. Old Zack, instead of retiring to the Rio Grande with the 6,000 mostly volunteers Scott had left to him, had taken on 17,000 Mexican regulars and smashed them. The casualty figures were 4,000 Mexicans compared with 600 Americans.[108] Taylor's unsought future election to the White House thereby became a virtual certainty.

Meanwhile, the likelihood of Santa Anna arriving to try to raise Scott's Veracruz siege had obviously decreased. Scott proceeded to cut off everything flowing into Veracruz, including a vital aqueduct, and emplaced cannon to batter the city. He wanted a quick surrender, and for an urgent reason: the Mexican coast's lethal yellow fever season was to start on May 1. By then Scott wanted to have marched his men into the higher and healthier Mexican interior.

He brought up more heavy guns and on March 23 sent a surrender demand to the Mexicans. On the twenty-fifth, consuls from Britain, France, and Prussia asked Scott to suspend his cannonading long enough for the city's women and children to be evacuated. Scott said no. The cannon having opened a considerable hole in the city wall,[109] the Mexican commander asked for terms. On the twenty-ninth, in a formal ceremony repeating Taylor's leniency at Monterrey, a resplendently uniformed Scott allowed the 5,000-man Mexican garrison to march out, stack muskets, and go to their homes. He also issued orders that residents of Veracruz, as well as their property and churches, were not to be damaged.

The siege had cost the Mexicans 1,100 casualties, the Americans just 17 killed and 60 wounded.[110] Scott now was free to ready his invasion. Yet prestigious military observers in both the New and Old Worlds—including the British Empire's Duke of Wellington—would forecast doom as the scheme unfolded. The plan was to keep all of Scott's troops with him in striking out for Mexico City, rather than siphoning off significant numbers of them in dribs and drabs to maintain and guard a supply line back to the coast. As the campaign proceeded, Wellington would declare Scott "lost. He cannot capture Mexico City and he cannot fall back upon his base."[111]

But Scott knew his plan had a New World military precedent. Three centuries earlier, the victorious Spaniard Hernán Cortés had taken virtually the same route to Mexico City that Scott intended to follow. Many enlistments in the little American army were soon to expire, but Scott knew that the Mexican military had been diminished and disheartened by the U.S. victories at Buena Vista and Veracruz. Within barely more than a month the two battles had cost the Mexicans more than 5,000 casualties, not counting another 5,000 captives and nearly 400 cannon at Veracruz. Santa Anna would need time to recover, days that Scott could use to refill his ranks and march toward Mexico City.[112]

Scott wasted little time in putting the Gulf Coast behind him—and, through Colonel Garland, burdening the Fourth Infantry's temporary quartermaster with his hardest job yet. The root of the difficulty was underfoot. Grant had to get the regiment's wagons, animals, and supplies across ten ankle-deep miles of sand before hitting the National Road. The expedition began on April 13 in intense heat, which worsened the ordeal. When horses gave out, Grant had to have men pull his wagons, and when the men went down with heatstroke, he had to replace them with others and meanwhile see that physicians cared for the sickened in patches of shade where they awaited supply wagons returning to the coast. Six of those so afflicted died.

Grant apparently did his job on that hellish day as well as any man could have, because it turned out not to be thankless. On April 14 Colonel Garland informed the hitherto-temporary quartermaster that his position from then on would be permanent.[113]

Scott's first objective, sixty miles rising west of Veracruz, was Jalapa. It graced a fertile and verdant region 8,000 feet above sea level, where the American troops could live healthily and well off the land. But to get there Scott had to get them past the forbidding pass at Cerro Gordo, which Grant remembered vividly in his *Personal Memoirs*. "Cerro Gordo is one of the higher spurs of the mountains some twelve to fifteen miles east of Jalapa," he recalled, "and Santa Anna had selected this point as the easiest to defend against an invading army. The road, said to have been built by Cortez [*sic*], zig-zags around the mountain-side and was defended at every turn by artillery. On either side were deep chasms or mountain walls. A direct attack along the road was an impossibility. A flank movement seemed equally impossible."[114]

On such terrain, a monumental surprise was as obviously called for as it was improbable. Clausewitz wrote that "by its very nature"—since it is an integral aim of warfare, and thus always expected—"surprise can rarely be outstandingly successful."[115] Cerro Gordo, thanks to Scott and his exceptional employment of his engineer staff, was one of the rare contrary instances.

Twiggs's division was Scott's vanguard, and First Lieutenant P. G. T. Beauregard had charge of engineers scouting Twiggs's front. A subordinate lieutenant showed Beauregard a path he had found leading toward the Mexican left, around the heavily guarded pass, and Beauregard followed it all the way to the summit of a slightly smaller hill just to the right of Cerro Gordo. Scott, arriving on the field the next day and recognizing the high and certain cost of assaulting the pass, ordered another engineer, Captain Robert E. Lee, to reconnoiter Beauregard's route. Lee in intrepid fashion did so and went farther—all the way to the Mexican rear, where he had to lie for several hours amid insect stings near a spring frequented by Mexican soldiers.[116] Under cover of darkness over two nights, Lee and subordinate fellow West Point–trained engineers sufficiently widened this precipitous and strenuous trail to accommodate troops. "This was accomplished," Grant later wrote, "without the knowledge of Santa Anna and his army and over ground where he supposed it impossible."[117]

Worth's division had brought up the rear of the march from Veracruz, so Grant could do little at Cerro Gordo except look on with wonder. While Lee and his crew were at work, Scott had other engineers direct the hauling of cannon by ropes up cliffs to points where they could enfilade Mexican gunners guarding the pass. Then on the morning of April 18 he sent Tennessee general Gideon Pillow's volunteers forward to distract Santa Anna's 9,000 dug-in Mexicans while Twiggs's division quietly climbed Lee's new "road" around the enemy left and attacked the Mexicans' flank and rear. Pillow, a highly conceited Tennessee attorney who had done much to get Polk his presidential nomination, took the wrong route to his objective, got too close to the Mexican guns, and left the field mid-battle with a minor wound while his men bled and died their way through heavy fire because of his mistake. Grant agonized in his position of inactivity. In a letter to an unknown correspondent, he wrote,

> While it was a most inspiring sight, it was a painful one to me. I stood there watching the brigade slowly climbing those ragged heights, each minute nearer and nearer the works of the enemy with our missiles flying over their heads while white puffs of smoke spitefully flashed out in rapid succession along the enemy's line and I knew that every discharge sent death into our ranks. As our men finally swept over and into the works, my heart was sad at the fate that held me from sharing in the brave and brilliant assault.[118]

The inauthentic-sounding words notwithstanding, Grant proved in black and white that he was insistent on experiencing, whenever possible, the same combat his fellow soldiers faced. Around this time he tried again to resign his quartermaster post. One wonders if one of his peers or superiors had complained about his habit of galloping away from his job into battle at every chance, because his attempted resignation was accompanied by a statement saying he was "amenable to court-martial should any loss occur to the public property in my charge by reason of my absence while in action." He complained of unfairness in the army's seeming ultimatum that the only way he could rid himself of his quartermaster duties was to resign from the army itself. He insisted that he "*must* and *will* accompany my regiment in battle." Again, though, his superiors rejected his resignation.[119]

He was plainly outraged. And it was not the outrage of a high-born gentleman demanding the privilege of fighting and bleeding in furtherance of future promotion and political ambition. Rather, it was that of a still young man who almost religiously disliked war and its suffering but was resolved to do his duty in it, if not to the country then to something even higher. He was determined to endure the dangers the other troops had to. There is no indication that he lusted after higher rank, and if he did so to any extent at all it was probably to better care for the family he hoped to start with his long-dreamed-of marriage. Grant was the rare army officer who did not plot for promotion. This trait was possibly rooted in his mother's piety and an accompanying skeptical view of worldly advancement.

The fighting at Cerro Gordo was over by 10:00 A.M., delivering to Scott some 3,000 captives, 43 cannon, and 5,000 muskets. The Mexicans had sustained between 1,000 and 1,200 casualties, while the Americans lost 63 killed and 368 wounded.[120] The battle's careful planning helped Grant realize that Scott, dubbed "Old Fuss and Feathers" because of his maximally grand style of dress and insistence on military exactitude, was as worthy of soldiers' admiration as "Old Rough and Ready" despite being Taylor's virtual opposite. Grant wrote home that Scott's victory at Cerro Gordo was "almost equal to Bonaparte Crossing the Alps" in snow to defeat the Austrians at Marengo in 1800.[121]

REACHING MEXICO CITY'S EDGE— AND "SPECIAL DISTINCTION"

Winfield Scott covered himself in pomp and plumage, yes, and used majestic language in his egotistical orders and proclamations, but underneath the vainglory he was a much more exact and exacting chief than Taylor. His discipline was tighter, his reconnaissance rarely missed much, and his hoarding of lives, so precious to achieving his goals while isolated with a small force in a far country, was generally diligent. By Scott's approach to both Veracruz and Cerro Gordo, Grant had been reminded that only a masochist attacks an entrenched, better-positioned, and ready foe if there is an alternative.

From Cerro Gordo, Scott hurried most of his troops on to beautiful, temperate Jalapa. Then he awaited replacements after considerately starting his 3,000 retiring enlistees homeward on May 6, before the yellow fever season could settle into Veracruz.[122] On that same day, he sent Worth's (and thus Grant's) division—half of the 7,000 men Scott had left—sixty miles ahead to the environs of Puebla, another beautiful city and one of Mexico's largest, home to 50,000 people. Knowing Santa Anna's army to have been whipped and scattered at Cerro Gordo, Scott soon brought many more troops forward from Jalapa. He then hunkered down in Puebla—for three months, it turned out—waiting for replacements of the 3,000 whose enlistments had expired and dealing with myriad other problems. These included marauding guerrillas, increasing malaise fomented by the jumpy and high-strung Worth, restraint of his own jealous ego to accommodate the arrival of Polk emissary to Mexico Nicholas Trist, and uncomfortable dealing with what turned out to be an abortive Santa Anna solicitation of a million-dollar bribe to end the war.[123]

The eventual arrival of new troops—the awaited replacements plus some reinforcements initially sent elsewhere—brought the total U.S. force under Scott's command to 14,000, of whom more than 3,000 were down with mostly tropical illnesses. The new units' arrival had been delayed because Polk, who was at least as interested in acquiring California as Texas, was supplying an army headed for the Pacific coast. The president also diverted Scott's original replacements to Taylor, who was still near the Buena Vista battlefield deep in northern Mexico and thought to be in worse danger. By the time Scott could get going again, it was August.

Just one highway departed Puebla toward Mexico City. After leaving the mountains it descended into what was called the Valley of Mexico, where it branched into three smaller roads to the Mexican capital. Each made its way along an elevated causeway between lakes, swamps, and beds of hardened volcanic lava sharp enough to cut troops' feet.[124] Ten miles east of the city, Santa Anna had entrenched 7,000 troops in a strong position high on a hill, El Peñon, to meet the American invaders. Scott refused to accommodate the Mexican. The U.S. commander marched around El Peñon.[125]

The road Scott selected to the Mexican capital, though, was not the one Grant would have chosen. Grant's route, he said in a letter home, would have been to swing around to come in from the north, where Grant thought the ground was harder underfoot and the city's defenses weaker.[126] He later wrote a friend that he had "communicated the knowledge I had acquired" from a map and "Mexican scouts in our camp, and others I met at Puebla who were familiar with the ground, to such of my superiors as . . . seemed proper, but I do not know whether General Scott was put in possession of the information."[127]

If Scott *was* given Grant's idea, he was not sufficiently impressed to take it to heart. Instead, he approached Mexico City from due south, passing through the little town of San Agustín. From there, he sent Worth's division north on a road to demonstrate at another little town, enemy-occupied San Antonio, on the eastern side of a three-mile-wide lava bed called the Pedregal. He meanwhile dispatched Twiggs's division westward around the southern side of the Pedregal to roll up what Scott thought was the lightly defended Mexican right wing at a town Scott's map mistakenly designated as Contreras. The "Contreras" Scott targeted was actually an extensive farm called Padierna. On the morning of August 20, fighting broke out there and got hot.

Scott, not having anticipated heavy Mexican resistance at "Contreras,"[128] decided he could meanwhile employ a lesser flanking move to eject the Mexicans from San Antonio. In addition to directing Twiggs's wider route around the all-but-impassable Pedregal, he sent Grant's unit on an arduous trek through the edge of it. If the tactic succeeded, Scott believed, General Worth should be able to chase the Mexican retreat from San Antonio northward to another town, Churubusco, just beyond which lay the Churubusco River and Mexico City. Grant, from an elevated lava rock in the Pedregal, could do nothing but watch as Twiggs's men fought the battle of "Contreras" at the Padierna farm and then pursued the defeated Mexicans around the western side of the Pedregal on a road that rejoined the San Antonio thoroughfare just beyond Churubusco.

"Contreras" turned out to be only half of a larger battle whose remainder occurred a few hours later at Churubusco. There Worth's men, after chasing the outflanked Mexicans out of San Antonio, had to capture a heavily defended convent as well as fortifications protecting a bridge over the Churubusco River. By day's end, Scott would kill, wound, or capture more than 5,000 Mexicans—but would have to report his own loss at 1,053, including 139 killed.[129] It was a costly victory, particularly for a remote army with no supply line and no prospect of timely reinforcement.

Among the fortunate survivors, though, résumés had been made or padded, especially officers'. But not Grant's. Despite having taken a combative part whenever the chance had materialized for more than a year, his combat affinity had seemingly gone all but unnoticed. When a superior undertook to praise by name the performance of each officer of the Fourth Infantry following "Contreras" and Churubusco, the final entry was about as paltry approbation as could be had: "And Lieutenant Grant, regimental quartermaster, who was usefully employed in his appropriate duties."[130] Thirty-four members of Grant's West Point class who were still alive and in the army included six captains, nineteen first lieutenants (among them his future brother-in-law Fred Dent), and nine second lieutenants. Grant was one of the nine.

The twenty-five-year-old westerner who had won such little notice since his father sent him east to West Point eight years earlier had had no ambition or expectation of becoming a general. Good thing, too, because he was well on a course not to. This time, even accustomed as he had been to lack of recognition, he may have been a bit resentful. He hints as much in a passage in his *Personal Memoirs*: "I had gone into the battle of Palo Alto in May 1846 a second lieutenant, and I entered the city of Mexico sixteen months later with the same rank, after having been in all the engagements possible for any one man and in a regiment that lost more officers during the war than it ever had present at any one engagement." Grant often employed wryly humorous self-effacement to refer to himself, but this sentence has a bitter whiff to it, as if this time he held his superiors, rather than himself, more responsible for the lack of notice given his extracurricular combat contributions. If so, he relieved the moment nicely with grim gallows humor in the three sentences immediately following. "My regiment lost four commissioned officers, all senior to me, by steamboat explosions during the Mexican war," he wrote. "The Mexicans were not so discriminating. They sometimes picked off my juniors."[131]

If he was going to advance in rank at all, he would have to do it soon. The capture of Mexico City would doubtless herald the end of the war. But last-minute opportunities were at hand . . . perhaps. Before Grant and the rest of Worth's division could enter Mexico City, it would turn out, they would have to first get past a fortified mill called Molino del Rey, then a high hill occupied by a castle called Chapultepec, and finally a couple of

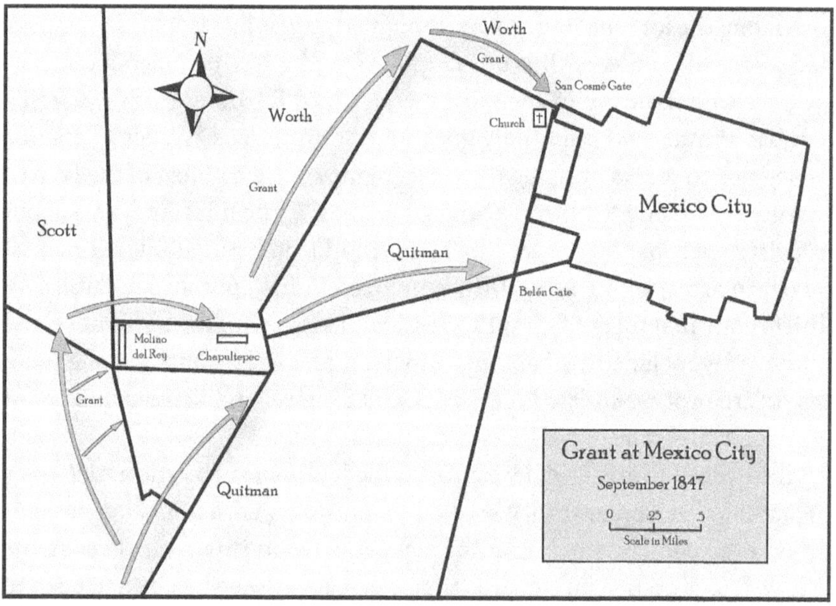

Lieutenant Grant, having participated in every Mexican War battle it was possible for one man to be in, finally won the approbation of superiors in the climactic conquest of the Mexican capital. He distinguished himself in the fighting at Molino del Rey and the city's San Cosmé gate.

city gates called San Cosmé and Belén, not to mention the Mexican soldiers waiting behind those gates.

They would have to do all that, that is, if peace had not already broken out. The latter was a strong possibility. Scott believed his victories at "Contreras" and Churubusco might be sufficient to take the fight out of the Mexicans. He also feared that immediately pushing into Mexico's capital might harden national resistance to a point where its people might never want to quit fighting. So when prominent Mexican and international officials came to him on August 21 to plead for a cease-fire and to assure him that Santa Anna, too, wanted it, Scott—nearly as eager for peace as President Polk—took it upon himself to formally request an armistice from Santa Anna. "Too much blood has already been shed in this unnatural war between the two great Republics of this Continent," he wrote in his message.[132]

Many U.S. troops believed Scott was squandering momentum they had accrued at "Contreras" and Churubusco—momentum they would have to regain at expensive human cost if permanent peace did not result. Nevertheless, negotiators for both sides met from late August into early September, to no avail. When Santa Anna stopped allowing U.S. quartermasters to buy food in the city, as the armistice had sanctioned, and was discovered to be enhancing the city's defenses, which the armistice forbade, Scott castigated the broken agreement and abandoned the armistice.[133]

Grant likely agreed with the men in ranks who felt the armistice was nothing but a postponement and ramping-up of suffering to come. So he may have learned something from Scott's disappointment at the gates of Mexico City, or what was learnable there may already have been part of his nature. During the Civil War—from Belmont, Missouri, in 1861 to Appomattox, Virginia, in 1865—his obsession was to never stop, never pause, never give the enemy a chance to rest and recoup. Destroy him.

Meanwhile, the Mexican War resumed. As was his wont, Scott went about trying to find and take the safest route into the capital. The Mexicans were seen reinforcing troops and strengthening fortifications at the gate to the city entered by the San Antonio road from Churubusco, so Scott veered to his left and came at the target from the west instead of the south. Also influencing this decision was information that to the left the Mexicans were melting down church bells and turning them into cannon in the long adjoining buildings of the huge mill, Molino del Rey. The mill was the rear, lower anchor of the hilltop Chapultepec fortress complex. Half a mile to the mill's front stood Chapultepec proper, which was Mexico's military academy, a former royal residence. From 200 feet above, it overlooked roads leading to the San Cosmé and Belén gates to the city.

To capitalize on the church bell intelligence and stop the cannon making, Scott hastily ordered an assault on the mill, which he thought was lightly defended. It was not. It and its environs were populated by probably 10,000 Mexican riflemen and 4,000 cavalry, as Grant himself soon discovered. His division commander, General Worth, sent the whole unit forward before dawn of September 8 behind a puny bombardment of just ten cannon shots, which Worth perhaps rushed in his haste to ply the gloried bayonet. Whatever his aim, he then ordered forward the first 500 of his men. They were swiftly shot to pieces by Mexican cannon and musket fire, 10 of their 13 officers and half of the men going down. A captain, sobbing, jabbed a finger toward the meager remains of his regiment and told an arriving officer, "There's the Fifth."[134]

Grant and the Fourth had been to the right as Worth dispatched the Fifth into the inferno. The Fourth then surged forward behind a battery. Enemy fire quickly cut down the artillery horses. The cannon had to be pulled a hundred yards farther by man rather than beast. But the cannon began pouring canister into the mill buildings and trenches fronting them, and the Fourth got farther than the Fifth. Grant saw Fred Dent, his fiancée's brother, dash in behind four companies that overran a Mexican battery and sweep on through a gate into the buildings. Grant and the vanguard of the Fourth were following so closely that he was one of the first inside the mill. Seeing the Mexican defenders begin to run away and up the hill toward Chapultepec proper and hoping to capture some of them, Grant ran out behind the mill buildings. Mexicans were still on the roof, and he commandeered a few soldiers to help him go after them. He spied a nearby farm cart, leaned it against the wall of the building with its handle shafts upward, and climbed it like a ladder onto the roof. There, as at Resaca de la Palma, he discovered that the enemy he had seen up there had already been captured—by a lone private who, he humorously says in the *Personal Memoirs*, had them "surrounded." He took over for the private and disarmed the captives and then had his little makeshift squad wreck the enemy muskets by bashing them against the wall before throwing them off the roof.[135]

Molino del Rey was a bloodbath. A total of 758 Americans were killed or wounded in an operation that many participating U.S. troops believed could have been accomplished by artillery bombardment alone, had the glory-hungry Worth not been so eager to see his own men charge. No molds for casting cannon were found inside the mill, and less than a mile in the distance the heights of Chapultepec remained unconquered. "A few more such victories and this army would be destroyed," one officer wrote in his diary.[136]

Another officer, possibly the erratic Worth, halted the Americans' pursuit of the fleeing Mexicans—wrongly, Grant appeared to believe. But Grant refused to fault his superiors. "Had this victory been followed up promptly," he later wrote,

> no doubt Americans and Mexicans would have gone over the defences of Chapultepec so near together that the place would have fallen into our hands without further loss. The defenders of the works could not have fired upon us without endangering their own men. This [pursuit] was not done, and five days later more valuable lives were sacrificed to carry works which had been so nearly in our possession on the 8th. I do not criticize the failure of the troops to capture Chapultepec at this time. The result that followed the first assault could not possibly have been foreseen, and to profit by the unexpected advantage, the commanding general must have been on the spot and given the necessary instructions at the moment, or the troops must have kept on without orders.[137]

Grant likely wrote this passage in 1884, surely recalling in the process how his own army had "kept on without orders" at Chattanooga twenty-one years earlier. There, he had ordered the taking of Confederate trenches at the foot of Missionary Ridge to discourage Confederate reinforcement of troops fighting Major General William T. Sherman, whose men were attacking from the left end of the ridge. But in taking those trenches his own troops put themselves under heavy fire from Confederates above them on the ridge. With their only alternatives being advance or retreat, they swept on up the mountainside on the heels of the retiring Confederates. The Southerners above could not fire on Grant's Union troops "without endangering their own men," and the unordered Federal onrush gave Grant one of his most improbable victories.[138]

The incident involving the "surrounded" Mexican captives on the mill roof at Molino del Rey is the only personal "exploit" Grant recalls of that battle in the *Personal Memoirs*, but there obviously were others. In 1864 Winfield Scott, when asked if he remembered Grant from the Mexican War, said that he did, adding that Grant had "attained special distinction" at the mill. Further, superiors soon officially lauded Grant "for gallant and meritorious conduct at the battle of Molino del Rey." James Longstreet later said that he had had occasion to see his West Point schoolmate under fire in the battle and had been impressed with his "superb courage and coolness" in combat.[139]

What Grant also did during the battle and in its aftermath seems notable, too. As had happened at Monterrey and likely at other battles in Mexico, instead of surrendering to the weariness of battlefield adrenaline-drain after the fighting, this officer, who had a deep aversion to the sight of blood, nonetheless repeatedly sought its company. As the battle raged, Grant saw and aided a wounded Fred Dent, plying him with water from his canteen and dragging him to a place where medical personnel would see him. After the fighting had ceased, according to another soldier, Grant was so solicitous about other wounded troops that he was described as no less than a "ministering angel" with a "kind heart."[140]

Even his superiors were finally, despite the slightness of his pedigree, taking more notice. They had to. As previously noted, he was serving, as he himself put it, "in a regiment that lost more officers during the war than it ever had present at any one engagement."[141] He was one of the handful left unhurt.

CHURCH YIELDS KEY TO THE CITY—AND A BREVET

Five days after Molino del Rey, to clear the approaches to Mexico City's western gates, Winfield Scott went after Chapultepec.

It was an unnecessary operation, in Grant's view. He believed the western gate of the city, San Cosmé, could be reached in a less bloody fashion by swinging wide westward around the hill-crowning castle. This would have outflanked the castle and forced its defenders to surrender or abandon it and make a fighting retreat to the city.[142] Scott, though, had been told that Chapultepec's guns could cover the city's whole northwest exurbs, and he also feared that if the fortress were left undisturbed in his wake, the U.S. forces would be vulnerable to assault from the rear.[143]

He first loosed a daylong artillery barrage on September 12 to soften the defense of the fortress. The American shells only minimally damaged the thick walls but saw better success on the tile roofs. Scott continued the barrage the next day from dawn until 8:00 A.M. and then sent his infantry forward—at first without vital scaling ladders, which seem to have been forgotten by Grant's least-respected opponent of future years, Major General of Volunteers Gideon Pillow. The Mexicans' fire, an element of which struck Pillow in the foot, was so heavy that it panicked the general into calling for reinforcements. But when the ladder deficiency was corrected, the Americans went up the hill and over the towering walls. Before 10:00 A.M. they had raised the Stars and Stripes on the Chapultepec flagstaff.[144]

Worth's division was on the right, assigned to aim for the ultimate goal two miles beyond: the San Cosmé gate. Worth's men reached the northeast corner of the Chapultepec complex just as Mexican defenders were retiring from it toward the city. The Americans fired some shots at the retreating foe[145] and continued north toward where their elevated road, after proceeding almost due north and skirting a marshy area for more than a mile, intersected another, shorter road whose right-hand fork led to the gate.

At the intersection, the new road not only took a sharp right turn toward the gate but also toward cannon fire protecting it. Before the attackers could even reach the turn, other Mexican guns overlooking the junction started making forward progress difficult. An aqueduct supported by ten-foot-tall masonry arches, which helped supply the capital's water, ran down the center of the highway, and Garland's—that is, Grant's—brigade of the advancing Fourth Infantry took cover behind the arches, dodging from one to another as they moved up. Canister from the Mexican guns at the turn, as well as bullets from snipers on surrounding housetops, slowed the progress of all of Garland's men except Grant. He and a trio of other lieutenants were in the vanguard, and the other three, including the one in command, were content to let the enemy fire stop them and wait for Garland to bring up the main force.

Not Grant. The wilderness farm-boy lieutenant was not good at waiting when there was work to do—or anytime, really. Here, in a reflex that appears to have been habitual, he saw something that needed doing and set about getting it done. Crossing the causeway alone, he continued to the left and found a route that took him to a portion of the San Cosmé road running behind the Mexican battery guarding the intersection. Then he returned to the aqueduct arches and said that if a dozen men would volunteer to follow him, they could compromise the battery so that the rest of the party could charge and take it. The requested volunteers came forward. In short order, in the company of about a hundred other Americans who joined them on the way, Grant and his volunteers neutralized the Mexican position. Their move outflanked and dislodged the defenders, whom Grant's party, along with the Americans at the aqueduct, chased to a barricade halfway down the San Cosmé road.

Beyond the barricade stood the gate, protected by a redoubt, two cannon, and thousands of Mexicans. The Americans pursued the Mexicans routed from the intersection and crossed the barricade, but the generals then pulled them back to join some howitzers for a main attack on the gate. To clear the road for this attack, the first thing they had to do was retake the barricade, which they did. Grant and another lieutenant were the first men over it. Then came another pause as commanders brought up more guns to train on the gate.[146]

Once again, Grant did not wait. He set off, looking this time for a way to outflank the San Cosmé gate. He crossed to the right of the road and stole past houses, through fields and woods. Eventually, at a distance off to his left, he saw the gate—and a church that appeared to overlook the area in its rear. He hurried back to get his little party again and, with a howitzer in tow, returned to the San Cosmé church. He directed the men to take the howitzer apart, carry its pieces to the belfry, reassemble them, and open up on the thousands of Mexicans manning the gate. The unexpected cannonade from hardly 300 yards to a rear flank "created great confusion" among the foes and apparently rattled them. "Why they did not send out a small party and capture us, I do not know," Grant wrote later. "We had no infantry or other defences besides our one gun."[147]

Worth, from his position with the Americans in front of the gate, saw the destruction being wrought by the Grant-bossed bell tower gun. After inquiring as to who commanded it, the general sent for Grant, who at first told the messenger he was busy. He went along, though, when the officer—John Pemberton, who sixteen years later would surrender Vicksburg to him—insisted. Peeved, Grant worried that he "might be under arrest." Instead, Worth highly commended him, told him that "every shot was effective," and sent him back to the belfry in charge of a captain who commanded another howitzer. Worth expected Grant to take along the captain's howitzer, too, but he did not, since the belfry had no room for it. Shrewdly, though, he did not mention that fact to the touchy Worth ("he probably would have looked upon such a statement as a contradiction from a second lieutenant").[148] Another American gun began firing from a rooftop on the opposite side of the road from the church. Then a horse-drawn cannon directly in front of the gate opened up, too. Other Americans who had tunneled through the houses came out on more rooftops, and the Mexicans began a fighting retreat from the gate. That night, American troops slept in houses inside the gate, while others, including Grant, kept tunneling so as to be able to outflank more street barricades in the morning.[149]

Unnecessarily, it turned out. Mexico City itself was now breached at both the San Cosmé and the Belén gates, and all organized fighting between Americans and Mexicans abruptly ceased. Santa Anna, implored by the capital's residents, swiftly withdrew his troops to prevent further municipal destruction. The next morning, September 14, Colonel Garland led the brigade's triumphal advance to the interior of the city—until guerrilla sniper fire cut him down. A first lieutenant in the Fourth Infantry named Sidney Smith suffered the same fate, except that whereas Garland recovered, Smith died two days later. Grant was quickly promoted to replace him.[150] At the same time, at the recommendation of General Worth he was brevetted captain for his work under fire at the San Cosmé gate.[151]

Thus on the war's final day of combat, after almost a year and a half of having participated to varying degrees in virtually all of the fighting in Mexico, Grant made his first, sudden, and dramatic advancement in rank.

REFLECTIONS ON VICTORY AND LEARNED LESSONS

Grant would remain in Mexico ten more months. Negotiations for the end of hostilities dragged on to an ignominious end for the Mexicans.

Grant had time not only to develop a love for Mexico but also to begin seriously pondering a future in this profession on whose ladder of success he had at the very conclusion of active fighting climbed a couple of rungs. There was time, too, to reflect on the abundance of knowledge he had accumulated in furtherance of that future.

Most important for his performance in the Civil War—and for its effect on America then, later, and now—was a sense of the grandeur of vision and matching fearlessness implicit in the ambitious aims of the Taylor and Scott campaigns. To attack and capture Monterrey, Zachary Taylor had taken his troops up the Rio Grande some distance before cutting loose from his base at Camargo and plunging 150 miles into the interior of hostile Mexico. Similarly, Scott followed by pushing nearly 250 miles from Veracruz into unfriendly territory to take Mexico City. Both generals were vastly outnumbered, yet each hesitated barely long enough to make the necessary tactical plans.

To a young officer paying attention and having a fidgety predilection to advance—as Grant did—these actions provided unforgettable evidence that taking the risk to lunge into unwelcoming regions could reap great rewards. The very magnitude of these undertakings also encouraged a widening of the perceptive student's vision and urged him to examine the whole of the map before him, not just the small sector immediately in front.

In the Civil War, such memories of aggressiveness doubtless had a significant effect on Grant, accentuating the restlessness that from boyhood had kept urging him to look farther down every road. Such considerations—or something—made him almost eager to challenge the unknown, and with workmanlike tenacity he did so again and again at Belmont, Fort Henry, Fort Donelson, Vicksburg, Chattanooga, and eastern Virginia. Grant possessed a farmer's consciousness of the urgency of getting jobs done in the proper season, and the examples of the Taylor and Scott campaigns helped give him the breadth of vision to do it. They also led him to encourage similar jump-offs into the unknown by his friend Sherman.

This breadth of vision, as evident as it would seem to have been in the Mexican campaigns, turned out to be the rarest of qualities among Civil War generals on either side. Perhaps the tenets of Jomini, in which so many of them were steeped, tended to limit their preoccupation to details rather than encouraged the wider view. For whatever reason, even the great Lee did not seem to have this sense of the true scope of the struggle. Time and again, he rejected calls to give his attention to more than his native eastern Virginia. In contrast, Grant—from Fort Donelson forward—never seemed to forget that the war was a whole encompassing wherever Confederates were concentrated.

Also, the experience of more or less abandoning supply lines so as to retain all of his troops (rather than sapping strength by leaving detachments behind to guard important points along the way) suggested to Grant the efficacy of not only living off the country he was passing through but also, as enmities in the Civil War grew bitterer, of denying the enemy the agricultural and industrial fruits of the country by destroying them. Grant began to actively advocate this in earnest at Jackson, Mississippi, during the Vicksburg campaign when he and Sherman entered the state's capital in 1863 and discovered a factory manufacturing Confederate uniforms. He sent the mostly female workers home with all the cloth they could carry and then directed Sherman to burn the plant.[152] Soon after the capitulation of Vicksburg, he ordered Sherman to march from the surrendered city to the Mississippi rail hub at Meridian, destroying the rails and all rolling stock as well as anything else of potential use to the Confederates.[153] This order was the obvious model for Sherman's later, fierier march from Atlanta to Charleston.

The easiest Mexican War lessons, though, were the elemental ones, commonsense matters of military course, such as, in the words of Clausewitz, the scent of cook fires "in the enemy camp at unusual times" suggest "that he is about to move," and "intentional exposure of troops in combat indicates a feint." Clausewitz also cited fundamental tactical principles: "Except in emergencies, cavalry is not to be used against unbroken infantry; firearms should not be used until the enemy is within effective range; in combat, as many troops as possible should be preserved for the final phase."[154] Such battlefield lessons were hard to miss. Mexican combat also quickly taught American officers that the new, fast, horse-drawn, and horse-killing light artillery was lethal to cavalry and that the bayonet could carry trenches manned by half-hearted Mexican soldiers, men who were all but enslaved in a society that gave them little to fight for.[155]

A number of more specific lessons were available, too, from the many moments Grant had spent in harm's way. From the first—for example, the crossing of the Little Colorado River on the initial march to the Rio Grande, when fighting was still only in prospect—bugle calls from the Mexicans gave the erroneous "impression there was a large number of them and that if [Mexican troops] were [present] in proportion to the noise, they were sufficient to devour General Taylor and his army."[156] Grant here also had to deal for the first time with the probability of imminent physical danger, and Taylor's dismissal of Mexican threats, bugled or written, and his determination to drive straight ahead surely reassured the young lieutenant. So must have the Mexican retreat.

At Palo Alto, Grant came closer to war's essence, seeing men mangled gruesomely near him, while Taylor vanquished the foe primarily with superior artillery. The next day, at Resaca de la Palma, Grant finally got into full combat, leading men in a charge and learning that for him, as he informed Julia in one of his myriad letters, flying bullets had "less horror" in actuality than in anticipation. He saw Taylor throw most of his 1,700 men onto a small sector of Santa Anna's mile-long, 6,000-man line and overwhelm the attack site—another lesson, this one in elemental tactics.

In contrast, while idling at Matamoros he also learned the complex, vexing, and danger-filled problems associated with controlling men amid an enemy population. But the lull there following the battles of Palo Alto and Resaca de la Palma also afforded time for other reflections on the importance of good officering. Many of the enemy officers exemplified how not to do it. "The officers of the lower grades," Grant later wrote of the foe, "were but little superior to the men," who were "poorly clothed, worse fed, and seldom paid." Nonetheless, "I have seen as brave stands made by some of these men as I have ever seen made by soldiers."[157]

Implicit in that is Grant's realization that an officer's primary responsibility is to lead. Most Mexican enlisted men, who tended to be conscripts, came from the country's lowest classes, especially the poorest Native Americans. These classes, in Grant's view, were treated by their nominal betters like slaves serving brutal masters in the American South.[158] Without freedom, they had little else to fight for.

Perhaps Grant's single most foundational lesson in generalship began at Camargo. There, amid Taylor's trek from Matamoros to Monterrey, the Fourth Infantry saddled Grant with the least loved yet most fortunate assignment of his Mexican career: regimental quartermaster. Here he learned to gather and manage the myriad items required to feed and clothe many hundreds of soldiers and to get such supplies to them in time for proper use. Although hardly glorious work, it was enormously important, the kind of toil without which an army can hardly exist, let alone fight. The job required extensive use of mathematics, patience, and inveterate enterprise—all qualities Grant possessed to high degree.

There was also good and bad role modeling. In Taylor's epic three-day conquest of Monterrey, Grant witnessed up close two obvious and monumental mistakes by generals, one on each side. A Taylor error cost many unnecessary American casualties by allowing the intended demonstration on the city's east side to become a full-fledged assault. At the same time, Mexican general Ampudia sapped his troops' morale by withdrawing them into the municipality's interior after they had successfully and valiantly defended the city's east side. And after the surrender, Grant saw Taylor give the defeated enemy generous terms—which, because the Americans already had their hands full, were especially advantageous to the victors.

On the march back from Monterrey to Camargo, General Worth gave Grant a lesson in how not to manage troops on a march. Worth wore out his division without "the least reason for haste," as Grant later wrote. By contrast, certain other generals "move[d] troops so as to get the maximum distance out of them without fatigue."[159]

At Veracruz, Grant participated in a grand amphibious landing, in which he saw Scott employ history's first landing craft specifically designed for such operations. There he also saw his commander besiege a city and batter its walls with artillery to save his army the human cost of an assault. Afterward, Grant witnessed a victorious Scott accord the surrendering enemy generous terms that also benefited his own purposes, reemphasizing Taylor's example at Monterrey.

At Cerro Gordo, Grant again paid attention as Scott husbanded his manpower by refusing to attack a high, forbidding target head-on. Instead, he used his engineers to find a flanking route from which to surprise Santa Anna with a surprise attack on the Mexican rear. At Molino del Rey he saw just the opposite: the carnage that could result from inadvertently profligate use of men. There Scott had uncharacteristically rushed to avail himself of a seeming opportunity without doing adequate reconnaissance—and Grant learned that a great advantage can be lost when a commander is not in position to direct the hot pursuit of a fleeing enemy.

He also discovered soon after this battle something he seems to have begun to despair of: that his army's hierarchy could finally notice even him.

MEXICO'S INDISPENSABLE BENEFITS

San Cosmé gate was the site of the most consequential of Grant's Mexican battlefield performances. It was also the most *deserving* of consequence. It most perfectly showcased his individual resourcefulness, his relentless bent toward enterprise and efficiency, his understated fearlessness, and his incessant drive to win.

While other officers were content to await the arrival of more troops under the arches of the causeway, Grant had headed off on his own to find a way to outflank the Mexican guns guarding the junction of the highway from Chapultepec with the one leading to the San Cosmé gate. Then he persuaded some soldiers to go with him to do it. After that, he was in the vanguard of Americans penetrating the last highway barricade that stood between that intersection and the gate. During yet another lull, as American leadership brought forward troops and artillery for the final push on the gate, he went off again on his own to look for a way to enfilade the Mexican defenses guarding the gate.

He recognized what he was looking for in the belfry of a church. He then found a gun and gunners to accompany him into the belfry to again strike the Mexicans from an unanticipated quarter. Many officers of his day—especially the gentlemanly ones—likely would have dismissed out of hand the idea of using a church for such a worldly purpose, had Grant's idea occurred to them at all. But the fact that it occurred so readily to Grant illustrates his unfailing concentration on the big picture and the grim singularity of purpose of his work under fire.

Also, his flat and sometimes humorous description in his memoirs of opening a cannonade from a church belfry with "no infantry or other defences" besides the one gun modestly obscures the daring nature of the act, but Grant's stated wonder at the Mexicans neglecting to "send out a small party" to capture him and his little band unmistakably attests to the move's inherent danger.[160] It is hardly surprising that he was brevetted captain for this exploit.

Significant indication that he had been learning his lessons lay in his observations of the performance of non-infantry branches of the army, especially the artillery. At Palo Alto and Resaca de la Palma, the Americans' gunnery—boasting longer range, superior accuracy, and, in some cases, singular "flying" mobility—won the day. It was particularly destructive of Mexican cavalry, which in Mexico's prior wars had been accustomed to defeating less mobile guns. These lessons were worthwhile for the Civil War, where continued advances in technology made artillery even more lethal, especially against cavalry.

Grant's required performance of the duties of regimental quartermaster during most of the Mexican War, meanwhile, was doubtless vital to his later rise. He not only had to continually amass huge amounts of whatever the regiment needed to maintain its ability to fight, but he also had to get all of it transported—on time—to wherever the regiment went. The difficulties of the latter were myriad but are perhaps best summed up by his problems with pack mules. Beginning with the march to Monterrey, during which the army departed early each morning, the problems were endless. "After they had started, the tents and cooking utensils had to be made into packages, so that they could be lashed to the backs of the mules," he recounted in his memoirs. "Iron kettles, tent-poles, and mess chests were inconvenient articles to transport in that way. It took several hours to start each morning, and by the time we were ready some of the mules first loaded would be tired of standing so long with loads on their backs. Sometimes one would start to run, kicking up until he scattered his load; others would lie down and roll over; others with tent-poles for part of their loads would manage to run a tent-pole on one side of a sapling while they would take the other."[161]

It is little wonder that he fled into battle from the fret of this assigned job at every chance imaginable. Less but importantly notable is the sensitivity that allowed this officer to identify not only with his burdened men but even with his burdened mules. It is just as little wonder that the animals would tire "of standing so long with loads on their backs" and perhaps unusual that an officer would have the sensibility to understand their wearying of it.

Consequential also was the firsthand personal knowledge Grant gained of many officers he would later encounter, under circumstances friendly or otherwise, in the Civil War.

Simon Bolivar Buckner, who would surrender an army to him at Fort Donelson in 1862, was among those with whom, after the Americans' last battle in Mexico, he climbed Mount Popocatapetl. The officer sent to bring him to General Worth from the church belfry at the San Cosmé gate was John Pemberton, who in 1863 would surrender another Confederate army to him at Vicksburg. And the engineer most relied upon by Winfield Scott for his masterful flanking maneuvers, Robert E. Lee, would all but end the Civil War in 1865 by surrendering a third army to Grant at Appomattox.

But there were many others. They notably included George McClellan, the conceited dandy who as Union general-in-chief would abortively sanction firing Grant after the Fort Donelson surrender if rumors of his drinking proved true. Grant's close friend and relative by marriage James Longstreet would become Lee's Confederate "warhorse." Braxton Bragg, the sour dyspeptic whose Confederate army would be routed by Grant's troops at

Chattanooga, vaulted from first lieutenant to lieutenant colonel in Mexico thanks to his steel-nerved handling of blazing and highly mobile field guns. Don Carlos Buell, who would be Grant's rival general during the first several months of the trans-Appalachian Civil War, progressed from first lieutenant to major in Mexico.

Ethan Allen Hitchcock, a colonel in Mexico, would nearly be given Grant's army during and after the Fort Donelson battle. Gideon Pillow, a volunteer general in Mexico, would be a Confederate general at Fort Donelson—and the one Confederate on whom Grant would heap most of his rare public scorn. George Meade, who would become nominal commander of the Army of the Potomac under Grant, was Zachary Taylor's chief engineer in Mexico. George H. Thomas, who would serve under Grant at Chattanooga, was promoted from first lieutenant to major as an artillery officer in Mexico.

Altogether, in Mexico Grant served under or alongside more than fifty men who became Union or Confederate generals in the Civil War. He later wrote in the *Personal Memoirs* that having known them "was of immense service to me."

> I do not pretend that all movements [in the Civil War], or even many of them, were made with special reference to the character of the commander against whom they were directed. But my appreciation of my enemies was certainly affected by this knowledge. The natural disposition of most people is to clothe a commander of a large army with superhuman abilities. A large part of the National army, for instance, and most of the press of the country, clothed General Lee with such qualities. But I had known him personally, and knew that he was mortal; and it was just as well that I felt this.[162]

Finally, Grant's long lack of advancement did not prevent him, like soldiers of lower rank from time immemorial, from assessing the performance and abilities of men who *were* generals. However, he did it with more charity than most, and his observations, like his on-the-ground impressions, appear more thoughtful and detailed than those of the average soldier. His memo to superiors on how to attack Mexico City was offered well before the final fighting. Two days before the national capital fell on September 14, he wrote to an unidentified recipient saying he had submitted his views and what they were:

> Much more hard fighting may be expected, as I foresee, before the city is captured. My observations convince me that we have other strong works to reduce before we can enter the city. Our position is such that we can not avoid these. From my map and all the information I acquired while the army was halted at Puebla, I was then, and am now more than ever, convinced that the army could have approached the city by passing around north of it, and reached the northwest side, and avoided all the fortified positions, until we reached the gates of the city at their weakest and most indefensible, as well as most approachable points. . . . It seems to me the northwest side of the city could have been approached without attacking a single fort or redoubt, we would have been on solid ground instead of floundering through morass and ditches, and fighting our way over elevated roads, flanked by water where it is generally impossible to deploy forces.

He added, though, that what he wrote was "entirely confidential" and that "the opinion of a lieutenant, where it differs from that of his commanding general, *must* be founded on *ignorance* of the situation."[163]

His opinions also showed that he was no mere automaton, doing the bidding of superiors without giving their orders serious thought. Additionally, he paid much attention to his superiors themselves, not just to their views. He had been so powerfully affected by Taylor's low-key directness and aplomb under fire that the example seems to have helped mold his own military deportment for the rest of his life. Much of the reason, of course, was likely that the Taylor model fit Grant's homely essence and rustic background far better than Winfield Scott's. Grant could never, because of his parental and environmental molding, have been an "Old Fuss and Feathers": vain, showy, and theatrical. But he could and did learn much from Scott's habits of meticulous military preparation, planning of battles, decisiveness, and careful husbanding of the lives put in his charge.

Grant would learn, though, that neither general was as all-knowing as Grant himself believed at the time. For example: "[Scott] divided his force of 10,000 men into four columns starting a day apart, in moving from Puebla to the capital of the nation, when it was known that an army more than twice as large as his own stood ready to resist his coming," he recalled in his memoirs.

> The road was broad and the country open. . . . General Taylor pursued the same course in marching toward an enemy. He moved in even smaller bodies. I never thought at the time to doubt the infallibility of the two generals in all matters pertaining to their profession. I supposed they moved in small bodies because more men could not be passed over a single road with their artillery and necessary trains. Later I found the fallacy of this belief. The [Confederacy] never could have been suppressed if larger bodies of men could not have been moved at the same time than was the custom under Scott and Taylor.[164]

One other observation about this period of Grant's military education seems warranted. Both as lieutenant and as general he more resembled the kind of infrequent officer who wins his commission under enemy fire rather than at a desk at a military academy. Such men tend to be scruffier, more aggressive, and more grounded in the grit of reality. Grant's superiors may have regarded him as that kind of officer: so plebeian and boringly adept at his most elemental of jobs that no superior thought of rewarding him with a promotion until it could no longer be denied. This was perhaps a holdover result of his western-ness and lackluster performance at West Point. He might almost as well have stayed in Ohio and enlisted in the Mexican War as a volunteer. In that case, though, he would never have become a regimental quartermaster—and probably would have risen faster.

And, of course, he would have been far less ready for his role in the Civil War.

Above, Brigadier General Simon Bolivar Buckner, a friend and West Point schoolmate who would surrender to Grant at Fort Donelson, here exhibits hints of his aristocratic roots and personality. *Library of Congress, Prints & Photographs Division, LC-DIG-cwpb-07434. Left,* Henry W. Halleck, Grant's commander for much of the war's first half, was nicknamed "Old Brains," but Admiral Andrew Foote termed him "a military imbecile." *Library of Congress, Prints & Photographs Division, LC-DIG-cwpbh-01124.*

"Hardscrabble," the home Grant built with his own hands in Missouri in 1856 while struggling to feed his family, disappointed Julia—which, after all that labor, must have disheartened her husband. *Library of Congress, Prints & Photographs Division, LC-USZ62–110714.*

Julia Dent Grant provided her husband with the overtly affectionate home life to which he was unaccustomed in youth—and which he cherished for the rest of his life. *Library of Congress, Prints & Photographs Division, LC-USZ62–101867.*

Above, Grant's father, Jesse, was an up-by-the-bootstraps, self-made businessman who exuded pride in his son's Mexican War record—until Ulysses resigned from the army. *Library of Congress, Prints & Photographs Division, LC-DIG-cwpbh-00916.*

Left, President Abraham Lincoln, like Grant, sprang from humble, practical beginnings. The Union was lucky to have had such an extraordinary war leader. *Library of Congress, Prints & Photographs Division, LC-DIG-ppmsca-19305.*

George B. McClellan, the Union's top commander early in the war, snubbed Grant's 1861 attempt to reenter the army and was a haughty, pluckless leader. *Library of Congress, Prints & Photographs Division, LC-DIG-ppmsca-41848.*

Above, John A. McClernand, a congressman-turned-general under Grant and longtime acquaintance of Lincoln, continually tried to backstab his commander. *Library of Congress, Prints & Photographs Division, LC-BH82-4101. Right,* James B. McPherson, another lower-class Ohioan sent by Halleck to spy on Grant, soon became a Grant admirer and one of the general's most beloved subordinates. *Library of Congress, Prints & Photographs Division, LC-DIG-cwpb-07051.*

Gideon J. Pillow, a Tennessee politician highly instrumental in getting James K. Polk nominated for president, was unskilled as a general and a favorite Grant target for uncharacteristic derision. *National Archives and Records Administration, Photographs and other Graphic Materials, 111-B-4143.*

Right, This photograph hints at the turbulent personality of William T. Sherman, another fellow Ohioan and Grant's most important and loyal friend for most of the war. *Library of Congress, Prints & Photographs Division, LC-DIG-cwpb-06584. Below,* Zachary Taylor, one of Grant's two top commanders in Mexico, forever imparted his taste for informal dress and laconic manner to his young subordinate. *Library of Congress, Prints & Photographs Division, LC-USZ62–110067.*

Lew Wallace, an unloved Grant subordinate, never saw his chief forget Wallace's seemingly dallying march to the aid of Grant's army on Shiloh's nearly disastrous first afternoon. *Library of Congress, Prints & Photographs Division, LC-DIG-cwpb-06442.*

Maine-born Illinois congressman Elihu Washburne was Grant's staunchest—and sometimes only—ally in Congress when he was assailed on overblown drinking charges. *Library of Congress, Prints & Photographs Division, LC-DIG-ppmsca-26793.*

3.

PEACETIME: LIMBO OF HORRORS

★★★★

A LONG, VEXING ADIOS

Some, possibly many, combat soldiers have trouble with peacetime. They fret in the annoyance and boredom of humdrum spit and polish. They quickly, if utterly ironically, miss the adrenaline rush of mortal danger. They grow frustrated with the glacial pace of peacetime promotion compared to that during combat, where attrition of the unlucky creates continual need to replace troops of every rank. They brood over the inexplicable good fortune separating them from dead former comrades. All of which cause many of them to lose focus, drink too much, and otherwise dissipate, sometimes violently, when they return to "safety."

Grant's relentlessly itchy soul seems to have possessed some of these traits. And his military problems were compounded by domestic ones. Except when diverted by battle and the preparation for it, he was very lonely, thousands of miles from a fiancée he had not seen in more than three years. He also was not afforded by background and personality an inclination to look for substitutes closer to hand. Julia wrote him exponentially fewer letters than he wrote her. And in the background hovered the specter of her haughty father and the baronial Missouri plantation, worked by enslaved people, he bossed—not to mention the future father-in-law's antipathy for Grant's abolitionist parents, whose feeling for the father-in-law was mutual. Grant's father, meanwhile, was a problem, too. Candid correspondence with Jesse Grant, his son learned early in the war, would be hawked to newspapers to enhance Jesse's community standing—until the son found out and thereafter kept potentially print-worthy information more private.

His life between wars—in uniform and out—would be a dismal, dragging thing that prepared him well for the experience of fighting the long

Civil War without discernible reduction of resolve. The Mexican War had tested his courage and found it bottomless, but what followed was the kind of agonizing, seemingly endless episode that would have ground most men into hopeless defeat. Its very length and variety of mundane horrors both measured the depth of his aptitude for all-out commitment and helped perfect his capacity for dogged refusal to quit. The lonely individuality of his several hells surely multiplied his faith in the only entity he could rely on: himself. These would be the indispensable materials making up his generalship.

In the Mexican conflict, he had already acquired most of the strictly military knowledge needed of a general that could be gained without actually holding the rank. What he had yet to learn was the harder lesson: how to summon the fortitude to quietly bear months and months of unrelieved stress from inside and outside the army. For him, compared with these behavioral lessons, the military ones were easy. He would one day come to comprehend that his resignation turned out to be a lucky thing for him, because had he "stayed in the army," at the outbreak of the Civil War he "would have been still a Captain on frontier duty," with no chance for appointment to the mainstream colonelcy that became his springboard to generalship. But the seven years before he mounted that springboard would be a wilderness that tried and built his capacity for endurance of misfortune. For almost anyone else, they would have constituted a gauntlet of debilitating vicissitudes.

At the close of hostilities in 1847 his quartermaster duties continued to be substantial as the American forces remained in Mexico. In addition, as he had done at Monterrey following the battle there, he established a bakery and successfully sold bread to finance a regimental fund for the benefit of soldiers' off-time recreation—books, magazines, and other diversions—and provided a share of pay for the regiment's band.[1]

But such work was not enough to preclude extracurricular activities. He apparently played cards often with officers who included future president Franklin Pierce and others who, like himself and Pierce, were members of an informal officers' group called the Aztec Club.[2] Established after the Mexican surrender and headed by Major General of Volunteers John Quitman of Mississippi, it consisted of 160 officers of Winfield Scott's army who had served throughout the campaign from Veracruz through Mexico City.[3] In other activities, Grant attended one bullfight but left before its conclusion, repelled by the sport's cruelty to the bull and horses.[4] He also visited the racetrack and seems to have attended the theater too, but infrequently, mentioning in a letter that the stage dialogue was in Spanish,[5] of which his command was limited. With some other officers he participated in a climb up Mount Popocatapetl, although after being beset by a snowstorm he and some of the others gave up the quest for the crest in favor of exploring an enormous cave.[6]

Another post-combat recreation became more important for his future. At some point during the war, or perhaps earlier,[7] he fell under the lure of the bottle, and an eventual sporadic, binging pattern of alcoholism began to take hold. Mexico was a drinkers' paradise, and even had it not been, armies are hardly bastions of abstinence. Too, heredity may have rendered him especially susceptible to thirst for the vine. As biographer Ron Chernow has noted, Jesse Grant's father was ruined by drink to such an extent that his family could not afford to raise its progeny, depriving Jesse of a home before he reached manhood.[8]

Hereditary or not, the same problem—although of much lesser proportion—dogged Jesse's eldest son. Of him, a fellow Ohio soldier wrote to his wife from Mexico, "I think he drinks too much, but don't you say a word on that subject."[9] Less believably, another fellow soldier told early Grant biographer Hamlin Garland that by the time Grant left Mexico he was beset by delirium tremens and other problems associated with heavy drinking.[10]

As his departure date neared, he incurred a large financial loss that was particularly troubling because its sum was not his to lose. The bakery he had founded to pay for recreations for the regiment had yielded a profit of $1,000—worth many times that in today's money—for the regimental fund, and he had taken pains to safeguard it. At Jalapa on the long trek from Mexico City back to the port at Veracruz, the money—whose total slightly exceeded Grant's annual pay—was in a chest in the tent of a captain. Grant had put it there because he had suffered a smaller loss from a chest of his own a year earlier[11] and thought that an officer not known to have charge of the money would be an unlikelier target for theft.

The chest nevertheless turned up missing, and Grant's loss became the subject of a government report whose existence in Washington must have been mortifying to a person of Grant's unusual degree of honesty. He was found blameless by a board of inquiry but was nonetheless expected to reimburse the government for the money. It was a nagging matter that followed him for years.[12]

Beneath this uncomfortable cloud, he left Mexico from Veracruz with the Fourth Infantry around mid-July 1848. He arrived in East Pascagoula, Mississippi, on July 23.

HOME?

Grant no doubt believed he was headed home, but finding a real one in the next few years would be an elusive and equivocal quest.

His parents were now in Bethel, Ohio. Julia's parents, by contrast, still lived on their plantation near St. Louis, political light years from Bethel. The two communities' prejudices, at least those of the elder Dents and Grants, were diametrically opposed. The fires of the oncoming war that Ulysses would contend the United States' Mexican aggression had brought on were already heating up sectional tempers within the nation and its individual households. For the rest of his life, Grant would find himself caught between the flames of two extremes with which his nature did not identify: the all-out abolitionism of his parents and the imperious inclinations of his slave-driving soon-to-be in-laws.

From Camp Jefferson Davis in Mississippi he naturally headed first, and fast, to Missouri to see the fiancée on whom he had not laid eyes in three years. She turned out to look the same as he remembered, but Ulysses, deeply tanned by the Mexican sun and newly minus a longish, reddish beard he had gotten used to wearing in Mexico,[13] looked and acted more like the typical combat veteran of any war, quieter and even more economical with words than he had been before. After a few days at the Dent plantation, where Julia set the wedding date for August 22 in St. Louis, he left for his parents' home in Ohio. There Jesse preened with pride as his now-distinguished son satisfied insistent neighbors with insightful descriptions of Mexican battles. Friends addressed the former "Ulys" or "Lyssus" as "Captain" in recognition of the brevet rank to which his exploits had raised him. Jesse informed the hero, however, that he and Hannah would not be attending the wedding. He said Hannah's shyness could not endure the prolonged conviviality sure to characterize Julia's Southern-style nuptials.[14] That, though, likely was an excuse to cover their contempt for the slave-based society in which the bride had been rooted.

Thus, minus his proud parents and with Dent relative James Longstreet as his best man, on August 22 Ulysses Grant formalized the most important human connection of his life. The former Julia Dent is best known in historical quarters for having been the most effective manager of Grant's unsteady hand with decanters. But, despite being snickered at behind hands in eastern intellectual and political circles for appearing unpolished and ignorant (as also was her husband),[15] she was far more than a bottle smasher. She provided Grant with the demonstratively loving domestic environment he had been without since birth and had, consciously or otherwise, always craved.

It was likely Julia's hearthside manner, rather than just her presumably sharp eye and practiced sense of smell, that kept her husband for most of his life in the neighborhood of the straight and narrow. For a man whose will was remarkably muscular in other realms but infamously puny in choice of beverage, Julia supplied that all-but-indispensable element in her husband's most dangerous psychological sphere. It may have been possible for Grant to become a general while also being a full-fledged drunkard—certain other Civil War generals seem to have managed it—but there is unquestionably no way he could have been such and become America's greatest one. Which he very arguably did.

The day after the wedding, the new couple set out by steamboat for Bethel so Julia could meet her in-laws. On the way, they stopped at Louisville to visit a wealthy Grant cousin named James Hewitt, to whom Grant hinted that he would be willing to leave the army if a promising business connection materialized. Hewitt ignored the hint, and Julia resented him for it for the rest of her life.[16] At Bethel, the elder Grants appeared to accept the new bride and pressed her to stay with them if the army posted Ulysses inconveniently. They remained not fond, however, of what they knew of her family or its lifestyle. Privately, they dismissed the Dents as lazy slave masters.[17]

Interfamily tension continued. Despite a four-month leave, Grant was still in the army and expected to report for duty in November to the Fourth Infantry's new headquarters at Detroit. Julia's father tried to prevent his favorite daughter, the new Mrs. Grant, from accompanying her husband, but Grant proved himself stubbornly equal to the old man's challenge. In front of his father-in-law, he asked Julia if she preferred to remain with her family rather than to go where the army was sending him, as she had repeatedly promised to do in letters to him in Mexico. She said she wanted to go with him.

When they reached Detroit, Grant found that higher-ups who had not been in Mexico thought his regimental quartermaster appointment did not apply in the United States. While he was on leave, they gave another officer his regimental job and assigned Grant, when he arrived, to that officer's company position, a remote one on the shore of Lake Ontario at Sackets Harbor, New York. Grant and Julia had to make a hard winter stagecoach journey to Sackets Harbor. Grant was not the kind of man who would scheme to get a post, as the other officer apparently was, but he *was* the kind who would stoutly defend his rights. His protest went up to the division commander, accompanied by a superior's note that "in my judgment . . . Lieut Grant has, unquestionably, been hardly & wrongfully dealt by." Four months later, the wronged lieutenant—or, actually, brevet captain—was ordered back to Detroit to assume his deserved place.[18]

From 1848 into 1850, Grant and Julia inhabited the same two army posts twice—Detroit very briefly, then Sackets Harbor for six months, then Detroit again when he recovered his regimental position, and finally Sackets Harbor yet again when the whole Fourth Infantry was ordered there. The couple handled military society together apparently very happily, insulated from extended family dissension, even though Sackets Harbor was tiny and rustic and Julia, for the first time in her life, was without the domestic help of enslaved people. On her own, she seems to have enjoyed arranging and keeping their house. Grant, meanwhile, passed some of his off-duty hours racing his horse up and down the street or, soon, doing the same thing in a buggy.

But in the early spring of 1850 Julia decided to return to St. Louis from Detroit to have their first baby. During her absence, Grant reverted to a depression he would almost always eventually experience when she was not around. This time he succumbed significantly enough to the bottle that he discussed the problem with their minister and, after attending a temperance lecture, helped found a Detroit chapter of the Sons of Temperance. Her husband's lurking penchant was not one Julia cared to discuss, but, returning to Detroit from childbearing, she was proud enough of his resistance to it that she hung his Sons of Temperance membership certificate in their parlor.

His head-on approach to his problem seems significant for a future general. Most notably, it signifies that Grant *was* approaching his problem—and in the fashion that would forever characterize him. Recognizing it for the mortal enemy it could be, he resolved to resist.

Soon, though, his resolve faced another trial. After their second stint at Sackets Harbor, the Grants had to separate again. In 1852, with national gold fever rising and Julia again expecting, the Fourth Infantry received orders to transfer to California via a long, hard journey. It was to be made by sea, except for an unusual interruption: a march across the Isthmus of Panama with nearly 100 military wives and children and a large number of other civilians.

Grant's taste for travel and seeing new places was moderated this time. For one thing, his regiment was now under the command of a lieutenant colonel—Benjamin L. E. Bonneville—who, a younger lieutenant in the Fourth later said, disliked Grant because of "something that had occurred in Mexico." Also, Grant was under a sour senior captain who was similarly unfriendly.[19] Worse, the Panama crossing was scheduled for the cholera season. Grant had seen too many men die this ugly death in Mexico and refused to allow Julia to chance the expedition, especially in her again delicate condition. He was just as fearful for his baby son, Fred—named after Julia's father to, no doubt, keep peace in that half of his contentious family. Not taking Julia and Fred, though, robbed Grant's immediate future of all prospect of joy.

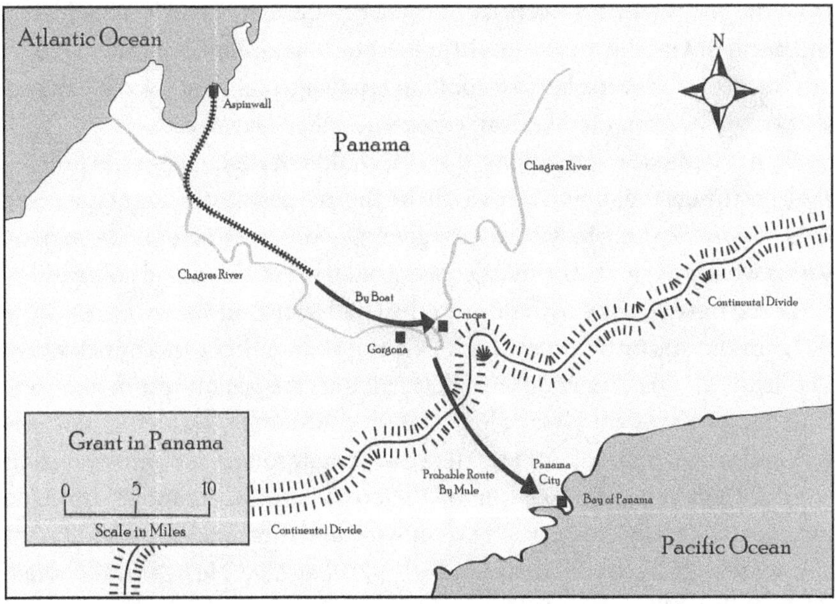

In 1852, in perhaps Grant's most impressive command achievement to that point, he shepherded sick soldiers and civilians on a hellish odyssey across the malarial and cholera-ridden Isthmus of Panama before proceeding to his ill-starred assignment on the U.S. west coast.

On July 5, 1852, he wrote "Dear Dear Julia" from New York a letter whose careless misspelling of the common word "by" may—or may not—indicate that it was jotted in haste before embarking. In haste or otherwise, he was an indifferent speller.

> We sail directly for the Isthmus. I never knew how much it was to part from you and Fred. until it come to the time for leaving. . . . You must be a dear good girl and learn Fred. to be a good boy. I think there will be an opportunity for you to join me in the course of next Winter in company with the other ladies of the Regiment left behind. . . . It distresses me dearest to think that this news has to be broken to you just at this time. But bear it with fortitude. Our separation will not be a long one anyway. At least lets hope so. Good buy dear dear Julia. Kiss Fred. a thousand times. A thousand kisses for you dearest Julia.[20]

The prospective length of absence involved in a move all the way to the West Coast prompted Grant, who rarely spoke idly, to talk of resigning from the army, fellow officers later recalled.[21] But in the end he shouldered the burden. He sent Julia and little Fred to his parents in Bethel and, as quartermaster, did the best he could to ready his regiment for the dangers that he knew, from the Mexican experience, likely lay ahead.

Even the Mexican privations, though, could not adequately steel him for the ghastliness that loomed. It would be the greatest test so far of the makings of American history's greatest general, compressing into six horrific weeks what was surely the most concentrated set of command tribulations he would have to cope with prior to the Civil War.

From the start it was a soldier's hell, not to mention a quartermaster's. The army, in typical fashion , had delayed until the last minute before contracting for a steamer already loaded with gold-hungry wannabe prospectors and some of their families. The vessel's staterooms and other housing were by then occupied, so Grant had to create accommodations sufficient for a vessel designed to carry 330 souls to suddenly take on an additional 700 soldiers and a few of their families, plus baggage. He had to supervise the building of bunk beds of several levels on deck for officers and men and, meanwhile, smooth over passenger feathers ruffled by the ill-humored Colonel Bonneville.[22]

The latter was no small task on a ship whose occupants' tempers were doubtless soon frayed by the grave overloading and widespread seasickness. But, as always seems to have been the case in times of tension, Grant appears to have done as good a job as possible. The captain of the vessel, a naval officer named Schenck who had not seen or heard of Grant before meeting him aboard ship, was impressed with the army lieutenant's quiet, round-the-clock steadfastness in watching over the passengers, military and otherwise. He said Grant calmed situations exacerbated by Bonneville and appeared to be "a man of an uncommon order of intelligence."[23] That man rarely slept and habitually paced the deck late into the night, and Schenck sometimes accompanied him to talk.[24] Having no idea of Grant's special problem, Schenck pressed him to employ the captain's liquor cabinet during his nightly rounds on the deck "and urged him frequently never to be backward in using it as though it were his own, and he never was. Every night after I had turned in, I would hear him once or twice, sometimes more, open the door quietly and walk softly over the floor so as not to disturb me; then I would hear the clink of the glass and a gurgle, and he would walk softly back."[25]

As quartermaster, Grant knew the expedition schedule, and he could only assume that the travelers' discomforts would worsen on arrival at the isthmus. On July 15, as they approached it, he wrote Julia the names of a few military wives who were aboard and added, "They[,] poor things[,] I fear will regret it [making the voyage] before twenty four hours. It is now in the midst of the rainy season and we have to cross the mountains on mules, through passes which are too narrow for two abreast, and the ascent and descent to[o] precipitate for any other animal."[26] The isthmian town where they disembarked—Aspinwall, now called Colón—was emphatically not inviting. Grant recalled many years later that its streets lay "eight or ten inches under water" and that pouring rain interspersed intervals of blistering sun. He recalled wondering "how any person could live many months in Aspinwall, and wondered still more why any one tried."[27] The annual rainfall in the isthmus was measured not in inches but in feet, from five to six of them in some parts and ten in others. The humidity eight months a year was 98 percent.[28]

Before their expedition could reach the mountains of the Continental Divide, where they would have to mount the mules, they first had to ride a new railroad for the eighteen miles its tracks had so far been laid—by Irishmen who were said to have died of cholera at a rate of one per crosstie. At tracks' end they had to navigate the Chagres River a half-dozen or more upstream miles to a place called Gorgona, in dugout boats mightily muscled against the current by near-naked Native Americans. Each boat held about thirty people, along with six crewmen. To describe the process as primitive in the best conditions would hardly convey truth.

And these were nowhere near the best conditions. The army had been warned of the cholera risk but expected the expedition to move quickly enough to outrun the disease. It did not. Plans went awry. Land transportation that the ship had contracted for had been snapped up by gold-frenzied civilians willing to pay more than double, and getting out of the isthmus for part of the contingent—Grant's part—became a nightmare. The other part, all but one company of the regiment, took the boats up the Chagres to Gorgona and then "marched to Panama," Grant later recalled, "and were soon comfortably on [a] steamer anchored in the bay" at Panama City on the Pacific coast. Grant, though, was not so fortunate. As quartermaster, he was left by Bonneville in charge of the remaining company to guard the regimental camp equipment and the civilian co-travelers. "I, with one company of troops and all the soldiers with families, all the tents, mess chests, and camp kettles, was sent to Cruces, a town a few miles higher up the Chagres River than Gorgona. There I found an impecunious American who had taken a contract to furnish transportation for the regiment at a stipulated price per hundred pounds for the freight and so much for each saddle animal. But when we reached Cruces there was not a mule, either for pack or saddle, in the place."[29] Grant ended up having to take charge, dismiss the contractor, and make arrangements with a native to supply mules at more than twice the original price.

Doing all this and gathering the mules took days, during which cholera broke out in Cruces. Men began dying with dizzying speed. They would be in good health one moment but then start writhing with cramps and die within hours. Grant, "to diminish the food for the disease," as he put it, sent his company of soldiers and the physicians on to Panama City, leaving himself "alone with the sick and the soldiers who had families. . . . I was about a week at Cruces before transportation began to come in. About one-third of the people with me died, either at Cruces or on the way to Panama [City]. . . . Altogether, on the Isthmus and on the Pacific side, we were delayed six weeks. About one-seventh of those who left New York Harbor with the 4th Infantry . . . now lie buried on the Isthmus of Panama or on Flamingo [Flamenco] island in Panama Bay."[30]

In all, the military corpses numbered about 150.[31] People died on the road to Panama City, and the survivors found cholera when they arrived at the coast. Notwithstanding all the problems, Grant showed his charges, civilian and military, the same solicitude and succor he had shown wounded soldiers on Mexican battlefields. A fellow officer on this hellish trek recalled that Grant "seemed to take a personal interest in each sick man. . . . He was like a ministering angel to us all." Seldom sleeping more than two or three hours at a time yet always managing to get supplies where they needed to be and in sufficient quantity, Grant, the same officer said, "was like a man of iron."[32] As usual, though, there is nothing heroic in Grant's own description of his performance, in fact little description of that performance at all, either in the *Personal Memoirs* or in letters to Julia at the time.

"I wish I could only know that you and our dear little ones were as well as I am," he wrote her from a California-bound ship on August 9. "I have enjoyed good health. It has been the province of my place as Quarter Master to be exposed to the weather and climate on the Isthmus, while most of the others were quietly aboard ship, but to that very activity can probably be ascribed my good health. . . . We have been out from Panama [City] over four days and no sickness has broken out aboard. All are healthy and every minute brings us towards a better climate."[33]

But climate, he already knew, is not everything.

CHEERLESS

Aboard a craft called the *Golden Gate,* Grant and what was left of the Fourth Infantry arrived in San Francisco Bay in mid-August. It was the beginning of what may have been Grant's most miserable year on earth, although several other hard ones were to follow.

After marking time for a week, the Fourth steamed north to a permanent post in the Oregon Territory: Fort Vancouver. It was a primitive, heavily forested riverside location with little besides quartermaster duties to occupy Grant's time. He and a fellow soldier often took long horseback rides, but Grant, a half continent away from Julia and his growing family and too rarely reached by the mails, quickly grew all but morose. A fellow resident of the fort described him as seeming "always sad," unlike most of his fellow officers. Once he visited the home of a sergeant to bring an official appointment he had obtained for the man to a federal ordnance position. While there, he shared with the sergeant and his wife a letter of his own that had arrived in the same mail. With hands that shook, he showed them a drawing that it included, a tracing of a hand of his newborn second son. They said he then quickly refolded the letter and left with tears in his eyes.[34]

Grant apparently loved children, and none more than his own. Most of his letters home abound with questions as to what his two little boys were up to. What were they doing and saying? Had their grandparents spoiled them? He was desperate to bring them and Julia to the Oregon Territory, but a lieutenant's salary and the appropriate allowances amounted to just $677 a year,[35] a sum nowhere near sufficient to support a family in the high-priced, gold-crazed Far Northwest of 1853.

By the onset of spring, he was gathering partners to try to make extra money. Having grown up farming, he settled on that as his principal vehicle and, with a trio of associates, rented a tract of land from the nearby Hudson's Bay Company. The group cleared enough to plant a huge field of potatoes, a crop that grew exceptionally well in Oregon. But, Grant later recalled, a number of other people decided to plant potatoes, too, and the fabulous crop that the Oregon soil raised for Grant and his partners turned out to be all but worthless. As he put it, he and his three associates were lucky when a Columbia River flood relieved them of the task of carrying the unsalable crop away.[36] True to his nature, he persisted with other similar schemes—shipping ice to San Francisco and trafficking in cattle, hogs, wood, and chickens, but each project came to less than nothing.[37] Rather than earn extra money, he repeatedly lost his original investment.

These reverses only increased his inclination to quit the army. He invited a couple who had shared the horrors of the Panama crossing, a Sergeant Sheffield and his wife, to move in with him, and Delia Sheffield was stirred by his longings for his family. She later recalled that often, when reading letters from Julia, "his eyes would fill with tears" and "he would look up . . . and say, 'Mrs. Sheffield, I have the dearest little wife in the world, and I want to resign from the army and live with my family.'"[38]

Amid his many ill-starred ventures, as if he did not have enough troubles, the reputedly brilliant but snobbish and insufferably egotistical Brevet Captain George B. McClellan arrived at Fort Vancouver in May 1853 with a surveying expedition tasked with finding a railroad route across the Cascade Mountains. McClellan's party had to be outfitted, and Fort Vancouver's quartermaster had to do it. It was a big job. Grant told Julia in a letter on June 15 that he was "very busy now being both Depot Qr. Master and Depot Commissary and having two expeditions to fit out for the great Pacific Rail Road Surveying party. . . . They require a large number of pack animals and many articles besides that have to be purchased, all of which has to be done by me."[39]

The fitting out of the surveying party may well have produced long-term future effects. A fellow lieutenant and friend of Grant who had been assigned to accompany McClellan as the party's quartermaster recalled that McClellan became "exceedingly" "annoyed and offended" because before the outfitting was completed, "Grant got on one of his little [drinking] sprees." The lieutenant said that in his opinion McClellan "never quite forgave Grant for it, notwithstanding the necessary transportation was soon in readiness."[40]

By the time Grant wrote the June 15 letter to Julia, he had learned through the army grapevine that he at last would soon receive a promotion to actual (not brevet) captain, succeeding a prominent soldier who had died. The advancement would return him to California to command a company at Fort Humboldt, 250 miles north of San Francisco. Delia Sheffield was happy for him, terming Fort Humboldt "a more desirable station,"[41] but Grant himself was not elated. He said he wanted to quit the army and, with his eye still on bringing Julia and the boys west, perhaps go into the lumber business.

He left Fort Vancouver on September 24. His new post was a gathering of log barracks and officers' cabins housing a desertion-reduced post population that originally had numbered 126. Nearby was a sawmill and a few harborside cabins for lumberjacks. The new assignment was the worst kind of combination of duties for any veteran of prolonged wartime combat—not to mention the thirst-plagued Grant. His new duties as commander of a company, according to a contractor who supplied Fort Humboldt with beef, were fewer and less taxing than his quartermaster labors had been, but the discipline was far more "rigid and irksome," according to a longtime friend and fellow officer.[42] The latter was largely the fault of the post commander, Colonel Robert C. Buchanan, who apparently had nursed hard feelings against Grant since the two were stationed at Jefferson Barracks outside St. Louis before the Mexican War. There Buchanan, then president of the post mess, and Grant had clashed over Grant's repeated lateness in returning to dinner from visits to the Dent plantation.[43]

None of the few officers at Humboldt was among Grant's sizable circle of longtime army friends, and Buchanan's spit-and-polish discipline made loneliness for Julia decidedly worse. The Humboldt commander was, another officer said, "a martinet."[44] He ran such a tight and uncomfortable ship that he once was said to have excessively rebuked a subordinate for having a collar askew.[45]

Grant's Oregon Territory agricultural setbacks and the move to Fort Humboldt had not reduced his appetite for drink, and Humboldt offered no longtime confidants who could caution him about it. A friend who was not at Humboldt but who knew him well recalled later that Grant "was in the habit of drinking in a peculiar way": lining up the little finger of one hand with the bottom of a tumbler, setting the hand's next three fingers snugly atop that one, and then filling the tumbler to the top of the fourth finger.[46] Grant's workmanlike digits were none too thin, and soldiers of that place and time often countered suggestions that they dilute their drinks with water with a standard howl: "Do you take me for a camel?"[47] These two facts made for unfortunate outcomes in Grant's case. The wife of the Humboldt sawmill boss later recalled having seen an inebriated Grant topple off a shoreside boardwalk.[48]

That was apparently not the only sighting of a drink-impaired Grant around Fort Humboldt. There appears to have been at least one other, and that one seems vastly more important historically. A Grant friend who was not at Humboldt himself but gathered talk from other officers who *were* there said that on a certain military payday Grant showed up at his company's pay table "slightly under the influence of liquor," and the starchy Buchanan learned of it. Buchanan then apparently gave Grant a choice: resign or have charges lodged against him. He quit "at once," the friend said. Many friends, when they heard, encouraged Grant to stand trial, believing he would be acquitted, the story goes, but he refused, saying "he would not for all the world have his wife know that he had been tried on such a charge."[49]

Grant may even, in a rash first moment, have viewed Buchanan's edict as a godsend. He apparently had lost all hope of reuniting with his family while still wearing a soldier's uniform. Oddly, on the day that the official copy of his captain's commission arrived at Fort Humboldt (several months after the actual promotion had taken effect), he wrote the army adjutant general in Washington a brief acknowledgment of receipt, and, in another brief letter written the same day, he "very respectfully" resigned from the army.[50]

The latter was an untimely missive. He had lent most of the money he had saved, and his debtors were now unable to be found. Nevertheless, he boarded a ship for San Francisco, where he expected to find two more men to whom he had lent money.[51] Saying his goodbyes at Humboldt, he said he hoped in ten years to be a well-to-do Missouri farmer.[52]

Probably the last letter Grant wrote from Fort Humboldt was dated May 2, 1854, three weeks after his letter of resignation. It was to Julia and was untypically brief and abrupt. There were few of the many usual expressions of affection, as if the letter had been penned amid final preparations for departure and perhaps with some bitterness about her laggardly correspondence. It was also uncharacteristically evasive, not disclosing his resignation and saying only that he had "a 'leave of absence'" and that Julia could "discontinue writing because before I could get a reply I shall be on my way home. You might write directing [the letter] to the City of New York."[53]

The frightening specter of "poverty," he eventually wrote, had long kept him from resigning, and he now encountered it face-to-face. Leaving Humboldt for San Francisco in his financial situation was bold, even reckless, and likely resulted from his obsession with re-closing his family circle as soon as possible. His circumstances, though, turned out to be less buoyant after disembarking in San Francisco. There he found one of his two debtors unable to pay and the other missing. At age thirty-two, the new ex-captain soon was walking the city's streets in fast-worsening need. The chief quartermaster of the army's Pacific Division, Robert Allen, who knew and liked him, heard of his plight and set about finding him. It must not have been easy. By then, Grant had fallen to a level barely above homelessness. He was in a cheap hotel called the What Cheer House, where he occupied an attic room containing only a cot, a small table, and a chair. When Allen walked in, Grant was sitting at the table with his head bowed.

"What are you doing here?" Allen asked him.

"Nothing," Grant said. "I've resigned from the army. I'm out of money, and I have no means of getting home."[54]

Allen took care of these immediate problems. With his help, Grant obtained enough daily pocket money as well as transportation by steamer to New York,[55] which he reached in much the same unfortunate condition as he had San Francisco. In New York, his deliverer was another old army friend from Mexican War days, Simon Bolivar Buckner, then a commissary officer in New York. Learning that Grant's hotel was about to evict him for nonpayment of his bill, Buckner guaranteed the payment himself and helped Grant exist until money could arrive from Jesse Grant in Ohio.

All the vicissitudes leading up to and surrounding the resignation are passed over in the *Personal Memoirs*, which, with Grant's typically tight-lipped privacy about such matters, dispense with them in less than a paragraph:

> My family, all this while [that he was on the Pacific coast] was at the East. It consisted now of a wife and two children. I saw no chance of supporting them on the Pacific coast out of my pay as an army officer. I concluded, therefore, to resign, and in March applied for a leave of absence until the end of July, tendering my resignation to take effect at the end of that time. . . . I was now to commence, at the age of thirty-two, a new struggle for our support. My wife had a farm near St. Louis.[56]

"POORLY QUALIFIED" FOR PRIVATE LIFE

"My wife had a farm near St. Louis," he wrote. Well, not exactly.

What his wife had, more or less, was 60 acres of Colonel Dent's 900-acre plantation, supposedly given her as a wedding present by her father. But she did not own legal title to these acres; the colonel had kept that. And it was land that, to be cultivated, first had to be cleared of huge oaks and elms.[57] So, for Grant, farming in the Missouri of the mid-1850s, as opposed to the Ohio of his boyhood, would be a more complicated affair than plowing ground and dropping seeds.

Before facing it, though, he had to go to Bethel to see how cold the ashes of his home fires had gotten since he resigned from the army. Jesse Grant, once he heard about the resignation, mightily protested it to Secretary of War Jefferson Davis, seeming almost to treat it as an act of personal betrayal by a person incompetent to make his own decisions.

"I never wished him to leave the servis," the elder Grant wrote Davis. "I think after spending so much time to qualify himself for the army and spending so many years in the servis he will be poorly qualified for the pursuits of a privet life. . . . He has not seen his family for over two years

& has a son nearly two years old he has never seen. I suppose in his great anxiety to see his family he has been induced to quit the servis."[58]

Whether or not Jesse Grant was correct, his son spent the next seven years in a wilderness of the soul that was likely the greatest trial that predated his generalship. Carl von Clausewitz had had the vision to recognize that civilian life and its politics underlie most of a military's purpose and were in fact the military's sole reason for being, but even Clausewitz may not have reflected on the extent to which adverse prior civilian experience can lay the foundation for a great general's military hardihood. It doubtless helped immunize against countenancing defeat. That is apparently what happened to Ulysses S. Grant between 1854 and 1861. It was not so much a matter of learning military precepts or rules of tactics or strategy. It was more a matter of hardening the will.

Unable to persuade Davis to "reconsider and withdraw the acceptance of [Ulysses's] resignation" and substitute a six-month leave, Jesse Grant sent money enough to get his son home from New York but apparently then turned his back on this firstborn whose military exploits he had so trumpeted across Bethel. Jesse, personally worth a then-comfortable $150,000 dollars, and his pair of other male offspring, Simpson and Orvil, seem from then on to have begun to regard Ulysses as a supreme family disappointment.[59]

The atmosphere may not have been much more pleasant at White Haven, the Dent plantation in Missouri. Grant said to Julia at the time, "You know I couldn't come home without hearing from you," indicating he was uncertain how welcome he would be.[60] As badly as his father and brothers regarded him, he may have feared worse at White Haven. In her autobiography, Julia paints his Missouri homecoming in roseate hues, but beforehand he seems to have been more than a little nervous about it. And no matter how joyous was his reunion with Julia and the little second son he had never seen (who was frightened by their initial encounter) and the first (who did not recognize him at all), the rest of the White Haven reception must have been less so. Julia's father had been unimpressed with Grant as a low-level army officer, and now he was a *former* low-level army officer—who, despite his West Point engineering education, appeared to have few prospects for civilian employment. Uncharacteristic as it would have been, Colonel Dent likely would have agreed with Jesse Grant on one thing: the army had ruined Ulysses for gainful civilian pursuits.

Missouri was uninviting in other ways, too. Although its vegetation, crops, and climate were similar to those to which Grant had been accustomed in southern Ohio, its community atmosphere was emphatically more stressful. Slavery-induced Southern xenophobia immediately branded Colonel Dent's son-in-law "a Northern man," a designation connoting neighborhood suspicion at best. The neighbors were openly mindful of the Dent son-in-law's status as a sectional interloper, and their consciousness of that had to have been heightened by events in the territory adjoining Missouri to the west. There, in so-called Bleeding Kansas, the American Civil War was already unofficially opening with abolitionists and pro-slavers killing each other over whether their new state would legally allow human bondage.

With the grit that would come to be seen by history as the bedrock of his character, Grant set about making himself as useful at White Haven as he could, given his lack of funds to stock "his" farm or build a house on it. He worked in the Dent fields planting oats, corn, and vegetables and in the woods cutting cordwood that he initially sold to Dent neighbors.[61] Courtesy of Colonel Dent, Julia had three black house "servants," but Grant himself initially had none to help him in the field, no doubt prompting condescending grins among the neighbors.[62] Then he began cutting and hauling saplings for a nearby coal mine whose owners paid fifty cents each for poles with which to reinforce the mine's ceiling.[63] He hired free black workers to help with the cutting and hauling—and further nettled the neighbors by paying these laborers more than the going rate. In between all of these activities, he was cutting and trimming logs that, once they had "cured" for a year, would become the house he intended to build on Julia's sixty acres.[64]

Although he stood smaller than the average height of his day, Grant's frame was deceptively muscular, thanks probably to his youth in the fields. He was not overbearing, but he was also no shrinking violet when it came to enforcing seemly conduct where that appeared to him to be his military or civic duty. In California, he had once bodily removed a loud inebriate from the audience of a performance at a post theater because the man's behavior was causing a disturbance.[65] Again in Missouri, he is reported to have remonstrated with a man who was being "noisy and vulgar" at a dance that Grant attended with Julia. The man must have been decidedly so, because another man who was there recalled that when the offender refused to quiet down, Grant "kicked him out of the door and clear out to the gate."[66]

Grant's physical strength could only have increased with his hard labors on the Missouri farm. Because most, if not all, of his income came from timbering—and the gasoline-powered chainsaw would not begin to enter American forests for nearly another century—Grant had to rely on an ax and, when he could afford it, the axes of hired men. Ax work is powerful exercise, the kind boxers have long used to build strength for prize fights. In fewer than four years in Missouri, Grant probably worked himself into the illness that—along with poverty—finally drove him from the fields in 1858.

In the spring of 1855, he and Julia were invited to move temporarily into the home of a Grant brother-in-law who was in California. Called "Wish-ton-wish," which was said to be a Native American word for whip-poor-will, the house was a large one made of stone standing in a grove of oaks and seems to have been suitably grand enough for the son of a status-conscious plantation master. It was also about a mile away from the sixty humbler acres Grant was bringing under cultivation on the perimeter of the Dent land and must have contrasted sharply with the home Grant built in the summer of 1856. Perhaps to acknowledge its difference from other, more vaunted Dent residences and maybe to satirize them a little, Grant called his homemade domicile "Hardscrabble," which appears from pictures to have been apt.

The two-story structure was of logs, bookended with brick chimneys, and "raised," as the saying went, with the help of neighbors and their enslaved people. Its interior, divided by a central hall that separated the downstairs sitting and dining rooms, was finished off by Grant himself. He also set the stones for the foundation, laid the floors, built the stairs, shingled the roof, and dug the basement.[67] Julia's younger sister Emily, also called Emmy, told an interviewer much later that above the sitting and dining rooms were, on the second floor, "three small bedrooms, two [others] of good size, and a small front room over a portion of the hallway below. The kitchen and servants' quarters were in cabins at the rear." One of Julia's St. Louis friends said she envied Julia in that "no grand city home can compare with that log building," with its "engravings on the walls . . . bits of delicate color in furnishings . . . books, reviews, and magazines lying about."[68]

Emmy Dent claimed the cabin was planned by Julia. But the elder sister, accustomed to plantation houses, apparently cared little for the result. The place has a rustic, rugged appearance that can be considered attractive only in a frontier sense. It also suggests the great physical effort that building it—while still farming—required of Grant. His deep disappointment at Julia's displeasure with it can only be imagined. The couple and their children lived in it barely a season, from just after its completion in September 1856 to the following January. That month Julia's mother died, prompting Colonel Dent to move to St. Louis and invite the Grants to take over White Haven. The larger place's operational responsibilities then fell to Grant, but with precious few funds with which to meet them.

His letters of the period bespeak hard labor, desperate hope, hovering want, and gathering gloom. On December 28, 1856, he was still beneath the roof of Hardscrabble when he wrote his father that he had "been laboring under great disadvantages but now that I am on my own place, and shall not have to build [a house] next summer I think I shall be able to do much better."

> This year if I could have bought seed I should have made out still better than I did. I wanted to plant sixty or seventy bushels of potatoes, but I had not the money to buy them. I planted twenty however and have sold 225 bushels and have about 125 on hand, besides all that I have used. . . . I have in [the ground] some twenty five acres of wheat that looks better, or did before the cold weather, of any in the neighborhood. My intention is to raise about twenty acres of Irish potatoes, on new ground, five acres of sweet potatoes, about the same of early corn, five or six acres [of] cabbage, beets, cucumber pickles & melons and keep a wagon going to market every day. This last year my place was not half tended because I had but one span of horses, and one hand, and we had to do all the work of the place . . . all the hauling for my [house] building, and take wood to the city for the support of the family. . . . This year I presume I shall be compelled to neglect my farm some to make a living in the meantime, but next year I hope to be independent. If I had an opportunity of getting about $500.00 for a year at 10 pr. cent I have no doubt it would be of great advantage to me.

The same letter closes with a poignant recollection and question, saying that at the Planters House hotel in St. Louis Grant "saw registered 'J. R. Grant, Ky.'" Making inquiries, he learned "that J.R.G. had just taken the Pacific R[ail] R[oad] cars. . . . Was it you?"[69]

Whether the J. R. Grant of Kentucky in the Planters House register was his father (which it almost assuredly was) is probably unknowable today, but the younger Grant must have thought so and may well have discerned it from the handwriting. To think that his father would visit so near his home and not make contact must have been painful. It is not, however, so surprising. Jesse appeared to care nothing for the Dents and may well also have been dodging his son to avoid an anticipated monetary plea like the one forecast near the close of the letter. Grant apparently received no answer from his father to this broad hint at need for funds, so six weeks later he brought it up again—more baldly and with some seeming tinges of bitterness along with his careless spelling.

> Dear Father,
>
> Spring is now approaching when farmers require not only to till the soil, but to have the wherewith to till it, and to seed it. For two years I have been compelled to farm without either of these facilities. . . . I want . . . implements to cultivate with. To this end I am going to make the last appeal to you. I do this because, when I was in Ky. you voluntarily offered to give me a Thousand Dollars, to commence with, and because there is no one els to whom I could, with the same propriety, apply. It is always usual for parents to give their children assistance in begining life (and I am only begining, though thirty five years of age, nearly) and what I ask is not much. I do not ask you to give me anything. But what I do ask is that you lend, or borrow for, me Five hundred dollars for two years, with interest at 10 pr. cent payable annually, and with this if I do not go on prosperously I shall ask no more from you. With this sum I can go on and cultivate my ground for marketing. . . . I have now in the ground twenty five acres of wheat. . . . I am getting some ten or twelve acres more cleared this winter which will turn off about 300 cords of wood that will be valuable next summer and winter; but the chopping has to be paid for now.
>
> The fact is, without means it is useless for me to go on farming, and I will have to do what Mr. Dent has given me permission to do; sell the farm and invest elsewhere. . . . Do not understand . . . that if I had what I ask for my exertions wood sease; but that they would [be] directed to a more profitable end. I regard evry load of wood taken, when the services of both myself and team [of horses] are required on the farm, is a direct loss of more than the value of the load. . . .

> My expenses for my family have been nothing scarcely for the last two years. Fifty dollars, I believe, would pay all that I have laid out for their clothing. I have worked hard and got but little and expect to go on in the same way until I am perfectly independent; and then too most likely. . . .
>
> Julia wishes to be remembered. Please answer soon.[70]

A national financial panic in 1857 shut off sources of cash, affecting both lenders and debtors. Farmers were hurting. Grant's family's want drove him to what must have been embarrassing lengths to feed them. A column of soldiers headed for New Mexico in 1857 was overtaken fourteen miles west of St. Louis by a shabby-looking Grant seeking the job of commissary clerk to drive the expedition's cattle overland and issue rations during the trek. He did not get the position.[71]

That he spent virtually nothing for clothing is well attested to by soldiers and fellow ex-soldiers who encountered him on the streets of St. Louis during this period. A dozen or more of them, at one time or another, saw him in fading military clothing, minus its insignia, during his forays to sell wood and other goods in the city. One former acquaintance from the Mexican War on his way to Fort Leavenworth detoured to see Grant and stopped a seedy-looking farmer riding a wagon to ask where he might find him. "I am he," the farmer answered. The soldier was stunned. "Great God, Grant, what are you doing?" he asked. Grant replied with the sort of laconic stoicism for which he would eventually become famous. "I am," he said, "solving the problem of poverty."[72] Sometimes old acquaintances would invite him into a hotel bar to talk over past times, and he would go and might smoke a cigar but would drink nothing but water.[73]

His hard and slimly rewarded labor continued through most of 1858. In late March he wrote his sister Mary that the spring had "opened finely for farming[,] and I hope to do well but I shall wait until the crops are gathered before I make any predictions."

> I have now three negro men, two hired by the year and one of Mr. Dent's, which, with my own help, I think, will enable me to do my farming pretty well, with assistance in harvest. I have however a large farm. I shall have about 20 acres of potatoes, 30 of corn, 25 of oats, 50 of wheat, 25 of meadow, some clover, Hungarian grass and other smaller products all of which require labor before they can

> be got into market, and the money realized upon them. You are aware, I believe, that I have rented out my place and have taken Mr. Dent's. There is about 200 acres of ploughed land on it, and I shall have, in a few weeks, about 200 acres of woods pasture fenced up besides. . . . In your letter you ask when my note in bank becomes due! The 17th of Apl. is the last day of grace when it must be paid and I don't see now that I shall have the money.[74]

Fever and ague, a sickness that had periodically afflicted his childhood and was characterized by alternating chills and high body temperature, had returned and begun to hound him, along with migraine headaches. All of these were likely products of stress.[75] He also exhibited symptoms of malaria, likely contracted on the hellish trek across Panama.[76] Julia, too, came down with ague, and some of their children—who now numbered four—and Colonel Dent's enslaved people also fell ill.[77] The family's financial situation, and its appearance to their acquaintances, grew ever grimmer. Although he did not complain or whine, acquaintances thought he often appeared sad, although silently so. The whole family eventually sickened, with Grant so much so that he was increasingly unable to tend his failing farm.

That fall, having not acquired adequate operating capital from Jesse Grant or anyone else, he left the fields. For Colonel Dent, he sold all the livestock and tools of the plantation, along with a few hundred acres of the land itself, and tentatively accepted the proffer of a job with his father, which he told the elder Grant that he "would prefer . . . to any one of mere salary that could be offered." He did not care for a "salaried position," he said in the same letter, but instead "want[ed] the prospect of one day doing business for myself."[78]

The position with his father, though, quickly fell through. Julia and the elder Grants were not fond of each other, of course, but although that was undoubtedly an indication of the unease, it likely was not the root of it. The root, almost certainly, was slavery.

HITTING BOTTOM

In a letter to his father on October 1, 1858, shortly after selling extensive acreage on the Dent plantation, Grant wrote that he expected to go to Covington, Kentucky, where his parents lived, "towards Spring." He added that he would likely be accompanied by an enslaved young man, "but this matter I leave entirely to you." He said Colonel Dent had advised him to take along this teenager, whom Dent had given to Julia as a servant, and "let him learn the farrier's business." If Jesse objected, his son implied, the youth could be left in St. Louis, where he would be able to earn Grant "about three dollars per month . . . now, and more as he gets older."[79] Grant's outspokenly abolitionist father almost certainly balked at even the mention of appending an enslaved person to his extended family. The continued intrusion of slavery into the father-son relationship may well have been what soured it yet again.

So Grant was forced to return to the aid of in-laws. Colonel Dent helped him found a new real estate firm in St. Louis in partnership with one of Julia's cousins, a man named Harry Boggs. There, according to cards the two began passing out, they would serve as "general agents" who would "collect rents, negotiate loans, buy and sell real estate, etc., etc."[80] Leaving his family at White Haven and having scant means of renting hotel accommodations, Grant moved into a small, all-but-bare room in the home of the Boggses, where Mrs. Boggs would remember that Grant appeared to be "a sad man . . . almost in despair. I don't think he saw a light ahead—not a particle."[81] The temperance-advocating Boggses were wary of his drinking. Mrs. Boggs said his "worst temptation was in meeting some old army friend."[82]

Living with the Boggses must have been miserable for Grant. They were Southern in sentiment, and he, although typically quiet about it, was the opposite. Regarded by his neighbors as a "Northern man" who did not share their enthusiasm for slavery, he was also unenthusiastic about the abolitionism he had heard more than enough of from Jesse—and continued to hear about antagonistically from Boggs.[83] With partisan rage intensifying across America, Grant was a nonpartisan patriot coming to occupy a political no-man's-land. He later said it "made my blood run cold to hear friends of mine, Southern men—as many of my friends were—deliberately discuss the dissolution of the Union as though it were a tariff bill. I could not endure it."[84]

While living with the Boggses he walked the twenty miles to White Haven each Saturday to see his family, returning to St. Louis the same way on Sunday. In early spring of 1859 he brought his family to St. Louis, installed them in a small house, and continued to try to collect rents and do his other dismal duties for the lackluster firm of Grant & Boggs. During March, the same month of the move, he took another significant step, which perhaps illustrates how the pressure of national dissension led men to take a second look at attitudes they had been handed by their society at birth. Or perhaps, working in his fields alongside another five-foot-seven human—but one of another color—named William Jones, Grant was forced to contemplate what it must have felt like to be Jones. If so, it is safe to say he did not like the feeling. Neighbors later recalled that this former officer accustomed to giving orders to soldiers did not have the stomach for giving them to enslaved people and then resorting to the traditional whips and other instruments of torture to compel them to obey. "He couldn't force them to do anything," Louisa Boggs remembered, likely with condescension. "He was just so good and good tempered."[85]

Whatever the reason, Jesse Grant's eldest son proceeded that March to free William Jones, the only enslaved person he himself had ever held title to, although it meant forgoing Jones's market value that was significantly more than the $500 he had tried to borrow from Jesse.[86] He never explained—outside the family, anyway—why he freed Jones. Julia, long accustomed to slavery and perhaps a little shamed by it in her reminiscing years, never mentioned the transaction, either. The certificate of manumission in the record of the St. Louis Circuit Court mentions "divers good and valuable considerations me hereunto moving [to free Jones],"[87] possibly indicating that Jones had paid Grant something for his freedom. There was, however, little chance Jones could have amassed sufficient means to pay any amount approaching his market value of $1,000.

Grant pressed on with the grim business of rent collecting, one for which even his proudly loyal wife saw him as supremely unfit. "I cannot imagine," she later wrote, "how my dear husband ever thought of going into such a business, as he never could collect a penny . . . owed to him."[88] He obviously went into it because he was at the end of his rope. But he had hardly gotten his family settled and his children into school in the city before, in mid-1859, the rope broke. This business for which he was so mismatched tottered and died when Mrs. Boggs talked her husband into withdrawing from the partnership and seeking a more gainful pursuit. Grant was soon flailing for whatever else he could find. On August 15 he applied for the position of county engineer, submitting a considerable collection of recommendations, but he soon found that the position would not be filled before the following February.[89]

There was another problem, too. The county commissioners charged with filling the job were dominated by Free-Soilers, with whom his many Dent connections were inimical. The engineer's post went to a Dutch immigrant, prompting the downcast and briefly bitter Grant to begin a soon-aborted weeklong membership in the secretive and nativist "American" or Know-Nothing political party. In February 1860, perhaps having heard rumors that the engineer appointee was about to vacate the position, he renewed his application, but the city retained the Dutchman.[90]

A month later, Grant was in Ohio, apparently making arrangements to accept a clerkship with his father's firm, which he did that spring. Jesse Grant was now retired, his $100,000-plus net worth being the equivalent of some $3 million today.[91] His business had become almost a mini-empire, with approximately fifty employees and stores and tanning operations in Ohio, Wisconsin, and Iowa. The center of the enterprise was the then-bustling Mississippi River port of Galena, Illinois. Grant's next-youngest brother, Simpson, had headed the home office, assisted by the remaining brother, Orvil, but Simpson was now dying of consumption and staying with Jesse and Hannah in Covington, Kentucky.

It seems to have been assumed that Ulysses would at least temporarily take over for Simpson, but apparently not in an authoritative capacity.[92] A cousin indicated there was no boss of the office; instead, the brothers and cousin worked rather communally, living out of a pooling of some of the firm's earnings set aside for their use rather than on the $600-per-year salary they nominally received.[93]

In his new position, Grant did not project great confidence in himself. A fellow Galena shopkeeper thought he was "a very poor businessman" who disliked interacting with customers. If caught being the only member of the firm in the office when a customer entered, he would ask the customer to wait. If the customer was in a hurry, Grant would "very reluctantly" get the requested item "but hardly ever knew the price of it" and thus often "charged either too much or too little."[94] He did not force himself on the community at large, instead meeting it almost with seeming reluctance, down-at-the-heels world-weariness, and laconic wit. For example, on a December evening shortly after arriving in town he showed up at a tavern on the fringe of a group of attorneys surrounding the stove and discussing a current law case. At length, somebody noticed him. "Stranger here?" he was asked.

"Yes."

"Traveled far?"

"Far enough."

"Looks as though you might have traveled through hell."

"I have."

"Well, how did you find things down there?"

"Oh, much the same as in Galena—lawyers nearest the fire."[95]

Even with its obvious discomfitures, the leather business agreed with Grant. It was preferable to starving. "In my new employment I have become pretty conversant and am much pleased with it," he resolutely wrote to a St. Louis businessman friend in December 1860[96]—despite the fact that, according to his father's later recollection, Simpson had agreed to send Ulysses to Galena only until another opportunity presented itself for him.[97] But Ulysses grabbed *this* opportunity like a drowning man seizing driftwood. "I hope to be a partner soon," he told the St. Louis friend, "and am sanguine that a competency at least can be made out of the business."[98]

But as he wrote that letter, the thing that would take him away from his "new employment" was already bearing swiftly down on the wrought-up nation, ready to spin Grant into the center of its maelstrom. Yet even the process of getting swept up would require the kind of dogged patience that the previous seven years had demanded. This man who would become the Civil War's supreme soldier would have to all but beg to be included in the conflict at all.

Like anybody else in the republic who kept himself or herself even marginally informed of public events, Grant saw a horrible cloud on the national horizon. Also like virtually everyone else, though, he had no inkling as to how horrific it would be or how the oncoming cataclysm would relate so centrally to him. In the same December letter in which he related to the St. Louis friend his hopes to become a partner in his father's leather business, he inquired how the secession of some Southern states then in progress was affecting the friend's business and attitude.

"It is hard to realize that a State or States should commit so suicidal an act as to secede from the Union," Grant wrote, "though from all the reports, I have no doubt but that at least five of them will do it. And then, with the present granny of an executive [indecisive Southern-born president James Buchanan], some foolish policy will doubtless be pursued which will give the seceding States the support and sympathy of the Southern States that don't go out."[99]

Grant's feelings on the matter were unequivocal. Most of his friends were Missourians and Southern in sentiment, but he was deeply opposed to their politics. As he would put it in a letter a few months later, he felt it to be the particular patriotic "duty of every one who has been educated at the Government expense"—such as himself and many of his fellow officer veterans of the Mexican War—"to offer their services for the support of that Government."[100]

Onrushing madness was overwhelming the disintegrating nation. Grant, like almost all of his peers north and south, misjudged the magnitude of the accumulating fury. He later recalled that as 1860 was turning into 1861, he and the "solid substantial people of the North-west"—now the Midwest—all but ceaselessly

> discussed whether the South would carry out its threat to secede and set up a separate government, the corner-stone of which should be, the protection to the "Divine" institution of slavery. . . . It was generally believed that there would be a flurry; that some of the extreme Southern States would go so far as to pass ordinances of secession. But the common impression was that this step was so plainly suicidal for the South, that the movement would not spread over much of the country and would not last long. . . . My own views at that time were like those officially expressed by Mr. [and Senator William H.] Seward at a later day, that—if there was armed conflict—"the war would be over in ninety days."[101]

On April 12, Southerners fired at a U.S. garrison occupying Fort Sumter in the harbor at Charleston, South Carolina, with cannon confiscated out of Federal armories. Five days later in Illinois, outraged Galenians gathered at the Jo Daviess County courthouse in a mass meeting that was initially, and not popularly, chaired by the town's Southern-born mayor, a man named Robert Brand. The mayor said he favored compromising with the Southern threat, but the townspeople had had more than enough compromise with the South's wealthy slaveholders. Another prominent Galenian, Maine-born Republican congressman Elihu B. Washburne, came to the rostrum and introduced resolutions in support of the Union. Washburne was followed by local Democratic attorney John Rawlins, who gave a whoopingly applauded speech positioning himself dead opposite to the mayor. He closed to raucous cheers by proclaiming that "the time of compromise is past, and we must appeal to the God of battles."

Grant and a friend had attended the tumultuous meeting together. As they left, the friend said he thought the gathering had turned out "fine . . . after all."

Grant quietly and approvingly agreed. "Yes," he said, "we're about to *do* something now."[102]

Truly. Galenians, like the inhabitants of hundreds of other small cities and towns across the Northern and Southern no-longer-united states, were afire with passion to teach the other side a lesson. A few nights later, the Galenians met again to form their first company of volunteers. But they found they had a problem: none of their longtime neighbors knew how to construct such a company.

Eventually, somebody remembered their community's recent newcomer and nominated "Captain U. S. Grant" to take over leadership of the gathering. Pressed forward, Grant was so stage-shy that he could barely put into words the meeting's purpose and ask the crowd to choose a secretary to record their action. By the time the latter issue was decided, though, the new chairman had recovered his composure. In language as succinct and unmistakably clear as the Civil War dispatches for which he would become famous, he called on his past experience in advising the prospective enlistees that "what will be required of you" would be far more difficult than the patriotic parading they had been doing.

"First of all," he told them, they would have to give "unquestioning obedience to your superior officers. The army is not a picnicking party, nor is it an excursion. You will have hard fare. You may be obliged to sleep on the ground after long marches in the rain and snow. Many of the orders of your superiors will appear to you unjust, and yet they must be borne. . . . If you put your name down here, it should be in full understanding of what the act means."[103]

After the organizers had gathered signatures, Grant turned down the post of captain of this company-to-be, with thanks. He did offer to go to Springfield with them to help with completion of the enlistment process. He explained to friends that he already had been a captain and could not "afford" to be one again. He was probably alluding to the size of his growing family, which had over the past half-dozen years endured more than enough belt-tightening. He also said he thought his nine years' experience as an officer in the regular army entitled him to lead a volunteer regiment as its colonel. He did tell the meeting that he would aid the company in any way he could and intended "to reenlist in the service myself."[104]

Grant never went back to his desk at the leather store. He spent his waking hours drilling the forming company, picking out cloth for its uniforms, directing sewing of the material, and teaching the officers their jobs. Then, after they paraded through Galena's streets in late April, he followed them onto the train to Springfield.[105]

There he entered the office of Illinois governor Richard Yates with a letter of introduction from Representative Washburne. Washburne had urged Grant to offer his services to Illinois rather than to his native Ohio and expressed hope that the letter could get him some meaningful work. The governor, though, did not seem impressed with the seedily dressed, middle-aged man in front of him.[106] Grant's personal appearance may not have been the only reason. Yates and Washburne were not close, having once had a disagreement as fellow congressmen. Too, they may have each been jealous of the other because they were rival politicians in the same state and each had a close, long-term friendship with President Lincoln.[107]

In any case, Grant had already waited several days to see the governor, and his never-fat purse was nearly flat. Friends had advised him against going home, but he had resolved to head there anyway when Yates, awash in enlistees, encountered him one evening at the hotel where they both ate and asked him to stay and come to see him the next morning. The next day, at the behest of influential Galenians, the governor put Grant to work for two dollars a day in a bare anteroom of the governor's office.[108] The task was to bring some order to the chaos, but it was menial, filling out forms, even drawing up the forms themselves, and performing other duties connected with mustering in new troops. Once again, Grant had to be talked out of going home.[109]

By the end of April, though, Yates detailed him to inventory the muskets available to Illinois troops. This may have been because Grant's abilities were becoming more evident. Or it may have been because no other man with the requisite level of military experience was around. Most of Grant's fellow civilian officer veterans of the Mexican War were in Washington or elsewhere lobbying for the highest ranks they could wheedle, pulling every political string in sight. Such self-promotion offended Grant's ingrained

Methodist humility and sense of fair-play. He superstitiously believed that he was doomed to fail at any job schemed or connived for. Trained regular army officers such as Grant tended to give politics a wide berth and minimal respect.

Within another week, the governor named Grant the commander of Camp Yates. Located on the western edge of the Illinois capital, the camp was the primary assembly point for the state's new volunteer troops. As its commander, Grant now had a salary of $4.20 a day and replaced a Mexican War acquaintance, Captain John Pope. But although this new office got Grant addressed as "Colonel," he remained a civilian, turning down an offer from the well-connected Pope to get Illinois politicians to help secure him an *actual* colonelcy.[110] The scope of his duties nevertheless continued to expand. On May 9, the governor sent him to southern and western parts of the state to formally muster in new regiments. When he reached Belleville and found no troops yet assembled, he crossed the Mississippi River to his recent hometown, St. Louis, to see his relatives by marriage.

It was not a happy reunion. His father-in-law was strongly in favor of the new Confederate States of America and wanted Julia and the Grant children to stay with him at White Haven while Grant was soldiering. He also tried to persuade Grant to become a Confederate. When Grant said no, the old man said he would shoot any Northern troops who trespassed on his property.[111]

While Grant was in St. Louis, Union sympathizers in that city narrowly averted a national disaster. Federal units prevented pro-Confederates from seizing an arsenal containing the South's largest supply of muskets and ammunition.[112] Captain Nathaniel Lyon, a West Point and old army acquaintance of Grant, commanded the local Federal regulars, and a Union loyalist congressman and colonel, Frank Blair Jr., led the volunteers. Grant may have hoped to attract some sort of offer of a command position while he was in St. Louis, but it did not happen. All he got was a front-row seat as Lyon and Blair captured the camp of the secessionist Missourians, held onto the arsenal, and pulled down several secessionist flags that had flown around town. Grant did see Blair on a horse leading volunteers and introduced himself, declaring his sympathy with Blair's action.[113] But no offer of a position was forthcoming.

During his visit, he also showed to history, if not to Blair or Lyon, the emphatic depth of his patriotic sympathies. On a horse-drawn trolley headed for the arsenal, he heard a windy Southern sympathizer exercising his lungs in a sparsely occupied trolley car.

"Things have come to a damn pretty pass," the man grumbled loudly, "when a free people can't choose their own flag. Where I came from if a man dares to say a word in favor of the Union we hang him to a limb of the first tree we come to."

That the normally laconic Grant made a reply, and what he replied, indicates how offensive he regarded this Southern "Confederacy" carved out of the nation to which he had sworn allegiance and fought for in Mexico. So does the fact that he recalled the incident so vividly in memoirs written a quarter century later. He wrote that he informed his fellow passenger that he and his former neighbors in St. Louis were "not so intolerant . . . as we might be." Then he added that he had "not seen a single rebel hung yet, nor heard of one; *there were plenty of them who ought to be, however.*" The fellow, he recalled in his book, "subsided."[114]

Recrossing the Mississippi, he mustered Illinois units at Belleville and Mattoon and returned to Springfield. There his mustering duties ended on May 22 with the filling of ranks of the last Illinois troops authorized by the state legislature. Two days later from Galena, he wrote a letter to Adjutant General Lorenzo Thomas in Washington. "Feeling it the duty of everyone who has been educated at the public expense," he wrote, he was volunteering his "services, until the close of the war, in such capacity as may be offered." He went on to add that, "in view of my present age and length of service, I feel myself competent to command a regiment, if the president, in his judgment, should see fit to entrust one to me." He closed by noting that he had been serving on the staff of the governor of Illinois organizing volunteers. Years later he confessed that he had felt "somewhat doubtful as to whether I would be equal" to commanding a regiment, but having seen militia colonels who had been mustered in both Illinois and Indiana, he "believed that if they could command a regiment . . . I could also."[115]

It did not matter, as it turned out. His letter got lost, to be discovered in 1865 stuck inexplicably in a Washington desk drawer. Perhaps it had been mislaid in the 1861 rush to multiply the tiny prewar army. Or perhaps its misplacement was another of the long-continuing repercussions of Grant's undistinguished exit from the old army, the tale of which was likely still making the rounds in the highest military circles in 1861. Given the small size of the prewar officer corps and the prevalence of its gossip, the latter seems more than likely.

Surely Grant could feel time, along with any prospective role in the anticipated short war, slipping away from him. Before his trip to St. Louis he had gotten wind of a possible impending command. In Springfield at the end of May he had found "that I had been spoken of for the Colonelcy of a Regiment now partly made up," he wrote to Julia on June 1. But nothing panned out. Also receiving no reply from his letter to the adjutant general, he took a leave to visit his parents in Covington, Kentucky. His real purpose was to visit the headquarters of new major general George B. McClellan in Cincinnati, directly across the Ohio River from Covington. "I was in hopes that when he saw me he would offer me a position on his staff," Grant later wrote. But McClellan did not see him at all. The problem seems likely to have been that McClellan remembered him all too well—specifically, that time at Fort Vancouver in 1853 when Quartermaster Grant started drinking before McClellan's mapmaking expedition had been completely outfitted. McClellan later claimed that he may have been inspecting troops in Indianapolis when Grant visited his office in 1861, but Grant said that was not what he was told at the time.[116] He waited for two hours outside McClellan's office on two successive days before giving up and going to look up an old army friend, Chilton White, who by now was a state legislator from Cincinnati. Grant told White his troubles.[117]

"I've tried to re-enter service in vain," he said. "I must live, and my family must live. Perhaps I could serve the army by providing good bread for them. You remember my success at bread-baking in Mexico?"[118]

4.

1861–1863: LAST LESSONS

✵✵✵✵

BACK IN COMMAND

He returned to Springfield, where he arrived on June 16. The next day he wrote to Julia of a momentous event.

In his absence his fortunes had taken a dramatic, long-awaited turn, perhaps the one forecast in his June 1 letter to Julia. "In a few days," he had added then, "all will be determined and then I will either go home to stay or will know what I am to do."[1] As it turned out, on June 15 Governor Richard Yates had issued an executive order naming Grant colonel of the Twenty-First Illinois Volunteers, a regiment Grant had mustered into the state's service at Mattoon on May 15. Grant learned of his appointment at Lafayette, Indiana, on his way back to Springfield.[2]

His appointed colonelcy, though, was a secondhand one. The Twenty-First Illinois was no prize. It had been the source of community dissatisfaction in Mattoon and of unflattering newspaper columns there and in St. Louis. Members had left their camp to carouse nightly in Mattoon and had stolen from area farmers. They did, however, have ample reason for discontentment, although it was no excuse: they had received no uniforms, were housed in sheds or stalls designed for farm animals at the Coles County fairgrounds, and had gone several days without blankets. Additionally, when their first muskets arrived, the load was so deficient that only half the men got one.

The initial commander whom they had elected, a former Decatur city clerk named Simon Goode, could not keep order when he tried to, which was not always. Sometimes he led men who were nominally on guard duty into town on drinking forays, and in personal appearance he was ridiculous. He carried three pistols and a bowie knife, claimed he never slept, quoted

Napoleon, and threatened to dare Confederate president Jefferson Davis to do battle with an equal number of men on each side, giving Davis the choice of site.[3]

Perhaps Goode's final straw occurred on the Twenty-First's train trip to Springfield, during which its members again drew newspaper notice. They were rowdily undisciplined on the train, and, not surprisingly, the *Illinois State Journal* in Springfield reported that they "needed more . . . drill." The subordinate officers conferred about the situation with Governor Yates and voted to make Grant their new colonel—for whom they already had indicated esteem by naming their incommodious Mattoon base "Camp Grant" after he had mustered them there.[4]

The fact that Yates issued his executive appointment exactly a month after Grant had mustered the regiment into thirty-day Illinois service indicates the appointment was aimed at encouraging the regiment to reenlist in the Federal army for three years or for the duration of the war. Grant went out to Camp Yates on June 16, accompanied by John E. Smith, Jo Daviess County treasurer. Smith was also a leader of the local Wide-Awakes, a Unionist citizen defense organization that Grant had helped to drill. The new colonel arrived dressed so "clumsily," Smith later recalled—"an old coat, worn out at the elbows, and a badly dinged plug hat"—that the men of the waiting regiment, "though ragged and barefooted themselves, . . . began making fun of him." Some mock-sparred at him from behind, and one knocked off his hat. When he turned and challenged them with a look, though, they withered and shrank back, and one tried to apologize for them.[5]

Grant's appointment took effect the next day, June 17, and the day after that he returned to Camp Yates. A lieutenant saw him enter the tent of the adjutant and say, "I guess I'll take command"—and he quickly did, sitting down to write out an order announcing that he was doing so and that he *required* the cooperation of all commissioned and noncommissioned officers to "instruct" the command and maintain discipline. In the same order, very significantly, he *requested* "the hearty support of every enlisted man."[6] He then walked through the camp to look it over and quickly showed eminent confidence in his ability to handle the Twenty-First Illinois. He disbanded an eighty-man detachment armed with clubs that Colonel Goode had posted near the camp boundary fence to keep troops from making forays into Springfield. He said the detachment would no longer be needed for that duty because the men would be required to be present at roll-call formations held several times a day.[7]

The next day, June 19, he issued two orders formalizing what he had said. One provided that no passes out of camp would be given unless approved by the colonel, but during the day no passes would be required—unless the "leniency" of the order was abused to necessitate its retraction.[8] The other announced that there would be drills 6:00–7:00 A.M., 10:00–11:00 A.M., and 5:00–6:00 P.M.[9] Six days later, a lieutenant in the Twenty-First wrote home that Grant's new system was working well:

> We have certain hours for drill each day, and every man must be on hand. If he is not, as soon as he gets back, into the Guard House he goes pop sure, and hours that they [the men] are not required to drill they can go where they please. The guard house was not large enough for the first few nights and days, but yesterday there was but two or three in [it] and today none. No person is allowed out of camp after dark unless by permission of the Col. So you see we have the best of order, and everything moves off pleasantly.[10]

Meanwhile on June 19, nine weeks into the war, two Illinois congressmen visited the camp to urge the new recruits to reenlist for three years in the Federal army. The two, John A. McClernand and John A. (Black Jack) Logan, would shortly become generals and would play widely varying roles in Grant's future. They were both Democrats from the southern part of the state, which had been settled largely by former Kentuckians, but McClernand, at least, was well known for strongly supporting the Lincoln national government. Grant was skeptical of Logan, having read "denunciations" of him in Republican newspapers disapproving of him for staying mostly silent on the question of secession and its recent national result. Grant hesitated about giving permission for Logan to speak.

"It was but a few days before the time set for mustering into the United States service such of the men who were willing to volunteer for three years or the war," Grant recalled in his memoirs, and "I had some doubt as to the effect a speech from Logan might have; but as he was with McClernand . . . I gave my consent." McClernand opened the speechmaking, followed by Logan. The latter's address, Grant wrote, was "hardly equaled since for force and eloquence. It breathed a loyalty and devotion to the Union which inspired my men to such a point that they would have volunteered to remain in the army as long as an enemy of the country continued to bear arms against it. They entered the United States service almost to a man."[11] Logan's remarks urging his audience to reenlist included a memorable one that was unpretentious and humorous but hit home like a hammer.

"You can't fall out now," Logan told them. "If you go home now to Mary, she will say, 'Why, Tom, are you home from the war so soon?' 'Yes.' 'How far did you get?' 'Mattoon.'"[12]

The laughter evoked by that final, sarcastic word assured that virtually every member of this state militia regiment would enter its new incarnation as a unit representing the United States. As he closed the speech, Logan—black-haired, black-eyed, upright, and dynamic—introduced the little man in worn civilian clothes beside him as the unit's new colonel. The assembled military neophytes must have at least sensed that this officer was not yet prosperous enough to buy a uniform. Nevertheless, long accustomed to speeches from the notables on such occasions, the new troops called for one from this shabbily attired person being characterized as their new leader. They got no speech. Instead, they received five words delivered in a calm, commanding tone that said that the man speaking was no politician but instead a soldier who had already been where they were headed—and did not shrink from the bloody prospect of returning there.

"MEN, GO TO YOUR QUARTERS!"[13]

Surprised, they looked quizzically at each other. Then they complied with this initial order from the strange little man who obviously knew how to give one.

"So long as no acceptable theory, no intelligent analysis of the conduct of war exists," Carl von Clausewitz wrote of commanders, "routine methods will tend to take over even at the highest levels. Some of the men in command have not had the opportunities of self-improvement afforded by education and contact with the higher levels of society and government. . . . Their only insights are those that have been gained by experience."[14]

Clausewitz here almost certainly refers only to *military* experience, but this distinction, even if merely implied, raises a question essential to a military biography of Ulysses S. Grant. What did Grant's seven years in his post-resignation wilderness of public disappointment, embarrassment, and penurious struggle have to do with the extraordinary generalship that followed? Looking at his Civil War performance, one is tempted to answer: almost everything.

Grant *had* been "self-improved," to use Clausewitz's term, by an education—and at West Point, no less—although he did not relish it. On the other hand, he had hardly had much significant "contact with the higher levels of society and government." He *had* received the examples of two very different and yet variously worthy military commanders in Zachary Taylor and Winfield Scott. And, in Mexico, he had enjoyed—if that is the word—a war experience of dimensions rivaled by that of few other officers on his junior level. But these things, his years in the nonmilitary wilderness tell us, are nowhere near the sum of the kind of know-how, physical and psychological, he would be able to call on during his dogged and labyrinthine search for a key to the conquest of Vicksburg in 1863, his army's escape from a Confederate trap and its subsequent all-out rush to victory at Chattanooga that same year, or the long and bitter slog from Spotsylvania to Appomattox in 1864–65.

That Clausewitz missed or ignored the importance of a general's *civilian* experience at first seems a bit odd in an expert who, having begun as a twelve-year-old lance corporal of infantry and son of a tax collector,[15] surely himself possessed some of this kind of background and experience. On the other hand, it is perhaps natural in an author who had occupied only staff positions and had never seen great supreme commanders rise from Grant's level of society and who, by the time he was writing his classics, had himself become accustomed to extensive "contact with the higher levels of society and government" and had written books highlighting the exploits of two dominant commanders—Napoleon Bonaparte and Frederick the Great—whose careers had been born to and had inhabited and gloried in society's highest strata: commanders, in other words, whose lives had never plumbed such plebeian depths as Grant had occupied for much of his life. The kind of civilian experience Napoleon and Frederick had enjoyed would have embodied little to none of the stress that Grant had endured, particularly in trying to feed and clothe a family during his years between the wars.

Also, and perhaps pivotally, it should be noted that Grant's most celebrated opponent in his post-wilderness years *had* enjoyed—in spades—the benefit of all those glittering "opportunities" Clausewitz mentioned. Yet Robert E. Lee lost. As son of one of the most famed figures of the American Revolution (no matter how time later tarnished that fame) and related by marriage to none other than George Washington, Lee had long been a foremost member of Virginia's vaunted Tidewater—that is, high—society.

In the Mexican War, he had occupied much higher positions of responsibility than had Grant. And whereas Grant too had gone to West Point, Lee had not just gone there but had graduated with one of its most impressive records in history and had later been its commandant.

Yet, as we have noted, Grant defeated Lee in the Civil War. Why? What was the difference in what we now term the "skill sets"—attitudinal and physical—of Grant and Lee? What advantages could a commoner like Grant possibly have had over an aristocrat like Lee? If there were any, they certainly were not traits perceived to be advantages at the time. Yet they must have *been* advantages, because they are the most obvious differences in the two men's careers.

Confederate partisans no doubt will protest that the argument is pointless, that Lee lost and Grant won only because Grant enjoyed overwhelming strength in numbers of troops and weapons, whereas Lee's Army of Northern Virginia was worn out with casualty depletion by the time it had to face Grant. True enough, perhaps. But who wore it out? *Lee* did, rashly hurling his tattered and barefoot legions against George B. McClellan's guns during the Seven Days' Battles, against George G. Meade's guns over the three days at Gettysburg, and so on. He gambled his army away, mistakenly assuming that each great victory he won would impel the Union to quit the war. He disastrously misjudged not just his own strength but especially that of his enemy.

The most important point here, though, is perhaps that *Lee was almost right.* If the military fate of the Union had fallen to any other hands than Grant's, how much longer might the war have lasted? And how much more would the Northern public have endured before making peace?

So Lee can perhaps be forgiven his error. For the first three-quarters of the war, his battlefield opponents had been led by men from near his level of society, and he had whipped them spectacularly, often embarrassingly. But for the war's final year, by contrast, he was faced with a leader from a supposedly lower class whose measure he had not been required to take before—a measure that, before this moment, he would not have had to stoop to take. So he was utterly unaccustomed to seeing a man like Grant lead an army against him, especially such a man as Grant backed by another such—Abraham Lincoln—who, like Grant, had climbed out of society's basement. Lee can hardly be blamed. *He had not seen men like them lead armies and nations.* No one had.

By contrast, from the beginning Grant, unlike Lee, had understood that the North had every bit of the physical wherewithal to win if it had the mental will to use it wisely and to the fullest. Soon after the South took Fort Sumter, he had written his sister that "if the South knew the entire unanimity of the North for the Union and maintenance of Law, and how freely men and money are offered for the cause, they would lay down their arms at once." Interestingly, in the same letter he voiced profound disappointment in Lee's Virginia—especially the part of it in which Lee lived.

> The conduct of eastern Virginia has been so abominable . . . that there would be a great deal of disappointment here if matters should be settled before she is thoroughly punished. This is my feeling, and I feel it universal. Great allowance should be made for South Carolinians, for the last generation have been educated, from their infancy, to look upon their Government as oppressive and tyrannical and only to be endured till such time as they might have sufficient strength to strike it down. Virginia, and other border states, have no such excuse and are therefore traitors in heart as well as in act.[16]

Grant and Lincoln represented a far different breed from Lee and Confederate president Jefferson Davis. Both identified strongly with their sweating, laboring enlisted men. One has only to recall Grant's wish in Mexico to march afoot, rather than ride on horseback, with his company, since his men would have to do so, being infantry rather than cavalry.[17] The patricians Lee and Davis no doubt loved their men, but they most assuredly did not identify with them. The soldiers of the Army of Northern Virginia, for example, tended to regard Lee as a distinguished and almost immaculate all-but-god—and he, whether consciously or unconsciously, likely saw the gulf between himself and them as fully that wide. Grant was likely not far off the mark when he wrote in the *Personal Memoirs* that the South's prewar plantation aristocracy regarded the non-slaveholders who made up "the great bulk of the legal voters of the South . . . as poor white trash who were allowed the ballot so long as they cast it according to direction."[18] Most of the common soldiers of the South came from that class.

Thus Grant probably felt he had more in common with Lee's men than Lee did. In his memoirs he remarked that they were so dominated by the slavocrats that "they too"—like the enslaved population—"needed emancipation."[19] Grant's own men seem to have admired him as devotedly as the

Army of Northern Virginia did Lee, but more as an extraordinary one of their own: gritty, disheveled, stubble-bearded, unfashionable, and understatedly tough, by extension all but "poor white trash." Lee likely saw him the same way. To his men in ranks, though, Grant surely seemed less like a god and more like the respected foreman of their grim, hardy work crew.

Lee's defeat was only the final, historic indication of the importance of the hard civilian years that had bisected Grant's military career. Without them, Lee might have taken a somewhat different view of his scruffy 1864–65 opponent. And Grant might have been less driven to prevail.

"THE QUIET MAN"

They called him "the quiet man,"[20] and for good reason. His every action, characterized by understated efficiency, accomplished much. As Abraham Lincoln would approvingly observe in his homely fashion three years later, Grant was not often noticeable, but the feverish industry that accompanied him was. "He," Lincoln said, employing a rural expression for motion with which Grant himself would have been familiar, "makes things git!"[21]

Unlike so many other colonels at the outset of the Civil War, most notably the political ones soldiering for the first time, Grant already knew how to be an army officer. He had been one for years, in many instances under fire. He was accustomed to giving orders and seeing them obeyed. He also had led a company for a significant period as a captain, if only a mostly provisional one. Stepping into command of a regiment from that of a company would not have been terribly difficult, since day-to-day operational direction of the larger unit was not so different from that of the smaller one. Basically it entailed dealing with several companies instead of one, more subordinates, and more orders from higher-ranking commanders.

Other than during combat, perhaps the most significant difference was the requirement to deal more in person with military, and potentially civilian, politics. The realities of such would not have been foreign to Grant. The all-important place of politics in a soldier's life, even if unpleasant, would have been no stranger to Grant than to Clausewitz. Politics—inside the army and out—was the primary engine of soldiering. Grant had long taken an active interest in keeping himself informed about national affairs and had already, up close, seen blood shed and lives lost in that great political creation of President James K. Polk, the Mexican War. He had continued to follow the machinations of Washington ever since, seeing the agitation over slavery fanned hotter by the nation's new Mexican conquests, as slaveholders and abolitionists vied to reap political spoils from the vast new territories.

The maturation of Grant's political viewpoint had occurred slowly, however, and in fact was continuing to develop as he reentered the army. Its early submersion is perhaps evidenced, and was almost certainly influenced, by his attraction to a slaveholder's daughter. A similar influence was likely the muted tension with his abolitionist father. Because of his connection to Julia's family, some of his friends concluded that he was a dedicated Democrat,[22] the party that coddled slavery. But up-close familiarity with a plantation worked by those people evoked less than his all-out enthusiasm, illustrated by his refusal to "drive" enslaved people to perform labor he himself was doing and badly needed help with. This reinforced an opinion among others that he was a "Northern man" not in agreement with the prevailing sentiment in Missouri.

But well before he was appointed colonel of the Twenty-First Illinois, his fealty to the North—and his enmity toward the seceded South—was total. In a letter to his father almost two months before his appointment, he wrote that there were but two political parties now, "Traitors & Patriots, and I want hereafter to be ranked with the latter."[23]

On June 21, 1861, two days after Congressman Black Jack Logan's masterful speech, Grant left Camp Yates for a swift visit home to Galena. On June 24, he showed up back in camp in a colonel's uniform he had had made in the interim.[24] But he did not wear the whole thing, according to the regiment's chaplain, except when doing so could hardly be avoided: on dress parade. Such of it as he wore day-to-day was reminiscent of Old Zack, forsaking the look of gentlemen of military autocracy. It amplified the message in his first order to the regiment: "In accepting this command, your Commander will *require* the cooperation of all the commissioned and non-commissioned Officers in instructing the command, and in maintaining discipline, and *hopes to receive* also the hearty support of every enlisted man."[25] The simple blue tunic with no rank visible would have conveyed vast significance to most enlisted men, if not indeed to the rest of the world. It declared Grant's preferred kinship with "the men," among whom he, by implication, included his fellow officers. In his mind, he and they were all cogs in a huge human machine constructed to do a job, not show off. The symbolism among his fellow officers was as striking as among the ranks. *This* man chose to command by commanding rather than by wearing the *trappings* of command. Such a choice was very different from that made by virtually all his fellow field officers, whether "old army" veterans or ex-office-holding former civilians hoping to accentuate prewar careers. It was a declaration that Grant unabashedly identified with the mass of society, not its elite. The message was a near-religious one that no man, officer or enlisted man, had to be around him long to comprehend.

By June 24, he already had had a pronounced effect on his regiment of former hellions. On June 17, the day he formally took command after arriving on the sixteenth, the *Chicago Tribune* reported that the regiment's "insubordination is rapidly disappearing." On June 22, the *Illinois State Register* in Springfield wrote that the men "are good soldiers in camp and present the strongest evidence of a willingness to do their duty well at all times."[26]

The Twenty-First was earmarked for duty in Missouri to contend with Confederate depredations. Grant initially received orders to get there by way of Quincy, Illinois, where he was to await transportation down the Mississippi River by boat. The *Chicago Tribune* reported on June 22 that Grant wished to *march* the unit to Quincy, rather than have it transported there by train. "I thought for the purpose of discipline and speedy efficiency for the field it would be well to march the regiment across the country," he recalled in a later communication to the Illinois adjutant general's office.[27]

There was likely more to it than that. Masses of young men need occupation to keep their idle hands from finding more alluring workshops, and the more physical exercise involved in the occupation the better. Although Grant was probably twice as old as many of his men, he was not dissimilar in the need for something to do. He badly needed a project—or the presence of his family—on which to concentrate his thoughts and keep his thirst at bay. While back on the Dents' Missouri farm peddling wood in St. Louis, he had met old army friends on the street and went with them into bars, but drank only water.[28] While working at the leather store in Galena, whose river-town saloons numbered more than fifty, he apparently consumed no alcohol. On sales trips to little towns in Wisconsin, Minnesota, and Iowa, he often loosened up enough to allow himself a drink after dinner, but that was all.[29] A cross-country march would help keep him occupied and away from the bottle.

In letters to Julia in late June and early July, Grant seemed to obliquely address possible home curiosity about his own deportment and, more straightforwardly, that of the men in his new command. He said he was "very much pleased" with his subordinate officers, who included a lieutenant colonel and a major of whom "I think a great deal" but with whom "I can never have a game of Euchre. One is a preacher and the other a member of [the] Church. For the Field officers of my regt. . . . one pint of liquor will do to the end of the war."[30]

Of his men, after four days of marching he wrote that he did not think "there is a more orderly set of troops in the volunteer service. I have been very strict with them and the men seem to like it. They appreciate that it is all for their own benefit."[31] On July 9 he issued an order praising them as comparable to "veteran troops."[32] He wrote his father on July 13 that "the lesson" of the hike toward Quincy "has been a good one for them. They can now go into camp after a day's march with as much promptness as veteran troops; they can strike their tents and be on the march with equal celerity."[33]

The intended march to Quincy began on July 3[34] but was aborted two-thirds of the way there. New orders instructed Grant to hold the regiment at the Illinois River for transportation by steamboat to St. Louis.[35] When the steamboat that was to carry the troops grounded on a sandbar before reaching them, Confederate activity prompted other orders directing them to take a train to Quincy. They were then to cross the Mississippi to Palmyra, Missouri, and rescue another Illinois regiment that had been reported surrounded by Confederates west of Palmyra along the Hannibal and St. Joseph Railroad.[36]

Here Grant began to learn what he termed a "valuable lesson" for a leader of an army. He recalled much later that he initially felt "anything but agreeable" approaching what he expected to be his first battlefield as a commander: "I had been in all the engagements in Mexico that it was possible for one person to be in; but not in command. If someone else had been colonel and I had been lieutenant-colonel I do not think I would have felt any trepidation." This statement is remindful of his awed thought on approaching his first potential action in the Mexican War, where he sympathized with the stress of responsibility Zachary Taylor must have been feeling with 3,000 men dependent on his leadership. Grant's anxiety in 1861 in Missouri was soon relieved, however, when the supposedly besieged troops he had been ordered to find and help "came straggling" into Palmyra unpursued but apparently frightened.[37]

Less than a week later, he was ordered out to Florida, Missouri, to try to capture some 1,200 Confederate-sympathizing State Guardsmen under Confederate brigadier general Thomas Harris. Because the area was thinly settled, Grant had trouble gathering enough horses and wagons to move the regiment along with its equipment, supplies, and ammunition. But before leaving, he wrote his father that he believed Harris, whose troops were mounted, would not be catchable.[38] On the road, though, he became more concerned. The country through which he had to travel was deserted, he later remembered, except for two horsemen who fled on being seen. He became "anything but easy," he recalled in his memoirs, and by the time he neared the brow of a hill overlooking the creek bottom where Harris had been thought to be camped, "I would have given anything . . . to be back in Illinois, but I had not the moral courage to halt and consider what to do." On reaching the crest of the hill, though, he was relieved to see the Harris campsite deserted. "It occurred to me at once that Harris had been as much afraid of me as I had been of him," he wrote, adding that it was a "valuable" lesson he never forgot afterward. "From that event to the close of the war, I never experienced trepidation upon confronting an enemy, though I always felt more or less anxiety. I never forgot that he had as much reason to fear my forces as I had his."[39]

Grant's military career now suddenly, and seemingly coincidentally, took off. On July 24, five weeks after he had taken charge of the Twenty-First Illinois, his superior Brigadier General John Pope assigned Grant the command of all troops around Mexico, Missouri. Seven days later, Abraham Lincoln nominated him for promotion to brigadier general, seemingly at the urging of Congressman Elihu Washburne. Grant read of his good fortune in the *Missouri Democrat,* a St. Louis newspaper, on August 3, but the promotion did not become official until six days later—and apparently was not officially published until August 20.[40]

On August 5, Pope sent Grant to St. Louis to meet with the new western commander, Major General John C. Frémont. Pope entrusted Grant with informing Frémont "of the policy I am pursuing here and its effects upon the people." Perhaps miffed by Grant's initial refusal of his offer to use his political clout to get Grant a colonelcy, Pope was thought by some to have tarnished Grant's reputation early on as a prospective colonel by intimating to Illinois politicians the circumstances under which he had left the army in 1854.[41] Nevertheless, Pope now introduced Grant in a letter to Frémont as "an old army officer[,] thoroughly a gentleman & an officer of intelligence and discretion."[42]

During the next month, in a flurry of assignments, Grant was given command of three regiments besides his own at Ironton, Missouri, which were anticipating an attack by Confederates under Brigadier General William J. Hardee.[43] The attack never materialized. Nine days later, Frémont mistakenly ordered Grant replaced by Brigadier General Benjamin Prentiss, assuming Prentiss had seniority; he did not. When Grant went immediately to St. Louis to iron the matter out, Frémont resolved it by rushing Grant into command at the state capital, Jefferson City. Frémont apparently was thereby complying with a directive from Pope, the district commander, that the region of northeast Missouri "eminently needed" a "discreet prudent man . . . for immediate supervision of the disaffected counties north of the Hannibal & St. Joseph [rail]road."[44]

On August 28, Frémont ordered Grant to Cape Girardeau to supervise movement against Brigadier General M. Jeff Thompson of Missouri state troops. The movement did not happen because Prentiss again refused to serve under Grant, still apparently believing himself superior in rank. But rank may not have been his only reason. Prentiss also is reported to have told a fellow officer that he would not "serve under a drunkard."[45] The result, though, was that the accused drunkard—who from the outset had taken almost draconian measures to keep accessibility to alcohol away from his rapidly expanding command—was assigned on September 4 to command all troops in southeastern Missouri and southern Illinois. His headquarters would be a river town that Grant would quickly transform into the most strategic Federal army position in the western theater in the fall of 1861: Cairo, Illinois.

PADUCAH—"I HAVE COME AMONG YOU NOT AS AN ENEMY"

In the thirteen pages Clausewitz employed to discuss military strategy involving rivers, he gave twelve of those pages to waterways that run parallel to the enemy's line. Only the final page devotes a few lines to those divergent ones that point straight into the heart of what in Grant's time was termed "the seat of war": the area of impending combat.

"Generally speaking, a river's role as a means of transportation is its most favorable aspect as far as the attacker is concerned[,] provided it runs at right angles to the front: [but] his lines of transportation are longer and he therefore has greater problems moving up his supplies," the classic strategist wrote. "Water transport will, therefore, come as a relief and be an advantage."[46]

The renowned theorist likely gave such short shrift to a situation like Grant's in September 1861 because he could hardly imagine a panoply of strategic riches such as Grant found confronting him. Cairo, his new headquarters, was situated on the state of Illinois's southernmost point, one jutting arrow-like into the mingling waters where the Ohio River joins the Mississippi—and pointing fatefully toward the heart of the Confederacy. Other such seeming signposts were close by. Forty-five miles from Cairo up the Ohio lay the mouth of the Tennessee, and just beyond that the mouth of the Cumberland.

Back at the Missouri town of Mexico less than a month earlier, Grant had sat under a tree studying maps spread out before him, maps of not just Missouri but the entire western theater. As an aggressive soldier with common sense, he recognized that the Mississippi, the Tennessee, and the Cumberland all offered the best attack routes into the seceded South west of the Appalachian Mountains.

The Cumberland rolled down to Nashville out of eastern Kentucky before finally turning north again toward the Blue Grass State, crossing its west side and intersecting the Ohio. The Tennessee flowed all the way to the Ohio out of eastern Tennessee, meandering through northwest Georgia, northern Alabama, and a tiny portion of northeast Mississippi before it, too, took a sharp right turn due north to cross Tennessee and Kentucky and emptied into the Ohio. And the Mississippi, legendary Father of Waters, swept past Cairo southward to pass between Kentucky and Missouri, Tennessee and Arkansas, and Mississippi and Louisiana all the way to New Orleans.

Grant's actions within hours of assuming the Cairo command showed that his study of his maps had been no idle one. He very well understood the geography of the central South and those rivers' import for war—and ached to accept their spectacular invitation. It was as if fate, not Frémont, had picked him for this job. He had gone to Cairo in the first place because, to counteract increasing Confederate activity on the Mississippi, Frémont envisioned an operation southward along that wide stream. His ultimate goal was Columbus, Kentucky, a point so high and commanding on the Mississippi's eastern bank that if grabbed by the Confederates it would be a monumental obstacle; cannon well-placed there could control river traffic in both directions. As a preliminary, Frémont had planned a foray from Cairo to tiny Belmont, Missouri, just across the river from Columbus, and had chosen Grant to lead the expedition.[47]

Why he chose Grant, whom he had barely seen—and who he could not know did not much like him[48]—is somewhat understandable, despite Grant's old army reputation. A Grant acquaintance from the Mexican War persuaded Frémont that a well-occupied Grant would not be receptive to alcoholic temptation[49] and that he was the best man available. Most of Frémont's other brigadiers, such as Prentiss and McClernand, were after all former civilian politicians who almost certainly evinced more lust for glory than did Grant. And close proximity to other highly ambitious men was likely something the egotistical Frémont preferred to avoid.

Prentiss's prideful disruption of the aborted Jeff Thompson entrapment scheme turned out to be fortunate for Grant and the Union. Instead of taking him off into the interior of Missouri as the Thompson chase would have done, the Prentiss problem stymied that plan and prompted Grant to move his headquarters to Cairo—just two days before a naked Confederate power grab occurred in his front. One of the few military officers whom he had long ridiculed suddenly violated Kentucky's self-declared neutrality. Confederate brigadier general Gideon Pillow, ordered forward by western theater commander Leonidas Polk, not only beat the Federals to Columbus but now, according to Union intelligence, was about to march with 4,000 troops on critical Paducah, which controlled the mouth of the Tennessee.

Like many West Pointers who had served in the Mexican War, Grant regarded the militarily untrained, proudly upper-class, and highly egotistical Pillow as a cartoonish buffoon. In an infamous incident at Camargo, Pillow had ordered his troops to dig their supposedly protective ditch *inside* their breastworks instead of outside, causing widespread military merriment. Pillow was also the epitome of a political general, appointed to wear his splendid Mexican War uniform by his close friend President James K. Polk, in whose nomination for the presidency he had been singularly significant.

Pillow's main mission in Mexico had been presumably to spy for Polk on potential Whig presidential aspirants Zachary Taylor and Winfield Scott. Pillow thus personified everything about politics that Grant disliked, military or otherwise. To allow himself to be beaten to Paducah by Pillow, of all people, would have been little short of mortifying.

But in this situation any Confederate, not just Pillow, would likely have activated Grant's aggressive second nature exactly as Pillow did. On September 5, immediately on hearing of the Confederate incursion, Grant hastened to act. He dashed off a brief and cryptic wire to "Speaker House of Representatives" in Frankfort to inform the Kentucky state legislature that "Confederate forces in Considerable numbers have invaded the territory of Kentucky."[50] He also sent another dispatch to Frémont saying that if the commander did not reply to the contrary he would leave that evening to get ahead of the Paducah-bound Confederates. This Grant dispatch is lost to history. There remains only a second one he sent soon afterward noting that he already that day had "fully" telegraphed "all information" and informed Frémont that his Cairo force was "now nearly ready for Paducah on the strength of the information [previously] telegraphed."[51] He soon sent another, briefer one: "I am getting ready to go to Paducah. Will start at 6½ o'clock."[52]

He did not, though. Instead, he waited until after 10:00 P.M., when no forbidding reply from Frémont had yet arrived. Actually, Frémont *had* replied, but—seemingly oddly, in such pressing circumstances—he did it by letter. He also sent a telegram, but only after taking time to translate both it and the letter into the Hungarian language, which served as a code he used for secrecy. In the letter, he told Grant to go ahead to Paducah "if you feel strong enough," which again sounds somewhat offhand and vague in such a crisis.[53] It also sounds as if Grant had a better realization of Paducah's significance than Frémont did.

By the time Frémont's wire and letter reached Cairo, Grant had gone. He presumed he knew what Frémont's answer would be—or, at any rate, *should* be. With two regiments and a battery of four cannon on three transport vessels escorted by two gunboats, Grant steamed up the Ohio overnight and disembarked at Paducah at 8:30 A.M. the next day, September 6. Secessionist flags were flying and the local residents, who had been expecting the Confederates, "came out of their doors looking pale and frightened" to find Federals there instead.[54] Confederate brigadier general Lloyd Tilghman and his staff and a company of Paducah troops they had just recruited had hurriedly departed by railroad and taken all the cars that had been on hand in the city. At the depot, though, they had left behind "a large number of complete rations and about two tons of leather" intended for the Confederate army. Grant ordered the rations distributed to his soldiers, put detachments out to guard the roads and the town itself,[55] and issued a proclamation to the locals:

> I have come among you, not as an enemy, but as your friend and fellow-citizen, not to injure or annoy you, but to respect the rights, and to defend and enforce the rights of all loyal citizens. An enemy, in rebellion against our common Government, has taken possession of, and planted its guns upon the soil of Kentucky and fired upon our flag. Hickman and Columbus are in his hands. He is moving upon your city. I am here to defend you against this enemy and to assert and maintain the authority of your Government and mine. I have nothing to do with opinions. I shall deal only with armed rebellion and its aiders and abetors. You can pursue your usual avocations without fear or hindrance. The strong arm of the Government is here to protect its friends and to punish only its enemies. Whenever it is manifest that you are able to defend yourselves, to maintain the authority of your Government and protect the rights of all its loyal citizens, I shall withdraw the forces under my command from your city.[56]

By noon, he was headed back to Cairo, which he reached by 4:00 P.M., having left the troops at Paducah along with the two gunboats and a steamboat. As soon as he had wired Frémont a summary of his work he was gone again, this time to Cape Girardeau, Missouri, to bring forward the Eighth Missouri Volunteers to reinforce the troops at Paducah.[57] He had left the officer in charge there with instructions all but identical to those he had previously issued to his troops wherever he was; that these were directed at troops in potentially rebellious territory only made them more appropriate.

"You are charged to take special care and precaution that no harm is done to inoffensive citizens," he said in written orders to the officer. "That the soldiers shall not enter any private dwelling nor make any searches unless by your orders and then a detail shall be made for that purpose. Exercise the strictest discipline against any soldier who shall insult citizens, or engage in plundering private property."[58]

In the several such orders he had issued since returning to the army, he showed his deep consciousness of the Clausewitz principle that the military is inextricably connected to the surrounding civilian world and thus its every action is immediately political or potentially so. He also showed his instinctive and abiding identification with defenseless civilians, loyal or otherwise, with whom his troops had to interact.

For his hard day's work and extraordinary efficiency in grabbing Paducah, Grant got precious little thanks from St. Louis. Along with Frémont's tardy and then-irrelevant dispatch telling him to take Paducah if he felt "strong enough," he found at Cairo another message. It was from a Frémont staff officer, and, on Frémont's orders, it all but condemned him for having sent his telegram to the Kentucky legislature.

"I am directed by Major General Fremont to inform you that Brigade and other Commanders are not to correspond with State or other high authorities, in matters pertaining to any branch of the public service, either in initiating such correspondence or in replying thereto," wrote Major Joseph H. Eaton. "All such subjects are to be submitted to the Major General Commanding the Department for his information and action."[59]

Notwithstanding Frémont's obvious displeasure, Grant hardly seems to have been out of line with honorable military tradition. Perhaps Frémont was chagrined that he had not thought of notifying the legislature himself. Or more likely he was angry because Grant's message to the Kentucky legislature exhibited a concern for the feelings of potential enemies, which sharply contrasted with edicts Frémont himself had issued in Missouri exactly one week earlier. On August 30, Frémont had taken it upon himself to (1) declare martial law throughout the state, (2) announce the confiscation of property—including enslaved people—belonging to residents actively aiding the Confederacy, and (3) promise death sentences to all secessionist guerrillas caught within Federal lines.[60]

Whatever Frémont thought of Grant's message to the Kentucky legislature, sending it was a prudent thing to do, particularly in the wake of the Confederates' surprise disregard of the state's self-declared neutrality. It underlined, and capitalized on, the great political error the Confederates had made. And Frémont *had*, after all, put Grant *in command* of a Federal response that had to be made as swiftly as possible. Prudent also was the explanatory proclamation Grant issued to residents of Paducah, to which by inference the subordinate's dispatch could also refer and which even more starkly contrasted with Frémont's controversial announcement.

The indirect censure he received probably only confirmed Grant's opinion of Frémont. In 1856 Grant had voted for the indecisive James Buchanan for president against Frémont, the first nominee of the brand-new Republican Party. Grant later wryly explained that he had voted for Buchanan because he did not know him and against Frémont because he did.[61] There actually was more to it than that, and the gist of the situation illustrates how much thought Grant had been giving the impact of politics ever since the Mexican War. He had feared that the election of the Republican Frémont might trigger secession, whereas he thought that the election of the dithering Democrat Buchanan might give the heat of that moment enough time to cool down.[62]

The importance of the rebuff episode lies in the fact that Grant had better political instincts than Frémont, ones far more in harmony with those of the leader of his government as well as its people. Lincoln's inaugural address had emphasized that Southerners were fellow Americans—"not enemies, but friends"—and in his April call for troops to quell the "rebellion," he had emphasized that his intention was to engage in war limited to the repossession of "the forts, places, and property that have been seized from the Union." Otherwise, he wrote, "the utmost care will be observed, consistent with the objects aforesaid, to avoid any devastation, any destruction of, or interference with, property, or any disturbance of peaceful citizens in any part of the country."[63] When Lincoln saw Grant's proclamation to the people of Paducah, he highly approved of not just its message but its style. "The modesty and brevity of that address," Lincoln wrote of his first notice of this man who would eventually become his indispensable general, "shows that the officer issuing it understands the situation and is a proper man to command there at this time."[64]

Lincoln did not know it yet, but Grant already, more than the Union's other generals—*far* more for the most part—shared the president's sense of urgency about this job. His rush to take Paducah emphatically illustrated that. Like Lincoln, Grant was a man in a hurry who knew that in this situation he could afford to be nothing less. As the military historian Russell F. Weigley has put it, "excessive losses in battle might destroy the relatively fragile Northern will to continue the war." It was the ultimate Clausewitzian (that is, political) consideration. This war had to be as short as Lincoln could make it. And there was another reason for that, and it was just as important to Lincoln:

> The primary object of his government was the restoration of the Union, the achievement of which demanded that sooner or later the South must yield to the Union with some measure of voluntary consent. . . . The longer the war went on, however, the more bitterness it seemed likely to nourish, and the more difficult a true restoration of the Union might become. . . . More than that, the longer the war went on, the more likely it would become that accumulating Northern frustrations would push Lincoln's government into harsher and more vindictive policies, which might multiply the sources of Southern enmity. . . . Lincoln did not wish to defeat the Southern armies only to have an embittered South shift into guerrilla warfare, which might perpetuate itself indefinitely.[65]

It was perhaps easier for Lincoln and Grant, as commoners, to innately know such things than for slaveholders and other men from the top of society who presumed to be its masters. Lincoln and Grant could *feel* what was being felt by the middle and bottom of society, the levels from which they hailed—and by those whose opinions in a civil war, as opposed to peaceful times, were often the most critical ones.

Notable, too, is the fact that Frémont's rebuff of Grant's implicit consideration for the feelings of Kentucky legislators did not prevent Grant from continuing to do his military duty. Recognizing, apparently unlike his commander, that a soldier's first task is to obey his superior, he continued to follow Frémont's orders as best he could, even though some were plainly unworkable. As Frémont had suggested, Grant named an eminent West Point instructor of his, Brigadier General Charles Ferguson Smith, to take over command at Paducah as well as at Smithland, a hamlet a few miles farther east at the mouth of the similarly vital Cumberland. But Smith almost immediately reported to Frémont that one of Frémont's orders—to build a bridge across the Ohio between Kentucky and the Illinois shore—"will be exceedingly difficult of accomplishment, if at all, in any reasonable time," because the Ohio was "between 3/5 or 3/4 of a mile wide."[66] The latter would seem to be a fact Frémont should have known and considered.

By then Grant may have sensed that Frémont, then famously known as "the Pathfinder" because of his prewar explorations of the West, was living on borrowed time that was getting away fast. His August 30 Missouri decree and its potential effects on not just Missouri but other less radical states bordering the Confederacy, especially Abraham Lincoln's homeland of Kentucky, had repelled the president. When Frémont haughtily refused a Lincoln request that he rescind his harsh decree, Lincoln changed the request to an order, and Frémont had to comply.

Grant, having command of southeast Missouri and southern Illinois, must have known of the martial law decree and its rescinding. But how much more, if any, he knew of Frémont's Lincoln problem is questionable. Lincoln was, after all, the second presidential nominee of the new Republican Party, Frémont the first. Grant's correspondence for the period does not mention that. But it is easy to see that his instincts for handling the Kentucky legislators, as well as the residents of Paducah, conformed much more to the ideas of Lincoln, his fellow dedicated commoner, than to those of the pretentious Frémont. Grant and Lincoln understood how to mollify the citizens of Paducah.

The Pathfinder surely sensed that if he wanted to remain in command of the Federal Department of the West he needed to find a new path fast. He quickly nixed all offensive plans but his own and set to work trying to tame rebellious Missouri. Meanwhile Grant, seeing the Confederates consolidating their hold on the towering bluffs at Columbus, also saw a huge opportunity to reopen the commercially critical midsection of the Mississippi River slipping away.

BELMONT—WITH BOLDNESS

"A distinguished commander without boldness is unthinkable," wrote Clausewitz. "No man who is not *born* bold can play such a role, and therefore we consider this quality the first prerequisite of a great military commander."[67]

On September 10 Grant informed Frémont that, if it were up to him, "with a little addition to my present force I would take Columbus."[68] His superior did not respond. Two days later, Grant wrote him again about it, saying he believed a southward "demonstration" by Smith from Paducah, coupled with "two columns" marching down the Kentucky side of the Mississippi from Cairo accompanied by two gunboats and "a force" threatening little Belmont, Missouri, would compel the Confederates to withdraw from Columbus, "leaving behind their heavy ordnance."[69] Frémont ignored the suggestion.

Two weeks later, on September 26, he did have his adjutant write Grant that he was sending him two new regiments with which Grant and Smith should be able to "control the rebel forces on both the Kentucky and Missouri shores." He added that if the enemy exposed "a weak point on either side of the river you may inflict upon him a combined blow, but at present I am not in favor of incurring any hazard of defeat."[70]

That was because Frémont's attention was increasingly riveted on interior Missouri. Just three weeks after a terrible Union defeat at Wilson's Creek, the first major loss in the West and thus a twin to the eastern stampede of Federals at Bull Run in Virginia, a 3,500-man Union detachment ventured 125 miles up the Missouri River to the isolated town of Lexington, where 18,000 Confederates soon besieged it. On September 20 it surrendered, and Frémont's popularity went with it.

The Pathfinder knew he urgently needed to get it back. He gathered up most of the Federal troops in Missouri—38,000 men, almost 100 cannon, and several thousand wagons to haul their supplies—and set out in pursuit of the Confederate conqueror of Wilson's Creek and Lexington, Major General Sterling Price of the Missouri State Guard. Price, though, proved a hard target. Undersupplied with food, clothes, and ammunition, the Confederate knew he was in no condition to wage a campaign of any length against Frémont's legions, and he retreated sixty miles southward. Frémont was in mid-pursuit when his time ran out. On November 2 he received Lincoln's October 24 order relieving him of command.[71]

Grant had put his inactive interval to the best use he could. He imparted more training to his volunteers and improved their supply channels. He illustrated his strong identification with them by ensuring that their mail was speedily delivered, a familial godsend—as Grant himself so well knew—to men away from home contending with the privations of war. When Robert Allen, the old friend who had lent him money to get home from California in 1854, became chief quartermaster of the Department of the West, Grant's earlier supply difficulties vanished.

Grant's letters in the autumn of 1861 exhibit concern about being superseded in command of his army, which he wonderingly realized was a horde multiple times as large as Taylor's had been in Mexico. The letters also show a desire to fight a battle before he was replaced. On September 22 he wrote Julia that he "would like to have the honor of commanding the Army that makes the advance down the river, but unless I am able to do it soon cannot expect it. There are too many Generals who rank me that have commands inferior to mine for me to retain it."[72]

A chance for action began developing on November 1, the day before Frémont learned he was sacked. The doomed commander's headquarters in St. Louis ordered Grant to make a demonstration down both banks of the Mississippi to hold the Confederates at Columbus and prevent them from reinforcing Price. However, the order specified that Grant was to demonstrate only. He was to keep his "columns constantly moving back and forward . . . without, however, attacking the enemy." Headquarters also ordered him to send some troops to help Federals in interior Missouri drive secessionist cavalry leader Jeff Thompson "back to Arkansas."[73]

Grant sent the troops but revised the instructions that headquarters had issued. Instead of calling for the driving of Thompson into Arkansas, Grant's instructions to his officers went further, forecasting the pugnacity and totality of approach for which his generalship was soon to become known: "The object of the expedition is to *destroy* this force, and the manner of doing it is left largely to your discretion."[74] Grant's enduring idea was to eliminate an enemy if possible, not just chase him away to some point from which he could always return and attack. This was classic farm-boy logic; you do not half-do a job when fully doing it will prevent you from having to do it again. This was also, of course, classic Clausewitz, whose work Grant had never read: the militarily correct goal, according to both of them, was not to capture map points but, rather, armies.

Frémont had specifically ordered Grant *not* to attack, but by November 3 word of Frémont's dismissal was getting into newspapers, seemingly rendering moot the Pathfinder's injunction against aggression. Grant saw a chance to strike a quick blow. On November 5, he sent word to General Smith at Paducah that he was preparing to "menace Belmont" on the Mississippi's opposite bank from Columbus. He asked for help. "If you can make a demonstration toward Columbus at the same time with a portion of your command," he gingerly suggested to this old mentor, his junior in rank but his senior in age and experience by fifteen years, "it would probably keep the enemy from throwing over the river much more force than they now have there, and might enable me to drive those they have there out of Missouri."[75]

Grant and some 3,000 Federal soldiers, in a convoy of six steamboats and two gunboats, left Cairo under cover of darkness on November 6. They dropped eight miles downriver and tied up on the Kentucky side for the rest of the night, hoping to deceive Polk into believing they were heading for Columbus. At 2:00 A.M., Grant later claimed, he got "information" that Confederates from Columbus were crossing the Mississippi into Missouri. The next morning, still eleven miles north of Columbus, he cast off and moved down to three miles above Belmont, disembarking on the Missouri side out of sight of the Columbus cannon. In his memoirs, he unconvincingly asserted that as his men boarded the boats in Cairo he had had no plans to attack.

"But after we started, I saw that the officers and men were elated at the prospect of at last having the opportunity of doing what they had volunteered to do—fight the enemies of their country," he continued. "I did not see how I could maintain discipline, or retain the confidence of my command, if we should return to Cairo without an effort to do something."[76]

This was a pretty weak excuse. Grant had taken a wildly rebellious Twenty-First Illinois and quickly brought it to heel, so he knew he could enforce at least passable discipline in his ranks. And he would hardly be unduly concerned about retaining the "confidence" of a command he feared losing any day thereafter. So it was not the troops who refused to return to Cairo "without an effort to do something"; it was Grant.

That is made even clearer by his attempt to further justify his action by behaving well out of character. Concocting the highly suspect story of receiving 2:00 A.M. "information" that the Confederates at Columbus were sending troops across the Mississippi to reinforce comrades in Missouri, he thus fabricated an urgent need for his attack with a purported fact that was not only not true but also doubly *un*true. That very day, Columbus Confederate commander Polk was in the process of sending Pillow's division *eastward*, to reinforce fledgling Fort Henry on the *Tennessee* River.[77] Grant's made-up story to the contrary suggests how desperate he was to fight at least one battle with his important command—and to threaten the continually reinforcing enemy in whatever way he could. His 3,000 Federals were nowhere near strong enough to attack the fortified bluffs of Columbus, though, so he kept his eye on what had been considered the more logical prize from the beginning: the tiny and comparatively undefended Confederate camp across the river at Belmont.

All went well at first. From the river bank three miles above the Missouri hamlet, he marched his men through woods and cornfields toward the target. Soon he ran into Pillow's Confederates, who had been pulled back to Columbus and thrown across the river to Belmont when Polk learned of the Union presence. But Pillow, with an all-too-typical lack of prudence and military intellect, established his line in a cornfield, while woods covered Grant's men. Grant directed the fire of his half-dozen cannon onto the center of Pillow's line, blowing a hole in it. The hole prompted a retreat that soon degenerated into a panicked stampede. Pillow's men kept running right on through their camp to the river bank, where they cowered under its tall lip.

At the camp, the Federals lost interest in their pursuit and started celebrating their great supposed victory. Grant found that he was unable to push them farther or maintain the discipline he claimed he thought he would have lost control of if he had taken them back to Cairo without the fight. Enlisted men ran the national flag up the erstwhile rebel flagpole as regimental bands played. They began to sing and pillage the enemy camp.[78]

"Some of the higher officers were little better than the privates," Grant later wrote. "They galloped about from one cluster of men to another and at every halt delivered a short [speech] upon the Union cause and the achievements of the command. All this time, the [Confederate] troops we had been engaged with for four hours lay crouched under cover of the river bank, ready to come up and surrender if summoned to do so; but finding that they were not pursued, they worked their way up the river and came up on the bank between us and our [steamboats]."[79]

Grant's loss of control for a while was total. When he discovered some of his men playfully using captured Confederate cannon to take potshots at empty Southern steamboats downriver, he tried to get them to train the guns on two more steamboats coming straight at them across the river from Columbus, loaded to their roofs with Confederates. But, he wrote, his "efforts were in vain." And the two gunboats that had escorted the transport vessels bringing his troops to Belmont had pulled back upriver out of range of the heavier Confederate cannon on the bluff, so the Confederate steamboats crossed the Mississippi unopposed.

Finally, in a desperate attempt to regain his men's attention, Grant had his staff officers set fire to the camp, which evoked belated cannon fire from high above on the Columbus bluffs, where Confederate artillerists had previously seemed to fear hitting their own troops. The tumult and terror of that plunging cannon fire helped Grant gain sway over his ranks again, but he and they quickly found that some of the Confederate reinforcements had connected with Pillow's men—and the combined enemy forces had got between the Federals and the Union steamboats. Some of his officers, Grant recalled, thought they had been "placed in a hopeless position, where there was nothing to do but surrender. But when I announced that we had cut our way in and could cut our way out just as well, it seemed a new revelation to officers and soldiers. They formed line rapidly and we started back to our boats."[80]

They made it, too, by the skin of their teeth. But they left wounded on the field and a whole regiment, the Twenty-Seventh Illinois, that had got separated in the fighting. Grant's first offensive as a high-ranking officer had turned into a debacle. The return to the boats was less a counterattack than a frantic straggle. Once again, though, under Grant's direction Union cannon broke the Confederate line, and Federals poured pell-mell through the opening, leaving behind a trail of discarded blankets, haversacks, muskets, and the like. Grant, having lost his own mess chest and a horse that was killed beneath him, was the last man aboard the last steamboat, sliding his second mount down the steep riverbank and trotting it up a single plank run out to accommodate him as the vessel pulled away. The Twenty-Seventh Illinois had to be picked up later by a boat sent back for it. Some 600 of Grant's men were killed, wounded, or missing, compared to about the same number of Confederates.[81]

What happened at Belmont has been mulled over by historians ever since. Was it a battle or a raid? If it was a battle, as Grant later claimed, he most assuredly lost, pursued to his boats and barely escaping with his life. If it was a raid, though, the verdict is different. As a raid it succeeded in many respects.

Specifically, it put the fear of God—or perhaps of Grant—in Polk, the Confederate bishop-general. From then until Federal capture of Fort Henry flanked him out of Columbus three months later, he refused to send any of his units west, east, or anywhere else. It also tarnished the invincible image of Confederate soldiery that had widely prevailed across both the North and the South up to then. Again, as he had done as a junior officer in Mexico, Grant had shown all, including himself, that he could remain mentally cool in the cataclysm of combat and, when faced with calamity, could also devise an escape on the spot. And he had shown his men that he was one with them, unafraid to stand in their midst shoulder to shoulder when the fire was hot. When the chips were not only down but scattered to the wind, he had seen men rise to heroism under his direction and inspiration.[82]

"The two objects for which the battle of Belmont was fought were fully accomplished," an elderly Grant contended in his memoirs. "The enemy," he wrote, "gave up all idea of detaching troops from Columbus. His losses were very heavy for that period of the war. Columbus was beset by people looking for their wounded or dead kin, to take them home for medical treatment or burial. I learned later, when I had moved further south, that Belmont had caused more mourning than almost any other battle up to that time. [And t]he National troops acquired a confidence in themselves at Belmont that did not desert them through the war."[83]

These claims appear to have some substance, but they put a gloss to the "battle" that it does not deserve. Grant began creatively buffing its shine immediately after the fight. His first report to headquarters in St. Louis (whose order against attacking he had violated) said his force "met the rebels about nine o'clock this morning two and a half miles from Belmont, drove them step by step into their camp and *across the river.* We burned their tents and started on our return with all their artillery. . . . The rebels *recrossed* the river and followed in our rear to our place of embarkation. Loss heavy on both sides."[84]

His men did not drive "the rebels" to the other side of the river. Those same "rebels" did not "recross" the river and simply "follow" his troops to the boats; there was far more energy to the Confederate pursuit than that. The first casualty estimate he reported was 250, less than half the actual total. In what seems to have been a desperate attempt to introduce more purpose and triumph to the thing, he eventually made up the stories about the phantom 2:00 A.M. message and a similar figment of the imagination, a purported November 5 attack order from headquarters in St. Louis. No record of either has been found. Similarly, the recollection in his memoirs of hearing later in Memphis that Belmont "caused more mourning than almost any other battle up to that time" has a bloodthirstily boastful tone that is very unlike the Grant of the balance of history.

To make such exaggerated claims, he must have been abashed at his Belmont performance, as well he might have been. As a new general, he had made at least three glaring rookie errors. He had failed to pursue Pillow's men once he reached their camp, allowing his troops to assume too early that they had won the fight. He had not exerted sufficient control over his vital naval gunboats, allowing the Confederates at Columbus to send several more regiments unopposed across the Mississippi to lead the counterattack and the chase that drove his men wildly to their steamboats. And, perhaps most important, he did not appear to consider that the Confederates *could* counterattack.

In his memoirs he recalled that initial journalistic reports understandably "severely criticized [Belmont] in the North as a wholly unnecessary battle, barren of results, or the possibility of them from the beginning."[85] The sting of those early reports likely filled Grant with tormented determination to prevent Belmont from becoming his last fight with this command and, as years passed, a stain on his subsequently brilliant record—thus the elaborate, duplicitous, thoroughgoing attempts to improve the image of the "battle."

In any case, his ploys worked at the time. Congressman Washburne hurried to bring the best version of the Belmont story to the attention of Abraham Lincoln,[86] and that version soon got around. The *Cincinnati Gazette*, the *Chicago Journal*, the *National Intelligencer* in Washington, the *Philadelphia Daily Ledger*, the *St. Louis Republican*, and the *New York Herald* all praised Belmont as a signal (and badly needed) triumph. And the *New York Times* said it was "in high degree creditable to all our troops concerned in it, and the success of the brilliant movement is due to Gen. Grant."[87]

Grant, of course, had fuller knowledge of the particulars. Sensitive about Belmont to the end of his days, he had his staff revise his official report of it in 1865; therein he claimed to have gotten the "order" from St. Louis headquarters to move quickly to prevent the Columbus Confederates from reinforcing others in Missouri. And his memoirs, written in 1884–85, "disclose" his receipt of the 2:00 A.M. "information" on his way downriver of a major movement of Confederate troops from Columbus toward interior Missouri.[88] Perhaps the best reasons these less than admirable stratagems worked are, first, that the North badly needed a victory and, second, that they were employed to justify making *an attack*. The Union army already had, and would ever have, plenty of generals ready to create facts to justify *not* attacking.

To the end of his military life, Grant would be guilty of devoting far more thought to what he intended to do to the enemy than on what the enemy could do to him, but he quickly set about trying to correct his Belmont mistakes. Almost immediately, he improved his relations with the navy, although not entirely of his own volition. Before Belmont, he had broken a promise to Admiral Andrew Foote that he would keep the admiral advised of his combat plans. Out of a desire for secrecy, he had slipped away downriver with a Foote subordinate at the last minute. Foote, outraged, badgered the navy into giving him rank commensurate with Grant's so that the inconsiderate brigadier general could not afford to be so inconsiderate again, and Grant was not. He also never again lost complete control of his men on a battlefield.

In sum, Belmont is more of a plus than a minus on Grant's record because his behavior throughout exhibited iron-minded perseverance and a trait as old as heroism itself: boldness. Clausewitz said of boldness that "a soldier ... can possess no nobler quality; it is the very metal that gives edge and luster to the sword." Boldness, Clausewitz also asserted, is the root of the "noble capacity to rise above the most menacing dangers."[89]

Grant showed at Belmont that he possessed that rare noble capacity—one that, Abraham Lincoln was already beginning to sadly learn, was even rarer on the level to which Grant had so suddenly risen. But Belmont also showed that Grant's "edge and luster" needed polish.

NAVIGATING "MILITARY IMBECILES," PART 1

As 1862 opened, Grant had a few hard battlefield lessons still to learn. He obviously realized he needed to give more consideration to his naval assistants on the Cumberland, Tennessee, and Mississippi Rivers. And he especially had to pay more attention to defense without losing his dogged aggressiveness.

But there remained other difficult lessons, too, which became more important as he kept moving forward. These often had little to do with Confederates but concerned, rather, the *Union* army and getting past weak-kneed, nitpicking superiors and certain jealous subordinates.

Grant had barely survived Belmont when he was assigned a new commander. Major General Henry Wager Halleck had grown up on a farm in upstate New York, but as soon as he could he had bitterly fled plow handles and a cold, insensitive, domineering father for the halls of academia.[90] There he flourished and built an exalted opinion of his own brilliance. He attended Hunter Academy, graduated Phi Beta Kappa from Union College, and finished third in the class of 1839 at West Point. He traveled to France soon after graduation and became an authority—signally for his future mindset—on defensive works. During the Mexican War he was stationed in California, on the voyage to which he translated aboard ship Baron Jomini's massive *Political and Military Life of Napoleon*.

In California Halleck occupied various high civilian political positions as an army officer while studying law and then left the service to found California's leading law firm. He also wrote influential books on jurisprudence and acquired a significant interest in a silver mine that helped make him rich. Six years before the Civil War he married a granddaughter of Alexander Hamilton, and soon after the firing on Fort Sumter President Lincoln, at the suggestion of General of the Army Winfield Scott, appointed him the army's fourth highest-ranking officer (behind Scott himself, McClellan, and Frémont).[91] Halleck was, in sum, quintessentially eminent—and thus the antithesis of Ulysses S. Grant.

He also differed considerably from Admiral Andrew Foote, with whom Grant became friendlier after Belmont. Grant and Foote were intent on—in fact, obsessed with the necessity of—carrying war to the Confederates before the Confederates got fully prepared to meet it. Halleck, meanwhile, seemed preoccupied with risking his celebrated reputation as infrequently as possible. Foote soon became increasingly frustrated and privately termed Halleck a "military imbecile."[92]

Foote had concrete reasons for his frustration. He had been getting reports from gunboat captains whose vessels he had assigned to roam the rivers of the border states on reconnaissance missions, and he had decided Fort Henry on the Tennessee River was especially vulnerable. The contention was well-nigh inarguable, given the fort's current state. It had been foolhardily located on a floodplain into which the Tennessee was rising, and its best protection was theoretically on the other side of the river: a hill-crowning companion fortification still under construction, Fort Heiman, which at the moment possessed no cannon. So Fort Henry was in growing danger of both flooding and being captured as the rainy season progressed. Foote believed he and Grant "should ascend" the Tennessee with 6,000 troops and four gunboats and attack Fort Henry. According to the highly experienced naval officer, Grant favored attacking Fort Donelson on the Cumberland, some twelve miles to the east, but was happy, for aggressiveness's sake, to cooperate with Foote on the Tennessee if Foote could talk Halleck into letting them move.[93]

Grant had already tried on his own and been rudely rebuffed. On January 20, he had asked Halleck—for the third time—for permission to visit St. Louis and lay before him a plan that Grant and General Smith at Paducah had been devising. They too had learned from gunboat captains about the incomplete fortress across the Tennessee from Fort Henry and, realizing that its height held the key to Henry's defense, wanted to attack that facility and then Henry. But Halleck, whom Grant then venerated as one of the military's mental giants, did not take kindly to Grant's unwitting attempt to trespass on his commander's intellectual province.

"The leave [to come to St. Louis] was granted," Grant recalled in the *Personal Memoirs*, "but not graciously. I had known General Halleck but very slightly in the old army, not having met him either at West Point or during the Mexican War. I was received with so little cordiality that I perhaps stated the object of my visit with less clearness than I might have done, and I had not uttered many sentences before I was cut short as if my plan was preposterous. I returned to Cairo very much crestfallen."[94]

Why Halleck treated Grant so shabbily appears explicable. In addition to Grant's prevailing image as an abuser of the bottle (which was at that moment being reemphasized in new information reaching Halleck's desk), Grant's imprecision of dress and manner seemed to go along with what he had, between wars, become well-known as: a down-at-the-heels farmer. Halleck's youth had given him strong reasons for looking down on "country people," a sentiment he sometimes expressed.[95]

Despite Halleck's treatment of him, though, Grant did not remain "crestfallen" long; his ability to recover from disappointment was a personal trait that principally explains the dawning success of his generalship. He pushed his superiors almost as hard as he pushed Confederates. Less than a week after being virtually run out of Halleck's office—"when [your commander] wishes to consult you on [strategy] he will notify you," Halleck had coldly told him, before walking out of the room himself[96]—Grant united with Foote to send Halleck two simultaneous telegrams urging him to let them attack Fort Henry. The very next day, Grant sent another wire on his own sounding a familiar Foote theme: if they did not move immediately, the Confederates would "materially strengthen" Fort Henry, the unfinished Fort Heiman across the river from Henry, and Fort Donelson.[97] By implication, they warned that this strengthening of the forts would cost more Union lives the longer it proceeded.

Then destiny, the kind that too seldom rewards dogged persistence, interfered. Halleck, who too had been thinking of Fort Henry and Fort Donelson, had not intended to move on them so quickly. He believed that, to be successful, the kind of move that Grant, Foote, and now Smith were proposing would require 60,000 men, four times the number they actually had. On January 29, however, Halleck received a telegram that enlivened him. From General-in-Chief McClellan on the eastern front, the wire said that eminent Confederate general P. G. T. Beauregard, the conqueror of Fort Sumter and second in Confederate command at Bull Run, was rumored to be on his way westward from Virginia with fifteen regiments. Halleck—vying with Louisville, Kentucky, commander (and close McClellan friend) Don Carlos Buell for supremacy in the Union west—suddenly was compelled by his ambition to get ahead of Buell by beating Beauregard to the punch.

On January 30, Halleck sent Grant a curt telegram instructing him to "make your preparations to take and hold Fort Henry. I will send you written instructions by mail."[98] He sent this wire with deep misgivings—because he was then in the midst of trying to replace Grant. Little more than hours after icily dismissing the unloved, scruffy brigadier from his St. Louis office, Halleck had wired McClellan requesting that the general-in-chief persuade sixty-three-year-old retired brigadier general Ethan Allen Hitchcock to return to the army with the promise of a promotion to major general. McClellan had done so and put the promotion in the works.[99]

Halleck, now forced by circumstance to order Grant forward before Hitchcock could arrive, was not the only one who was surely feeling the need to move fast. Grant himself had, besides his own inner restlessness, another reason. He had just had scandalous, explosive charges filed against him in military channels. They were related to his old nemesis the bottle.

These charges, based on skimpy evidence and apparently largely unfounded, had been filed by a civilian supervisor of river transportation whom Grant had had arrested after the man refused to follow orders. The prisoner, William J. Kountz, was a prewar steamboat entrepreneur who was well acquainted with powerful politicians and top army officers, including brand-new secretary of war Edwin Stanton and General-in-Chief McClellan. Kountz had also ingratiated himself with an ambitious Grant subordinate, Brigadier General John A. McClernand, the Illinois congressman. McClernand had got Kountz named to his position as head of river transportation at Cairo and then praised the job the steamboat mogul was doing.

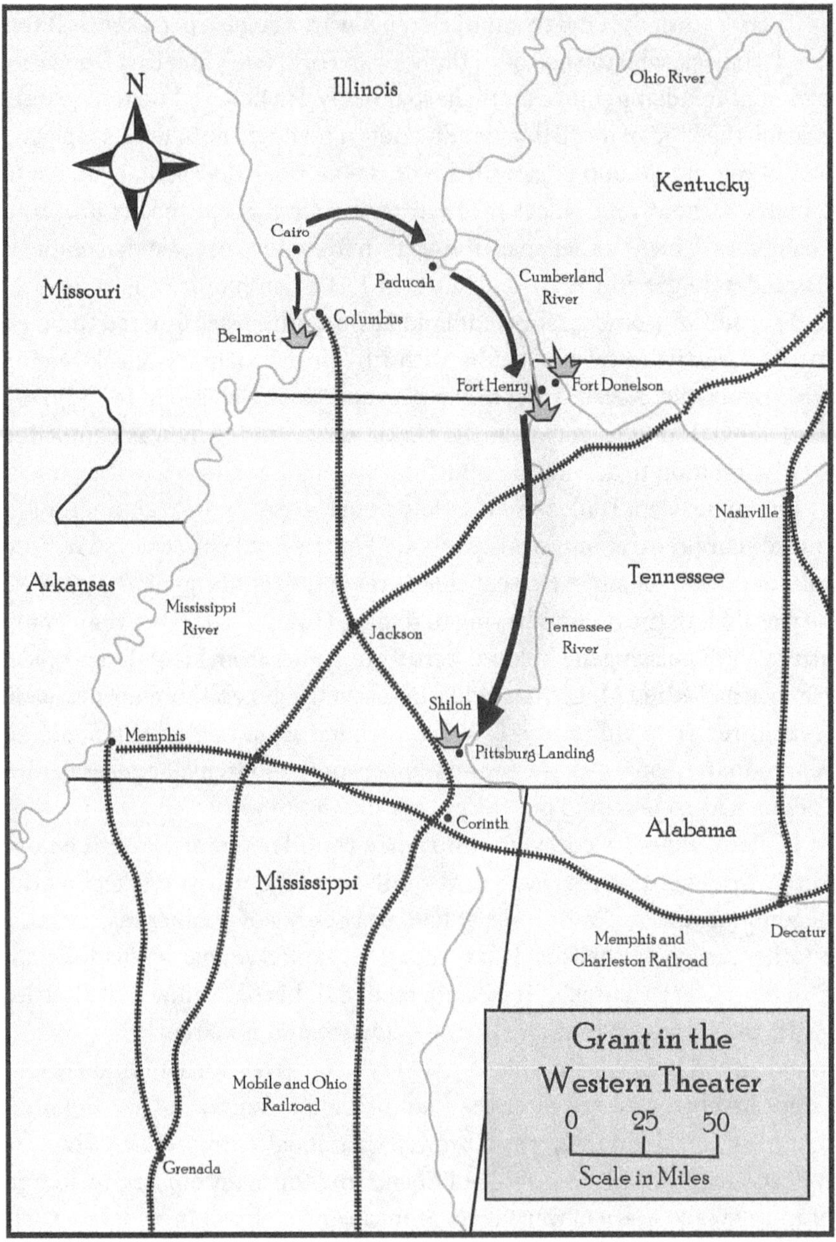

Grant's aggressiveness made him the most important commander in the Civil War's western theater. He beat the Confederates to Paducah, Kentucky, and then attacked Belmont, Missouri; captured a Confederate army at Fort Donelson; and prevailed at Shiloh in the war's then-bloodiest battle.

But Kountz had a reputation for being prickly, pushy, and fanatical on the subject of temperance. He became such a pest in Cairo that Grant had sent a complaint to Halleck and had moved his office to avoid the transport chief. Soon afterward, Grant placed Kountz under house arrest for discharging from government service a boat needed for military movements. Just days later, Kountz filed with Halleck's headquarters in St. Louis sensational charges that, had they become public, could have ruined Grant. They alleged that he had drunk with traitors and become "beastly" intoxicated aboard a flag-of-truce boat following the battle of Belmont; had since been "repeatedly and often openly drunk"; had drunkenly "vomited all over the floor" of a steamboat's kitchen; had drunkenly lost "his sword and uniform" at the St. Charles Hotel in Cairo; had visited a "Harlot" in her room at the hotel; had gotten drunk at a "Negro ball" along with his aides and others; had once got "so drunk that he had to go upstairs on all fours"; and had played "cards for money while he was . . . disbursing secret service money."[100]

The way Grant handled these charges is significant and perhaps instructive for aspiring officers. Halleck, nitpicking while declining to commit himself, sent the charges back to Cairo directed to Grant himself. They carried Halleck's notation that they had not been "sent through the proper channel." Exhibiting his steely nerve, Grant treated the document as if it were routine. He endorsed it to signify that it had passed through the Cairo headquarters and then sent it back to Halleck in St. Louis. He did that on January 29, the same day he sent his wire to Halleck saying that he, Foote, and Smith believed the Confederates would "materially" strengthen Forts Henry, Heiman, and Donelson if the Union did not move immediately. With lucky coincidence, it was also the day Halleck received McClellan's tip concerning Beauregard's move to the western front. The next day, January 30, Halleck gave the go-ahead to move against Fort Henry.

Thus, by the skin of his teeth, Grant remained in charge of the 15,000 members of twenty-three regiments who got jammed aboard steamboats departing Cairo for Paducah and the Tennessee River on February 3.[101] At Paducah, they were joined by four ironclad gunboats and three more wooden ones. Transport vessels on the western rivers were then in such demand that only half of Grant's army could reach its target at a time, 7,000 or so men in one load and another 7,000 more in a second one. And the cavalry had to get there overland, obeying a Halleck order to clear the roads of any Confederates who might otherwise attack from the Union rear once the troops reached Henry.

But at least they were underway. Grant had left behind almost nothing, taking with him not just all evidence of the Kountz charges but also every piece of paper that had come to his headquarters from Halleck. Well might Grant continually look over his shoulder, as aides said he did as they left Paducah, the last point at which orders to turn back could reach them. Although he had a bad cold, Grant suddenly slapped chief of staff John Rawlins on the shoulder almost like a boy headed out on a lark. "Now we seem to be safe, beyond recall," he said. "We will succeed, Rawlins; we must succeed."[102]

Seemingly so. The Kountz affair, as well as the as-yet-unknown but intended substitution of Hitchcock for Grant, would become less pressing with the onset of impending battles. His career-threatening problems were outdistanced by Grant's ceaseless urge to advance. The Kountz charges had likely been a long shot, anyway, because of Halleck's traditional soldierly prejudice against civilians presuming to tread on military turf, but publication of them would have stood Halleck in good stead in his wish to replace Grant. The Hitchcock matter would be decided in similarly short order by whether Grant proved to *need* replacing.

Grant's next lesson came from Foote. In a conference late on February 5, the night before the attack on Fort Henry, Grant rejected advice from the old salt as the younger and less-seasoned expedition chief laid out his plans. Grant's idea was to send his two divisions, Smith's and McClernand's, down opposite banks of the Tennessee while Foote's ironclads assaulted Fort Henry from the river. Smith would have the potentially harder task of reducing and capturing the artillery sites at Fort Heiman, provided it now boasted cannon. Then Smith was to bring his men across the river and lead the infantry attack on McClernand-surrounded Fort Henry.

Grant had set the starting time at 11:00 A.M.—and rejected Foote's suggestion that the boats wait and weigh anchor an hour later, since they had a shorter and less difficult distance to travel than the road-bound infantry. Foote wanted to allow time for the troops to fully invest Fort Henry before his gunboats opened fire and began the assault. He was doubtless conscious that the battle would be unusually historic and wanted it to end in victory. It would be the first time steam-powered ironclads would team with infantry to assail a riverbank fort.

Grant, perhaps taking Foote's suggestion as a challenge to his leadership from a member of a rival service branch, said no; they would all leave at the same time. Grant had been receiving false reports that the Henry garrison was being substantially reinforced, and by the night of the fifth he thought it was 10,000 strong.[103] Thus he may have believed it would be well to have Foote arrive in front of the fort early so the gunboat cannon could soften up resistance to his infantrymen. But Grant's rejection of his advice likely annoyed Foote.

"I shall take [Fort Henry] before you get there with your forces," the sailor warned.[104]

Overnight, the weather drowned Grant's plan. Rain poured. The roads that McClernand's men had to travel to reach and surround the fort turned into moats of mud and water. As Foote had predicted, he received the fort's surrender before Grant and his men arrived. The rising Tennessee River, further swollen by the rain, had all but flooded out the hapless facility before McClernand's men could surround it,[105] and on the river's other side Smith's men found Fort Heiman to be ineffectual, boasting no significant firepower because the Confederates were still without cannon to place there. The flood, nearly as much as Foote's guns, prompted Confederate commander Tilghman, before he struck his flag, to order all but some 100 members of the Henry garrison—the cannoneers—to escape and retreat twelve miles cross-country to Fort Donelson on the Cumberland.[106] Grant had to content himself with the empty Jominian pleasure of capturing a *place* rather than a significant number of the enemy—and Foote had done *that*.

Grant surely realized that a surrender accepted by the navy before he and his soldiers even arrived at Fort Henry—and after virtually all of its garrison had escaped—was not the sort of triumph that could banish his troubles. That night he wrote a brief report to Halleck beginning with "Fort Henry is ours." To his credit, he quickly mentioned that the fort had surrendered to Foote before the army arrived, but then he hastened on to a sentence that must have frozen Halleck's cautious blood: "I shall take and destroy Fort Donaldson [*sic*] on the 8th and return to Fort Henry with the forces employed unless it looks feasible to occupy that place with a small force that could retreat easily to the main body."[107]

The tail of the sentence was obviously intended to gratify Halleck's deeply defensive essence while promising even brighter results before Halleck could do much of anything to stop him. Grant knew he needed a quick victory that he could claim as his own, but there were other important things he could not know then. One was what a glory-grabber his commander was. In the two days following the fort's fall, Foote pushed his timberclad steamers hard—north to south across Tennessee into northern Alabama, the so-called Heart of Dixie, creating much credit that Halleck began trying his best to take. He rushed out a statement to reporters saying, "Fort Henry is ours! The flag of the Union is re-established on the soil of Tennessee. It will never be removed."[108] With Henry and its aftermath having given him a heavy leg up on Buell in their intra-army contest for western supremacy, Halleck was trying to use it to the fullest. This bought Grant a little time.

Something else Grant could not know was how faint a heart his commander possessed. Having supervised (in Halleck's own view) the lodging of a highly injurious wound—a smashing breakthrough—on the perimeter of the Confederacy, the St. Louis commander was desperate to hold this advantage and validate his new theater leadership. He beseeched Buell for reinforcements for Grant as well as a "demonstration" toward Confederate western headquarters at Bowling Green, Kentucky. But Buell, hardly blind to Halleck's motives and possessing similar ones of his own, replied that he could afford only to make real moves, not feints,[109] and grudgingly promised only a brigade. Sounding frantic, Halleck wrote Grant on February 8: "Shovels and picks will be sent you to strengthen Fort Henry. The guns should be . . . arranged so as to resist an attack by land. . . . Some of the guns from Fort Holt [in Kentucky, across the Ohio from Cairo] will be sent up. Re-enforcements will reach you daily. Hold onto Fort Henry at all hazards."[110]

NAVIGATING "MILITARY IMBECILES," PART 2

Halleck's message was too late.

By the time Grant got his chief's orders to entrench and hold on for dear life at Henry, he already had marched 12,000 of his 15,000 men on to Fort Donelson. And he had sent Foote's now much-feared ironclads back down the Tennessee River to the Ohio to head back up the Cumberland to Donelson. He also requested Halleck to send reinforcements there by water, rather than require them to march from Fort Henry.

Halleck had made no reply, yea or nay, to Grant's statement that he would "take and destroy" Fort Donelson on February 8. By the tenth Grant apparently was bothered by his chief's silence. For the first and only time in his career, he called an opinion-soliciting council of war that afternoon regarding the advance to Fort Donelson: Should they move now to get there before Confederate reinforcements did from Bowling Green, or wait for the Federal reinforcements promised by Halleck? First, he asked the judgment of the grizzled veteran officer, Charles Ferguson Smith, who gruffly said in one sentence that they should "move without the loss of a day." The leader of Grant's third brigade, Lew Wallace, took only one more sentence to agree with Smith. In between, Grant asked the opinion of McClernand, who took a prepared speech from a pocket and read it as if he had the floor amid a session of Congress. His remarks agreed with Smith but presumptuously told Grant in detail McClernand's view of how the march should be conducted.

Wallace thought the whole thing had all been for show and that Grant had already made up his mind,[111] which may well have been correct. The council would have provided cover had Halleck protested its decision later—or, in case of defeat, it could have provided insurance against a potential claim by the duplicitous McClernand that he had dissented.

On the subsequent march and in the days that immediately followed, Grant learned more hard lessons. He already had been delayed past his rashly asserted February 8 departure date. Rains had returned, continuing to swell the Tennessee and all but islanding Fort Henry. Flooding now covered much of the land around the fort for three miles eastward toward Fort Donelson. Because of the rain and its impact, Grant could not march to Fort Donelson before February 12. In the meantime, he had to deal with a discipline problem. At least 200 men of two of his Illinois regiments had been discovered "robbing and plundering most disgracefully," prompting Grant to ask their colonel for the names of the officers involved.[112] He recommended that these superiors be dismissed from the service without trial and the enlisted personnel punished. He also had Rawlins issue an order holding commanders of his brigades, regiments, and companies responsible for the behavior of their men. The order further said, "In an enemy's country, where so much more could be done by a manly and humane policy to advance the cause which we all have so deeply at heart, it is astonishing that men can be found so wanton as to destroy, pillage, and burn indiscriminately, without inquiry."[113]

Within months, Grant would significantly modify these opinions. The contrary influences would be the implacable and lethal enmity of Confederate guerrillas and probably also the views of Brigadier General William T. Sherman, who was soon to become Grant's closest military friend. Sherman's prior experience of war had been not in Mexico in combat but rather in Florida, vainly trying to chase down Native American warriors. As a result, Sherman had come to believe that the only successful method of defeating guerrilla-style foes who faded into the countryside after pillaging and killing soldiers and civilians alike was to "visit punishment upon the adherents of" their cause.[114]

At the same time, Grant issued other orders showing his deep identification with enlisted men, as well as his recognition that the overwhelming majority of those in his Civil War army were volunteers, not professionals. As such, they deserved consideration for their willingness to leave home and make the sacrifices of wartime. At minimum, such consideration meant having their officers endure their hardships with them. But many of the officers of Grant's units at Fort Henry had been escaping the rain and mud by billeting aboard the steamboats, and as soon as Grant realized it he issued orders forbidding it. Again siding with the military's lower classes against its "gentlemen," he directed all regimental-level officers to "immediately take up quarters with [their] commands and not on board steamers, as the general commanding regrets to see has been done."[115]

The February 12 march showed, though, that Grant's instruction of officers had not yet been as thoroughgoing as it needed to be, possibly because some of the volunteers had been so hastily gathered that there had not been time. The day of the march turned unseasonably warm for February in Tennessee, and the hike was either twelve or fourteen miles, depending on which of the two roads the units were ordered to take. The routes traversed rolling hills, which required considerable exertion to cross, but many and perhaps most of the troops were not overburdened with equipment. The officers of many units had not thought to order overcoats, blankets, and other seeming impediments brought along, and Grant had not, either. As always, he intended to move quickly[116] and perhaps thought light traveling was required. Even more likely, he probably did not think he had the luxury of the regular load while making a quick hit à la Belmont. The Confederates had fled Fort Henry, after all, and he hoped to get to Fort Donelson and make fast work of it before the Donelson garrison recovered composure from the Henry stampede. And since the journey from Cairo to Henry had been river-borne, there was a shortage of land vehicles anyway, so the marchers were accompanied by just four wagons per regiment. There was no room for tents and baggage.

Many of the officers apparently had not even ordered their men to bring minimum gear. "Thousands marched from Fort Henry as to a summer fete, leaving coats, blankets, and knapsacks behind them in camp," later recalled Brigadier General Lew Wallace, who was unhappy at being left behind to command a 2,500-man garrison guarding Fort Henry.[117]

Grant's plan proved overconfident in the extreme. With some cavalry, he had made a reconnaissance ride toward Donelson on the ninth, but he had not got within four miles of the fort.[118] So he could not see that Donelson would be a more formidable target than Henry. Unlike half-drowned Henry beside the wide Tennessee River, Donelson crowned a hill more than 100 feet above the narrow Cumberland. Although Grant never mentioned the results of this reconnaissance in any report—perhaps not wanting to further frighten Halleck—he did see and hear that more Confederates were arriving at Donelson. He may also have heard that trenches were beginning to stretch from in front of the hilltop fort southward all the way to the town of Dover just upriver. He definitely had heard that Brigadier General Gideon Pillow, the one officer whose abilities he had consistently derided ever since the Mexican War, was in command there, and that was apparently enough to sustain his optimism.

When his troops began arriving in front of Donelson, he soon found he did not have enough men to invest both the fort and Dover, which also required it. The little town, although a mile distant, was all but part of the fort, with two wharves welcoming Nashville steamboats that were rapidly making the place a Confederate supply depot. Grant, needing to extend his lines, sent back to Fort Henry for his third brigadier, Wallace, and the 2,500 hundred men he had left there. He not only needed them but also understood that Wallace, clout-possessing son of a former governor of Indiana, had been infuriated at not receiving a chance to lead men in the expected Donelson combat. Grant also informed Halleck of what he had done and asked him to send all further reinforcements to Henry because "there is now appearance that [Fort Henry] is in danger."[119] He continued to show his deep sensitivity to his subordinates' feelings by returning the 2,500 men from Fort Henry to Smith, from whose ranks they had been taken, and by planning to put Wallace in charge of reinforcements sent by Halleck.

The next four days were a tragicomedy of errors redeemed only by Grant's utter refusal to fail. On February 13, Smith's division on the Union left and McClernand's in the sidling center probed the Confederate defenses and reaped nothing but blood, Smith minimally (75 killed and wounded)[120] and McClernand more substantially (nearly 150 killed and wounded).[121] The single bright spot was the arrival of the first of Foote's ironclads. At Grant's direction it began firing, but even that, had the Federals known the results, would have evoked no cheers. The continual fire of the supposedly fearsome gunboats produced just one Confederate casualty, considerably boosting the Southerners' morale.[122]

Union misfortunes proliferated. That afternoon, the unseasonably balmy weather turned nasty. Temperatures plummeted, and sleet set in. Grant's men on the crest of the windy ridges began to wish for the overcoats left back at Fort Henry, as well as the tents Grant had been unable to bring because of the wagon shortage. Because of Confederate sharpshooters, the Union troops could not have fires, and the sleet turned to snow. Thermometer readings sank to twelve degrees. The men suffered so miserably that some ran in circles to keep from freezing.

Around midnight Foote and the rest of his gunboats, three more ironclads and two wooden ones, arrived four miles north of Fort Donelson. At 3:00 P.M. the following afternoon, February 14, with Grant desperately needing help, they attacked. What Grant wanted was for them to knock out Donelson's riverbank batteries and then steam past them to shell the trenches in front of Dover. That in turn would initiate an all-out McClernand assault on the Confederate left. Grant hoped McClernand could roll that end of the line back onto the center and then to the right and seize victory.

But, as noted previously, Fort Donelson was not Fort Henry. Crowning a hill, it was not flooded. As Foote's gunboats bore down on it, they continually had to raise the muzzles of their guns, and Foote was commanding not sailors but rather soldiers drafted to do temporary duty aboard the ironclads. It was hard and too often deadly duty. The Confederate guns above them loosed plunging fire that could hardly miss the ironclads, crowded as they were in the narrow river below. In a ninety-minute battle, the vessels were badly disabled and Foote himself twice wounded. At dusk, defeated, they drifted back downstream around a bend in the river as a roar went up from the Confederate trenches. It rolled from one end of them to the other.

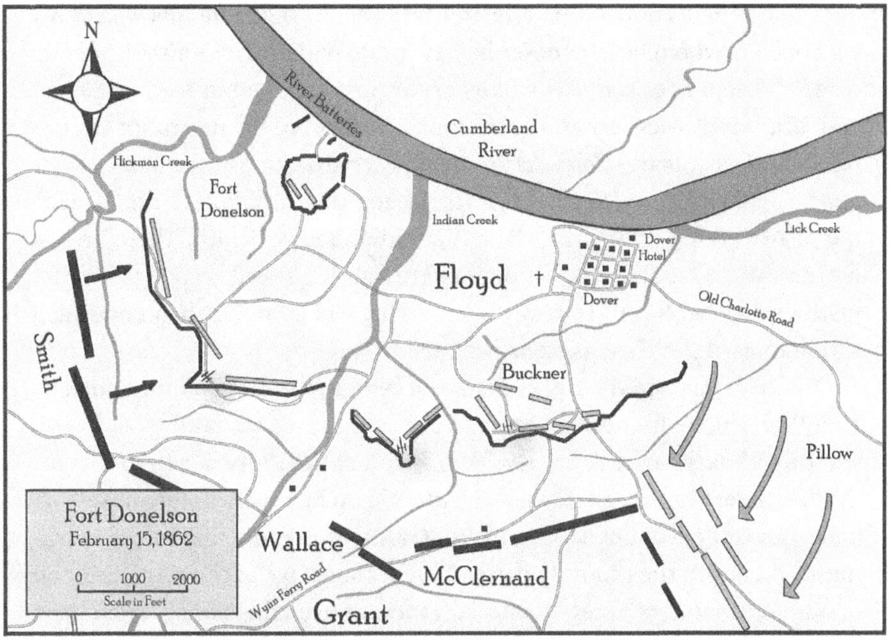

In the pivotal third day's fighting at Fort Donelson, Grant reacted to Pillow's overwhelming attack on the Federal right by throwing his left, under Brigadier General Charles Ferguson Smith, in an even more devastating assault on the depleted Confederate right, evoking the surrender hours later.

In the predawn hours of February 15, a downcast Grant received a message from Foote. The naval officer said he needed to see the general and was too severely wounded to come to headquarters. Grant already that evening had written Julia that "taking . . . Fort Donelson bids fair to be a long job"[123] and had ordered that picks and shovels be unloaded from the transport boats later in the morning. Then Grant set out on horseback across the four icy miles to Foote's mooring spot north of Fort Donelson. He left behind orders that brigade commanders Smith, Wallace, and McClernand hold their positions and display no aggression until they received further word. But, in an appalling lapse, he left no one in charge. He later recalled having "no idea there would be any engagement on land unless I brought it on myself."[124] Aboard Foote's boat, Foote handed him a cigar and told him the badly damaged ironclads needed to go back to the Cairo area for repairs. Further discouraging Grant, Foote said he would do his best to have them back in ten days.

When he left Foote's boat and arrived back on shore, he met one of his staff officers whom he later described as "white with fear . . . for the National troops." The officer said the Confederates had attacked in front of Dover and "scattered" McClernand's division.[125] So now, in the reverse of Grant's battle plan, it was the *Confederates* who were attacking and rolling up the *Union* line. Grant rode as hard as the frozen road would let him to reach the nearest point of his line, the left commanded by Smith. There he saw nothing amiss but, hearing the din of hard fighting ahead, leaped to his first instinct: he told Smith to ready his men for a charge. He then continued riding toward the right as signs worsened.

When he reached the right end of the center regiments commanded by Lew Wallace, he found McClernand's men fighting but falling back with cartridge boxes nearing empty. They had lost nearly two miles of front. Wallace later recalled that when Grant rode up he was "wholly unexcited" and "proceed[ed] at once to business." Grant later wrote that boxes of ammunition lay on the ground nearby, "but at that stage of the war . . . not all of our commanders of regiments, brigades, or even divisions . . . had been educated up to the point of seeing that their men were constantly supplied with ammunition during an engagement."[126] In other words Grant, the longtime quartermaster, had made certain that plenty of ammunition was available, but many of his subordinates (likely including the politician McClernand) had not been "educated," as Grant had been in Mexico, of the need to get it into the hands of men fighting too hard to have time to look for it.

Grant rode into knots of unsupervised infantrymen who were talking excitedly. They said that the attacking Confederates were carrying knapsacks, as well as haversacks filled with rations. Shaken by the momentum of the all-out onslaught, the men thought the knapsacks and haversacks indicated that the Confederates planned to fight as long as their rations held out. Grant's bigger-picture common sense told him otherwise: they were trying to save their army by breaking out of the Union siege. And his military instincts told him that in order to make such a powerful attack on the Union right, the Confederates must have borrowed many of their numbers from the other end of the line, the end opposing Smith. He could see that the Confederates had fallen back, which he thought meant that their attack had not fully succeeded and they were at least as "demoralized" as the retreating Federals.

Actually, the Confederates had fallen back to get the rest of the gear with which they planned to march to Nashville. They were indeed "demoralized," though, having seen their generals order the fort abandoned the day after they had all but sunk the previously terrifying gunboats. Grant rightly sensed that the critical point of the battle of Fort Donelson was upon him. He turned to a staff member and observed that men on both sides were discouraged and "the one who attacks first now will be victorious."[127] He then returned to the Union left and ordered Smith to attack the Confederate trenches in front of him, which he correctly sensed had been all but emptied to supply muscle for the attack on the Federal right. Smith's men surged forward and routed a skeleton force from the Confederate trenches. As dusk fell, they also hauled up artillery that they planned to put to use in the morning.

It turned out they did not have to, though. Overnight, two of the four Confederate generals facing Grant—commander John B. Floyd and second-in-command Pillow—unceremoniously boarded boats and departed for Nashville, leaving Grant's prewar friend and benefactor Brigadier General Simon Bolivar Buckner to make the capitulation that the four—seeing their line about to be enfiladed by Smith and noting Federal reinforcements arriving by the hour—had decided was the only alternative to annihilation. Buckner sent a party under a flag of truce and, in the high-flown and condescending language of a Southern officer and gentleman, proposed the naming of commissioners from both sides to draw up terms of surrender. Grant, heeding the growling negative reaction of the gruff and venerable Smith, sent the emissaries back with an ultimatum that further intensified the pressure and embodied Grant's aggressive get-it-done style.

"No terms except unconditional and immediate surrender can be accepted," his curt message replied. "I propose to move immediately upon your works."[128]

With no alternative, Buckner surrendered.

MAKING FRIENDS

Grant, now the sudden victor in the war's most decisive battle so far, had captured not just a fort but an army. Newspapers used his initials to dub him "'Unconditional Surrender' Grant." It was a triumph of colossal proportions, not least because his quick-thinking aggressiveness had vanquished myriad errors of his own making. Summarized, they are staggering:

After Fort Henry, he seemed to think that virtually all he had to do to beat the retreating Confederates was show up at Fort Donelson. Assuming Donelson would be a quick and easy conquest, he had ordered that no tents or other heavy baggage be taken on the march to get there—and he had not trained his officers sufficiently to prevent them from leaving behind their men's overcoats to protect against the unsurprising subsequent February snowstorm. He also found he had not brought enough men to adequately surround the fort and the vitally connected town of Dover. He presumed the ironclads would again, as at Fort Henry, be invincible, and they were not. He left his command on February 15 with nobody in charge and rode to the brink of defeat before he could return to his lines.

These blunders, though, were all correctable. They were mistakes of pre-fight attitude, the kind that are fatal mostly to indecisive, non-resilient, and fearful minds distracted by danger. More important were his unfailingly quick, cool, and correct decisions when he was under the pressure of minié balls and artillery shells. He may have advanced on Fort Donelson under considerable misapprehension, but his mind achieved clear focus as soon as he arrived. Most important, *the soberer reality he found did not dismay him*. Reception of Halleck's order to entrench at Fort Henry after he already was in front of Donelson only increased his dogged desire to take the Cumberland River fortress.

As much as Grant identified with his men, their coatless suffering from sleet, snow, and icy wind—to say nothing of the fire from cannon and rifles—did not deflect him from determination to end their sufferings the right way: by winning. In the crisis of the Confederate attack on February 15, when most commanders would have retreated or at least have stopped and entrenched at the point to which the Confederates had pushed them, Grant instead kept his eyes on the prize. He lunged to victory by ordering a charge, first on his left and then along his whole line.

Grant's quiet and fearless resolve not only achieved the Donelson victory but showed he had within him the means of making greater future conquests. While he battled for advantage in front of Dover, Halleck—desperate to get what he thought would be a more dependable man in charge of this operation whose outcome was vital to the success of Halleck's intra-army competition with Buell—tried to send forward Brigadier General William T. Sherman as Grant's replacement. Ethan Allen Hitchcock, after all, was too far away in St. Louis to be of immediate use. But Sherman resisted and, when ordered by Halleck to Paducah to replace the departed Smith, began rushing aid to Grant as swiftly as possible. He also sent forward a message that surely surprised and profoundly affected the recipient: "I . . . will do everything in my power to hurry forward to you reinforcements and supplies, and if I could be of service to you myself would gladly come, without making any question of rank."[129]

Grant knew Sherman, sort of. They were each Ohioans and West Pointers, but Sherman had been three classes ahead of Grant at the academy. And whereas Grant was sent to Mexico during that conflict, Sherman had been ordered to comparatively peaceful California. They hailed from different levels of society as well, Sherman being the foster son of a powerful U.S. senator and eventual presidential cabinet member. They had met once in St. Louis during Grant's between-wars agricultural struggles, which could only have given Sherman an unflattering view of Grant at a time when he was down and all but out. Yet now Sherman, who was senior to him among Union brigadier generals, not only worked hard to get indispensable supplies to him when the Donelson situation was in doubt but also offered to come to Donelson and serve beneath him if doing so would be helpful. Grant would never forget the offer. From then on, he would count Sherman one of his closest military friends.

He made another close and loyal friend during the Donelson campaign, too—another Ohioan who hailed from closer to Grant's societal level. Halleck, well knowing Grant's reputation with alcohol, had sent a spy along when Grant left Paducah for Fort Henry. Lieutenant Colonel James B. McPherson was also a West Pointer, although he had graduated a decade later than Grant. He was an engineer who finished first in his class, but the main task Halleck assigned him had only superficially to do with engineering: it was primarily to assess the truth of the Kountz report. McPherson's real job was to report to Halleck on "General Grant's habits," he would later tell another staff member. "It is said that he is drinking terribly and is in every way inefficient."[130]

In McPherson, though, Halleck picked the wrong prospective tattler. In the two and a half weeks between the army's departure from Paducah and the Fort Donelson surrender, McPherson apparently became a Grant admirer. Ill after undergoing the climatic hardships of the Donelson siege, McPherson returned to Halleck's St. Louis headquarters for treatment, and he wrote Grant a markedly friendly letter imparting good news: Halleck was "exceedingly gratified [by the Henry-Donelson victories] and says you could not have done better." McPherson even said that on learning of the surrender, Halleck "telegraphed Lincoln to nominate you for a Major General." But probably the best news for Grant, and perhaps an indication of just how close to Grant McPherson felt himself becoming, was that "you will not be troubled anymore by Kountz. His character is found out and I think he will be dismissed."[131]

Kountz, in fact, was not then banished for good. More than a year later, during the Vicksburg campaign, he would reappear briefly among Grant's troops—in McClernand's camps, invited by that general. By now surer of his ground, Grant had Rawlins send McClernand a sharp note inquiring "by what authority" Kountz was there. McClernand claimed to know nothing, except that Kountz had departed on a northbound steamer that morning. He would not be heard of in Grant's army again.[132]

But McPherson's well-intended letter also gave a false impression in a couple of important respects. Halleck was taking—in fact, soliciting—personal credit for the Foote and Grant victories. Halleck would have pointed out that, after all, his vaunted brain had supervised these feats from the comforts of St. Louis. He almost certainly would not have felt constrained to mention that he had ordered Grant to remain at Fort Henry and that he had not so much as commented on Grant's attack on Donelson while its outcome hung in the balance. But speaking to a crowd of 1,500 in St. Louis on receipt of word of the Donelson surrender, Halleck declaimed to great huzzahs, "I promised when I came here that with your aid I would drive the enemies of our flag from your state. This has been done, and they are virtually out of Kentucky and will soon be out of Tennessee."[133] The next day Halleck had indeed, as McPherson wrote Grant, sent a wire to Washington requesting that Grant be promoted to major general. But there was more to it than that. The wire's exact message: "Make *Buell,* Grant, and *Pope* major generals of volunteers *and give me command of the West.* I ask this in return for Forts Henry and Donelson."[134]

Halleck's celebratory mood was so sanguine that he even informed McClellan that he thought he himself might go to Tennessee and personally take command of Grant's army.[135] He swiftly came to his senses, however, and decided against submitting himself to the minimal niceties of Dover. Rather, he remained in St. Louis and assessed his situation. Some of Halleck's subsequent behavior seems at least partially motivated by jealousy of the subordinate with the new press-conferred nickname "Unconditional Surrender," but Halleck's most diligent biographer says no; Halleck simply regarded Grant as unworthy of a commander's respect, let alone his envy, because of "his bearing and personal conduct."[136] Whatever the motive, Halleck set about to cut Grant back down to a public stature below Halleck's own, whether that was his aim or not. To do it, he employed the same handy weapon for which McPherson had pronounced him ready to dismiss Kountz from the service for employing: talk of Grant's thirst.

After the Henry-Donelson conquest, Grant went to Nashville to confer with Buell, who was supposedly headed there to capture it and had been chosen by his friend McClellan for that honor. Grant, on the other hand, wanted to go there only in the interest of the work they all were supposed to be doing: defeating the Confederacy. He hoped to "learn what I can of the movements of the enemy," he wrote to Julia.[137] In the meantime, Grant was returning to Buell 7,000 reinforcements that Buell, in response to Halleck's shrill beseeching, had finally lent Halleck and Grant—too late—for the Donelson struggle. These troops at Grant's instruction now landed in Nashville while Buell, fearing that the place had not yet been evacuated by Confederates, sat on the other side of the Cumberland River. Grant himself then had to wait for Buell to decide to cross the Cumberland into the Tennessee capital to meet him for what proved to be a frosty exchange of views.

Halleck became enraged that Grant had gone to Nashville. He complained to McClellan, correctly, that his unloved subordinate had gone there without permission. Grant had written Halleck's chief of staff about his planned Nashville visit and, receiving no reply, assumed there was no objection. But Halleck told McClellan that Grant had "left his command without my authority" and, in wild overreaction, added that Grant's army "seems to be as much demoralized by the victory of Fort Donelson as was that of the Potomac by the defeat of Bull Run." Halleck complained that he could get from Grant "no returns, no reports, no information. . . . Satisfied with his victory, he sits down and enjoys it without any regard for the future. I am worn-out and tired with this inefficiency."[138]

The "inefficiency" was of course that of the cautious Buell, not Grant, who was restlessly itching to go forward. But McClellan, who had had history with another kind of Grant "inefficiency" at Fort Vancouver in the 1850s, wrote back—with the approval of Secretary of War Stanton—that Halleck should arrest Grant "if the good of the service requires it." The next day Halleck responded by putting into plain English what he and McClellan were really talking about: "A rumor has just reached me that since the taking of Fort Donelson General Grant has resumed his former bad habits. If so, it will account for his neglect of my oft-repeated orders. I do not deem it advisable to arrest him at present, but I have placed General Smith in command of the expedition up the Tennessee."[139]

In all likelihood, the "rumor" was nothing more than a convenient creation of Halleck himself. Halleck informed Grant of his dissatisfactions after telling him he was being replaced by Smith, but he made no mention of the "rumor." Grant wrote back that he was "not aware of ever having disobeyed any order" from headquarters, "certainly never intended such a thing. I have reported almost daily the condition of my command and . . . every position occupied."[140]

After receiving another reprimand from Halleck the next day complaining that he had "neglect[ed] . . . repeated orders" and not furnished headquarters with daily reports of "the numbers and positions of the forces under your command"—which Halleck falsely claimed had been requested by McClellan—Grant showed that the man who had snatched victory from disaster at Fort Donelson could be just as unyielding with superiors, although respectfully. He wrote Halleck on March 7 that he had tried his best to furnish all the information Halleck desired and that "evry move I made was reported daily to your Chief of Staff, who must have failed to keep you posted. . . . It is no fault of mine if you have not received my letters." Then he delivered a line that was a masterstroke of directness, brevity, and roll-of-the-dice courage:

> Believeing sincerely that I must have enemys between you and myself who are trying to impair my usefulness, *I respectfully ask to be relieved of further duty in the Dept.*
>
> U. S. Grant
> Maj. Gen.[141]

Likely Grant, or John Rawlins, went even further. Somebody sent to Congressman Elihu Washburne copies of the Halleck-Grant correspondence on the matter, and Washburne took it to Abraham Lincoln. On March 10 Halleck received a telegram from the U.S. adjutant general inquiring, at the behest of Lincoln and Secretary of War Stanton, whether Grant had done the things Halleck claimed and "whether he has committed any acts which were unauthorized or not in accordance with military subordination or propriety, *and if so, what*."[142]

A surely jolted Halleck, knowing McClellan had not actually "advised" him to arrest Grant, backtracked immediately to avoid upsetting his own apple cart. Just like Grant, he could see—despite his Jominian contempt for civilian concerns—that it would hardly do to countenance a transfer (and implied censure) of the general who had won the most celebrated Union triumph of the war to this point. Halleck rushed to clean up his mess, writing the adjutant general that he had investigated the Grant matter and that the general's purported errors had been explained. He recommended that "no further notice be taken" because "all . . . irregularities have been remedied."[143] Meanwhile, to a second Grant request to be relieved, Halleck replied no: "You cannot be relieved from your command. There is no good reason for it. I am certain that all the authorities in Washington ask, is, that you enforce discipline and punish the disorderly. The power is in your hands; use it, and you will be sustained by all above you. Instead of relieving you, I wish you, as soon as your new army is in the field, to assume the immediate command and lead it on to new victories."[144]

Grant was thus mollified. But, significantly for a study of his generalship, he felt he had a new problem. He had a strong attachment to Smith, the mentor assigned by Halleck to replace him at the suggestion of McClellan, and he was now reluctant to supplant his former teacher. He in fact wrote his old West Point instructor that although Halleck expected him—Grant—to command the army headed southward up the Tennessee River, "I think it exceedingly doubtful whether I shall accept; certainly not until the object of the expedition is accomplished."[145]

In other words, Grant would not think of upsetting any plans Smith had made for the immediate future, if ever. But Smith was happy to be replaced by this junior in whom he saw his aggressiveness mirrored. He obviously knew Grant idolized him, because Grant had consistently sought his counsel on matters ever since Smith had been assigned to Paducah. To assuage Grant's feelings, Smith wrote back that he probably would have to give up the command anyway because he had badly injured a leg in a freak accident that had left him virtually immobile. That turned out to be all too true. The wound refused to heal, and Smith died, deeply mourned by Grant, on April 25.

The mutual Grant-Smith affection, Jean Edward Smith observes in his excellent Grant biography, "contrasts sharply with the backbiting that afflicted less accomplished commanders."[146]

AGAIN REVIEWING BELMONT'S HARD LESSON

Grant had another hard lesson left to learn from the Confederates, one he had not taken fully to heart after the all-but-accomplished breakout at Fort Donelson: that his enemies would surprise him if they got the chance. They dispensed that lesson again at Shiloh a month and a half later.

General Albert Sidney Johnston, minus the estimated 15,000 men Grant had captured at Donelson but plus a lot of others desperately gleaned from across western Dixie, slammed into Grant's army near Shiloh Church in southwest Tennessee on April 6, 1862. Johnston's 40,000 riflemen constituted roughly the same number Grant had, but the Federals were scattered, camped willy-nilly to be near sources of water. And some of them were still breakfasting when the Confederates struck.

A primary reason Grant was surprised was likely that for more than two weeks he had been preoccupied with trying in vain to get Halleck's permission to launch an attack of his own against Johnston; Halleck predictably ordered him to bring on no battle.[147] So when Johnston brought the battle to *him*, Grant—as well as Sherman, who now commanded a division under Grant—disingenuously maintained forever after that the attack had not been unanticipated. They said they had seen Confederates spying on them for days beforehand, which was true. But they obviously had not expected to see as many of them at one time as emerged from the mist in yelling hordes early that April morning. In the bloodiest battle in American history up to then, the Confederates pushed the Federals almost—but, crucially, *only* almost—into the Tennessee River.

Grant spent some of that first day up front under fire—and, throughout that day, enduring mounting disappointment. Several people who saw him, though, detected no great concern. He had been scheduled to meet Buell in Savannah, Tennessee, that morning, but the balky Buell, although in the same town, had not shown up by 7:00 A.M. So Grant, having heard firing upriver, left for the battlefield, sending orders for Buell's lead division to march down the opposite side of the Tennessee and then ferry across to Pittsburg Landing. He also ordered another Buell division that was still on the march

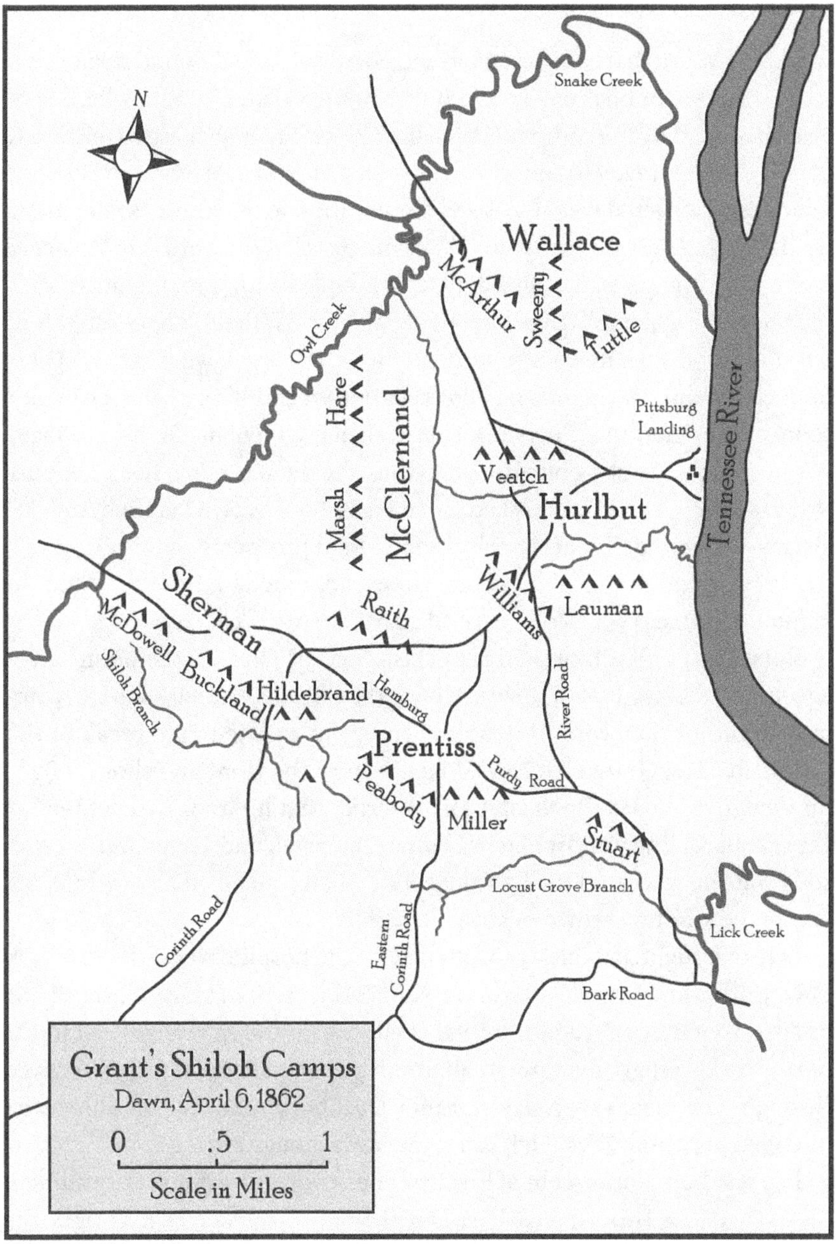

The Federal camps at Pittsburg Landing at dawn on April 6 were scattered to take advantage of water sources. The ensuing battle took its name from Shiloh Church, a log structure that Sherman's troops were camped around. The "Wallace" at the map's top right was Brigadier General W. H. L. Wallace, who would die of wounds incurred that day—not Lew Wallace, who did not arrive until dusk.

from Nashville to hurry to Savannah and board battlefield-bound steamboats. As his own steamboat passed a nearer landing called Crump's a little later, Grant stopped by the camps of Brigadier General Lew Wallace to tell him to get his division ready to move and await instructions. Arriving at Pittsburg Landing, he ordered wagonloads of ammunition forward and, seeing thousands of stragglers on the riverbank, immediately sent word for Wallace to come ahead "at once." He also detailed a couple of Iowa regiments to stem the tide of stragglers.[148] Then he rode forward and found his lines retreating. Around 10:00 A.M. he conferred briefly with Sherman, who had been shot in the hand but was managing heroically. Grant and his escort rode on and soon encountered an artillery fusillade. A shell fragment hit Grant's scabbard, momentarily separating him from his sword, but he was miraculously unhurt. When aide William Rowley asked him if the outlook was not getting "squally," Grant—expecting Wallace's arrival soon—said prospects were "not so very bad."[149] Around noon, with Federal troops approaching from the right, he animatedly observed, "Now we're all right. There's Wallace."[150]

But it was not Wallace. And back at the landing shortly after noon, Grant encountered a less-welcome subordinate than Wallace: Buell, who had come by boat rather than with his troops. Perhaps in an attempt to break Buell's formidable ice, Grant said he had just been to the front and showed Buell his dented scabbard. Buell later loftily wrote that he "took little notice" of the scabbard. The atmosphere was obviously cool, and Grant and his staff soon rode back toward the fighting, while Buell walked off to confront and berate the swelling crowd of stragglers.[151]

Late that night, outside a rain-drenched field hospital where doctors were sawing arms and legs off screaming wounded, Sherman found Grant sitting under a tree that afforded minimal shelter from the rain. Planning in the next breath to suggest a retreat, Sherman observed that they had just lived through "the devil's own day." Grant's legendary reply cut off Sherman's intended proposal: "Yes. Lick 'em tomorrow, though."[152]

In a reaction reminiscent of his surrender-aborted response to imminent disaster on the third day at Fort Donelson, he attacked at first light the next morning. Reinforced with fresh troops from Buell during the night, he pushed the unreinforced Confederates from the field. Grant had made a mistake, but the Confederates had made a worse one: they had underestimated him. In gentlemanly fashion, they assumed that almost defeating him was enough for one day and they could finish the job later.

They were wrong. Part of the reason was that they were unable to overcome their own errors of the previous day. Johnston had planned to drive Grant back from the west bank of the river before Buell could arrive on the east bank from Nashville with the Army of the Ohio, but bad weather and lack of sufficient training had delayed the Confederate attack more than a day. Then the fight ended up pushing the Federals two miles *toward* the river instead of away from it. And on the afternoon of the first of the two days of battle, Johnston bled to death on the field from a leg wound he did not realize he had suffered. Then his successor, Beauregard, demanded that his army waste hours capturing a knot of stubborn resistance known as the Hornet's Nest instead of simply surrounding it and rushing on toward the river. By nightfall they had enough time left to push Grant only to the brink of destruction, not over it.

That night with Sherman, Grant bared a little of his "Lick 'em tomorrow" reasoning. He compared the situation to the one on the climactic day at Fort Donelson: *both* sides had fought to the cusp of exhaustion, "and whoever assumed the offensive was sure to win."[153]

The comment and the thought process that produced it are classic Grant. When McPherson approached his chief around 10:00 P.M. of the first day, before the arrival of Sherman, he asked if Grant wanted him to "make preparations for retreat." Grant looked up as if he could not believe what McPherson had said. "Retreat?" he replied. "No. I propose to attack at daylight and whip them."[154]

The nucleus of Grant's generalship is encapsulated in just such lines. Retreat? No. I propose to attack at daylight and whip them. . . . Lick 'em tomorrow. . . . Whoever assumes the offensive will win. . . . No terms except unconditional surrender can be accepted; I propose to move immediately upon your works.

Confederate general Simon Bolivar Buckner, a proud Kentucky plantation scion, had resented Grant's unfriendly reply to his query regarding the possible convening of commissioners to work out terms of surrender at Fort Donelson. Buckner thought it ungentlemanly of Grant to respond that way to a past friend and antebellum benefactor. It might well have been, had they been in a drawing room at a country club. But they were not, and Grant, in contrast to Buckner, was completely conscious of it. They were amid deadly business on which lives of men and nations depended, and everything hinged on who won, not on chivalric pleasantry.

At Shiloh, Beauregard, another proud plantation product, likely would have recoiled with the same attitude as Buckner's at Donelson had he known of Grant's intentions the night after Shiloh's first day of fighting. He might even have laughed. He later said he "thought I had Grant just where I wanted him."[155] He obviously did think that, because that evening he telegraphed an even more erroneous message to Confederate headquarters in Virginia: "We this morning attacked the enemy in strong position in front of Pittsburg [Landing] and after a severe battle of ten hours, thanks be to the Almighty, gained a *complete victory*, driving the enemy from every position."[156]

Part of the reason Beauregard so misjudged Grant that night was because Beauregard was in the process of ignoring information from some of his own subordinates. Some of his cavalrymen had stayed awake and at work that inclement night, and they had reported seeing Federals by the thousand crossing the Tennessee to join Grant.[157] But Beauregard's headquarters had received word from Alabama Confederate commander Ben Hardin Helm, another plantation son who was Abraham Lincoln's brother-in-law, saying Buell's troops were headed there instead of to Pittsburgh Landing.[158] Helm's command had seen a fraction of Buell's army heading for Huntsville, and Helm assumed it was the whole thing.

SHILOH—"IF BUELL HAD COME IN BY THE FRONT . . ."

So much for Grant's Confederate enemies at Shiloh. He also had to deal with the Union ones.

First there was Don Carlos Buell, who appeared none too eager to rescue this questionably reputable upstart who now, after Buell's lengthy and fairly distinguished military career, suddenly outranked him. Sherman recalled in his memoirs that when Buell arrived at Pittsburg Landing, he "seemed to mistrust us and repeatedly said he did not like the looks of things, especially about the boat landing, and I really feared he would not cross over his army that night, lest he become involved in a general disaster."[159] Buell later stoutly disputed the much-quoted story from John Rawlins, Grant's chief of staff, that, on meeting Grant at Shiloh, Buell asked what arrangements Grant had made to retreat—to which Grant was said to have replied, "I have not yet despaired of whipping them, general."[160]

If Buell, not liking "the looks of things," *did not* inquire about retreat, one wonders—after reading his own account of nearing Pittsburg Landing on a steamboat—*why* he did not:

> We met a stream of fugitives that poured in a constantly swelling current along the west bank of the [Tennessee] river. The mouth of Snake Creek was full of them swimming across [that is, away from the battlefield]. We arrived at the landing about 1 o'clock. . . .[161]
>
> On the shore . . . the face of the bluff was crowded with stragglers from the battle. The number . . . would not have fallen short of fifteen thousand, including those who had passed down the river and the less callous but still broken and demoralized fragments about the camps on the plateau near the landing. At the top of the bluff all was confusion. Men mounted and on foot, and wagons with their teams and drivers all struggling to force their way closer to the river were mixed up in apparently inextricable confusion with a battery of artillery which was standing in park without men or horses to man or move it. The increasing throng presented a barrier which it was evidently necessary to remove, in order to make way for the passage of my troops when they should arrive.[162]

Buell's reminiscence also asserts that at that afternoon meeting "there was none of that masterly confidence [on Grant's part] which has since been assumed with reference to the occasion."[163] From the tone of that and Buell's preceding observations, the mood of their meeting and Buell's scorn and perhaps alarm seems evident.

Grant, in his own memoirs, recalled that Buell's

> attention was attracted by the men lying under the cover of the [river] bank. I saw him berating them and trying to shame them into joining their regiments. He even threatened them with shells from the gunboats nearby. But it was all to no effect. . . . I have no doubt that this sight impressed General Buell with the idea that a line of retreat would be a good thing just then. If he had come in by the front instead of through the stragglers in the rear he would have thought and felt differently. Could he have come through the Confederate rear, he would have witnessed there a scene similar

> to that at our own. The distant rear of an army engaged in battle is not the best place from which to judge correctly what is going on in front.[164]

He then, in a remarkable passage again underlining the extent of his empathy with his common soldiers, defended his skulkers against Buell's obvious contempt: "Most of these men afterward proved themselves as gallant as any of those who saved the battle from which they had deserted."[165] Buell, Grant added, "was a strict disciplinarian and perhaps did not distinguish sufficiently between the volunteer who 'enlisted for the war' and the soldier who serves in time of peace. One system embraced men who risked life for a principle. . . . The other includes, as a rule, only men who could not do as well in any other occupation."[166]

Grant of course knew all too well whereof he wrote. He himself had appeared to be one of the latter and, during his seven hard civilian years, had proved it to the satisfaction of many, including his own father and brothers. Buell, on the other hand, had never left the army to try his luck as a private citizen. After the Mexican War, in which he had been recognized for gallantry three times, he apparently mellowed. He served thirteen years in the adjutant general's department and had, in the words of historian Jean Edward Smith, "become a friend of detail. . . . A close friend of McClellan for many years, he came to share Little Mac's view that war involved maneuver, not bloodshed. 'The object is not to fight great battles,' Buell wrote in December 1861, 'but by demonstrations and maneuvering to prevent the enemy from concentrating his forces.'"[167] Buell had become a member of the military elite and thus, in his own mind, a soldier far superior to Grant and the unschooled volunteers with whom Grant identified. Grant and the volunteers saw war not as battles to be avoided but rather as ones that had to be fought and endured, along with all the horrors that went with them, in order to accomplish the mission and go home.

As after Fort Donelson, Grant became a hero for a day or two—until the casualty lists came in. Nearly one-quarter of the approximately 100,000 Americans who fought at Shiloh were killed, wounded, or captured. And more than 13,000 of these losses were Grant's Federals. Newspapermen, politicians, and a general public appalled by the horrific numbers began to emphasize the surprise element of the Shiloh story and to assume that the reason for it was that when Johnston struck, Grant had been not just unready but drunk. The *Cincinnati Gazette* published a widely circulated article apparently sourced by many of the first day's deserters saying that the dawn Confederate attack was so unanticipated that Union soldiers had not entrenched and had been bayoneted in their beds. Grant also was soon vilified for not pursuing the Confederates back to their base at Corinth, Mississippi, after the battle ended.

Not pursuing a retreating enemy violated Grant's personal military creed. The reason he did not do it this time was, once again, his strong identification with the men in ranks. He later wrote that he had "wanted to pursue [at Shiloh], but had not the heart to order the men who had fought desperately for two days, lying in the mud and the rain whenever not fighting, and I did not feel disposed positively to order Buell, or any part of his command [who were fresher, having mostly taken the field on the second day], to pursue. Although the senior in rank at the time, I had been so only a few weeks. Buell was, and had been for some time past, a department commander, while I commanded only a district."[168]

The *Cincinnati Gazette* article was widely reprinted and was the first of others that took similar tacks. Politicians from states heavily represented in Grant's army protested their losses loudly. Ohio governor David Tod asserted that two regiments from the Buckeye State that had infamously fled the battlefield were only victims of the "criminal negligence" of two Ohio natives, Grant and Sherman, as well as other Union generals. Ohio lieutenant governor Benjamin Stanton said Grant deserved to be "court-martialed or shot." Congressman James Harlan of Iowa said Grant had blundered at Belmont, Fort Donelson, and Shiloh, and that Buell, another Ohio native, had saved him at Shiloh. Soldiers in Buell's army claimed to be convinced that Grant had been drunk when the Confederate onslaught struck.[169]

Jealous subordinates, led by second-in-command McClernand, also took their shots. The recent congressman used his lengthy civilian acquaintance with Lincoln to sidestep the chain of command and send a personal report straight to the president. It exaggerated his own role in the fighting and blamed Grant for the extent of the slaughter as well as for the lack of pursuit of the Confederates on the battle's second day.[170] But Lincoln also heard Grant championed by longtime Lincoln friend Congressman Washburne, and he seemed to be already beginning to realize that Grant was a rare commodity among the gentleman generals of his army. A famous but possibly apocryphal story has it that to one Grant-detracting adviser who said Grant should be fired, Lincoln replied that he could not "spare this man; he fights!"[171]

Grant's endurance of seven years of civilian ignominy surely helped him bear up under this pall of national shame, whose proportions would have driven lesser men to quit and flee to obscurity. But Grant was no longer the sort of man to quit anything in mid-stride, especially when he felt he had done nothing wrong. He knew he had not been drunk or even drinking, and he, like many and maybe most veteran officers of his time, felt that entrenching sent the wrong message to the troops. Grant later said he had ordered his engineer, Colonel McPherson, to lay out a line for entrenchments, but McPherson had reported that the line would have to run farther away from water sources than where the division camps were already established.[172] And the initial reason for camping at Pittsburg Landing at all was just to establish a staging area for an impending, Halleck-led Union attack on the nearby Confederate base at Corinth.

"The fact is," Grant later wrote,

> I regarded the campaign we were engaged in as an offensive one and had no idea that the enemy would leave strong intrenchments to take the initiative when he knew he would be attacked where he was if he remained. . . .[173]
>
> . . . Up to that time the pick and spade had been but little resorted to at the West. . . . Besides this, the troops with me, officers and men, needed discipline and drill more than they [needed] experience with the pick, shovel, and axe. Reinforcements were arriving almost daily, composed of troops that had been hastily thrown together into companies and regiments—fragments of incomplete organizations, the men and officers strangers to each other. Under all these circumstances I concluded that drill and discipline were worth more to our men than fortifications.[174]

It is rarely mentioned (and Grant certainly did not mention) that Halleck had been expected almost daily since late March to come south and take command of the Union army *before* the Shiloh battle. The great man did not arrive, though, until afterward. The fact that Grant realized he was intended to be just a caretaker until the advance on Corinth was to begin is no excuse for his army's unpreparedness, but it does seem to be a consideration.

Halleck certainly did nothing to take Grant off the hook of national scorn, and the vaunted department commander finally did arrive on April 11.[175] Having never fought a significant battle or even seen where one had recently *been* fought,[176] Halleck was as shocked as a civilian would have been at the blasted Shiloh landscape littered with burned and stinking piles of dead horses, hundreds of wrecked military vehicles, and myriad human corpses partially washed out of shallow graves by rain. He swiftly set about instituting his ideas of how an army in the field should be commanded—and illustrating exactly the kind of officer Grant was not and never wanted to be: an armchair stickler for bureaucratic correctness. On April 13, 1862, Halleck issued orders to Buell and Grant specifying that each intra-army communication should deal with a single subject and "be properly folded."[177]

Halleck was a huge problem to overcome, as were the longtime Lincoln acquaintance McClernand and a few other Union generals, and Grant overcame them with an approach to military politics as careful, considered, and ego-swallowing as his fighting style was aggressive. That approach was patient, almost self-defensive until the decisive moment, and always immeasurably aided by his incessant battlefield bellicosity. It was probably assisted even further by his lifelong superstitious, semi-religious aversion to scheming against competitors for particular positions or assignments. Rather than make aggressive moves against intra-army foes, he tended to let these foes accomplish their own destruction. Then his decisions became swift and final.

Grant vanquished McClernand partly by letting the waves of the ex-congressman's wild ambition crash on the rocks of theater commander Halleck's deep Jominian contempt for civilian politicians. With some apparent justification, McClernand indiscreetly complained all the way up the chain of command to Lincoln that he was being victimized by the prejudice of a cabal of West Pointers. During the buildup to the Vicksburg campaign, Grant and Sherman, with Halleck's acquiescence, literally stole an army from McClernand. The ex-congressman aided them, though. He obtained a leave from Grant's army and at least tacit permission from the White House to go home to the Midwest to recruit masses of new volunteers. With these, he planned to lead his own campaign against Vicksburg, thus potentially outflanking a similar drive getting underway by Grant and Sherman. Unfortunately for McClernand, his recruits were directed by Halleck to Memphis, which was in Grant's assigned district of command.

Grant then coolly directed Sherman to take them on down the Mississippi toward Vicksburg,

He did this, though, only after informing Halleck of what was happening and asking whether the new troops sent into his jurisdiction were under his command. Halleck, having little respect for McClernand as an officer and perhaps wary of his relationship with Lincoln, said yes. He thus encouraged Grant to send Sherman southward with the recruits while McClernand, a widower, dawdled in Illinois getting remarried. When McClernand arrived in Memphis with his new bride, what he had presumed was his waiting army had vanished.

That, though, occurred in the fall of 1862. In the summer, Grant got and took excellent advice from Sherman on coexisting with Halleck. When the department commander exited his comfortable St. Louis headquarters to take command of the army following the Shiloh battle in April, his arrival relegated Grant, the next ranking officer, to second in command. It was a position that carried considerable prestige but offered no command responsibility—in other words, no command at all. In the view of historian Jean Edward Smith, second in command was a position whose duties Grant "was temperamentally incapable" of discharging, having "never served in that capacity. As quartermaster with the Fourth Infantry in Mexico he commanded the unit's supply train, and when he returned to the service in 1861 he commanded a regiment."[178]

Grant took umbrage at the new assignment, and Halleck apparently had no inkling why. As an armchair warrior, Halleck almost certainly assumed Grant would appreciate being honored with this leisurely job. Grant was not. He habitually ached to do meaningful work, not lounge. So he and Halleck once again clashed, with Grant complaining that the image the position gave him was one of *dis*honor, of an officer placed under arrest. The storm of public abuse he continued to suffer in Shiloh's wake likely heightened his sensitivity to the look of it.

Halleck respected Grant as a fighter, terming him "brave & able in the field."[179] However, Jominian to the core, Halleck regarded combat as something to be avoided wherever possible, rather than sought, and thus of secondary importance in generalship. He was markedly disrespectful of Grant's deficiencies in what Halleck regarded as major aspects of officering: immersing oneself peacetime-like in every detail of military administration (such as writing correctly folded messages), making an impeccable and vaunted appearance (*looking like* a general), and conducting oneself as, well, a gentleman.

A major Grant downside, in Halleck's eyes, was that he looked and acted much more like the soldiers with whom he most identified—the volunteer enlisted men—than a general. Grant also insisted on driving this identification home by wearing the standard enlisted man's tunic, usually rumpled, with his rank's stars just stuck on the shoulders. Halleck's friend Ethan Allen Hitchcock, chief of staff to Winfield Scott in Mexico before retiring to St. Louis to preoccupy himself with writing books and making "philosophical investigations,"[180] opined to Halleck that Grant was "little more than a common gambler and drunkard."[181]

Had Halleck any idea how *much* Grant empathized with common soldiers, he no doubt would have been further repelled. Halleck took pride in the victories Grant brought Halleck's department but otherwise regarded him with unease. Grant's aggressiveness was dangerous in Halleck's cautious view. Responding to a pointed letter, Halleck disingenuously reassured Grant that he was not Grant's enemy,[182] and Grant, mollified, unenthusiastically tried to adapt to his labor-less job.

"THE TURNING POINT OF THE WAR"

Meanwhile Halleck, with the Shiloh army now swelled to 110,000 men, began his great conquest of Corinth.

In his final approach to the town, he ordered his front ranks to entrench every night and be up before dawn so as not to be caught unawares, as Grant had been at Shiloh. Grant wrote that the roads leading south to Corinth were ordered improved and side roads constructed so that troops moving toward the city on any of the different routes could rush to each other's aid in the event of attack. "All commanders were cautioned against bringing on an engagement and informed in so many words that it would be better to retreat than to fight," he recalled in his memoirs.[183] Grant, left emphatically out of the decision-making, chafed and brooded. When he suggested to Halleck a sally around the right to the rear of Corinth, which would block any attempted Confederate retreat, "I was silenced so quickly that I felt that possibly I had suggested an unmilitary movement."[184]

In Halleck's armchair philosophy of war, Grant had done exactly that. Halleck did not *want* to block a Confederate retreat. Jominian theory, bent on the capture of geographical points rather than on the destruction of armies, suggested that if an enemy wished to leave the desired point without a fight, all the better. Grant, though, thought with the battle-hardened skepticism of the men carrying rifles. After Halleck's mighty monthlong movement captured a deserted Corinth, Grant eventually wrote, "our . . . officers and men . . . could not see how the mere occupation of places was to close the war while large and effective rebel armies existed."[185]

The profound disgust of the common soldier with the Halleck approach is perhaps reflected in the reaction of Brigadier General John "Black Jack" Logan, another rifleman's general, to Halleck's insistence on entrenching every night. "My men," Logan told somebody, "will never dig another ditch for Halleck except to bury him."[186]

Ditchdigging was not Grant's preferred style of war. He fought by feel and urgency, and his feeling was that Corinth could and should have been taken immediately after Shiloh (if not, indeed, in the wake of the fall of Fort Donelson), before the Confederates had time to recover from the troop trauma that had to have followed their cataclysmic loss of practically all of central and western Tennessee. But Halleck's fearful moves, like those of McClellan in the east, afforded the Confederates ample time to mentally and physically regroup.

Yet again, in the wake of the Corinth "capture," a despondent Grant decided to resign. Sherman heard about it at headquarters and rode to Grant's tent to find the occupant joylessly packing up letters and other papers. Sherman asked where he was going.

St. Louis, Sherman remembered Grant saying.

"Have any business there?"

"Not a bit."

Sherman asked why, then, he was leaving. Grant said he was "in the way here" and could "endure it no longer."[187] He alluded to his task-less job in adding, "If I can't command a brigade or division, I can carry a musket."[188]

Grant's fellow Ohioan reminded him of Sherman's own recent recovery from an earlier plummet from public grace in Kentucky, when newspapers had branded him insane. Sherman said now that if Grant left the army, he could miss a chance at the same sort of reputational reclamation. Sherman opined that Grant sitting at home would be miserable when "armies are moving."[189] He prevailed on Grant to postpone leaving for two weeks and to promise to let him know before he left.

Grant promised.[190] He was doubtless moved by Sherman's obvious concern about his welfare, which perhaps also included worry about the effect the departure of his influential fearlessness would have on the Union's officer corps. Sherman's concern not only helped keep the future savior of the Union in the army but also helped cement the most important military friendship of the war. Sherman and Grant were two very different men, but they obviously felt a closeness stemming from their mutual possession of at least three powerful traits. First, each was steel-nerved and skilled on the battlefield; second, each disliked pretentious showiness; and third, each admired, rather than was jealous of, those traits in the other. What one saw with either of them was not only what one got but also what these two generals preferred to see in their peers. Yet what they too often *did* see was that they were two of a kind and all but alone among the Union's elite warrior class, a clan top-heavy with greedy ambition, leeriness of fighting, rampant egomania, and privileged roots.

Sherman, whose bent toward outrageous rhetoric later led him to memorably declare that he and Grant had stood by each other when Grant was "drunk" and he himself was "crazy," contended flatly that his persuasion of Grant to stay with the army was "the turning point of the war."[191] The latter seems nowhere near as much of an overstatement as the former.

Grant had said, shortly before the battle at Fort Donelson, that despite his difficulties with Halleck, he thought the vaunted scholar of war was "one of the greatest men of the age."[192] It was a popular opinion held even more strongly by Sherman. But Grant's view of Halleck's military talents began changing with the "conquest" of Corinth. At the time Sherman, in another instance of his habitual over-the-top bombast, claimed to consider the "capture" of the Mississippi rail nexus "a victory as brilliant and important as any in recorded history."[193] Grant differed. He believed that the "victory" occurred about a month later than it could have—and, as already noted, that it did nothing to damage the Confederacy's primary western army, which *should* have been the target.

Halleck, though, unabashedly got about safeguarding this prize so bloodlessly won. He began fortifying it as if he expected Beauregard to assail him at any minute to get it back. Ninety miles south at Tupelo, Beauregard harbored no such intent. Rather, he busied himself reorganizing and replenishing his army and taking a personal leave, capitalizing on the respite Halleck provided him.

Halleck then enlarged upon his error. Instead of again ramping up pressure on the South's primary western army, he decided that *his* army needed reorganization. He began parceling it out to various points—*places*, as his Jominian studies had counseled—to take up guard duty. He put John Pope's Army of the Mississippi south of Corinth to protect that town's rail junction. He sent four divisions under Buell eastward along the Memphis & Charleston tracks with the useless task of repairing them all the way to Chattanooga. The repairs could be only temporarily effective with destructive Confederate cavalry perpetually lurking.

Halleck meanwhile gave Grant an active command again, assigning him to Memphis. There the former second-in-command showed his deep identification with Clausewitzian concerns having to do with the local populace. His predecessors had not just outlawed the local church practice of publicly praying for Confederate president Jefferson Davis but had commanded that prayers instead be lifted for Abraham Lincoln. Grant quickly reversed half of this policy, leaving in place the restriction against praying for Davis but refusing to demand that it be done for Lincoln. Grant had his adjutant general inform his officers, "You can compel all Clergymen within your lines to omit from their church services any you may deem *treasonable*, but you will not compel the insertion or substitution of anything."[194] At the same time, he took strict measures for the safety of his soldiers, thereby showing a crucial aptitude for adjusting to shifting civilian reality. The Union military's attempts to ingratiate itself and its cause with the secessionist populace had proved futile, and Grant abandoned the efforts. While refusing to make the locals pray for Lincoln, he shuttered the city's hotly secessionist newspaper, the *Avalanche*. He then announced that Federal supplies lost to guerrilla attacks and ambushes would be made up from personal property of local civilians—and, further, that captured guerrillas who were not part of the Confederate military would not be treated as prisoners of war but rather as high-priority criminals deserving long-term imprisonment or execution. Two weeks later, he took another harsh action, ordering that all relatives of Confederate soldiers or officials be evacuated southward into territory controlled by the flag to which they obviously felt more allegiance.

On July 11, 1862, meanwhile, Lincoln radically reduced Grant's Halleck problems. The president ordered the Jominian scholar east to become commander of all the North's armies, the title McClellan had previously held. As a result of the promotion, Halleck essentially *had* to give Grant the principal command of two of those armies: the one Halleck had commanded at Corinth as well as John Pope's former force, now headed by William S. Rosecrans. Halleck, however, retained overall command of the army led by Buell, in recognition of the cool relations between Grant and Buell. The forces Halleck passed to Grant numbered approximately 80,000, but they were so widely scattered doing Halleck's defensive duties that they were all perpetually in danger of attack by superior numbers of Confederates.

As commander of the principal Union troops west of the Appalachians, Grant had to cope with myriad problems. One was that growing gangs of indigent runaway enslaved people kept following his soldiers back into his camps. His reaction again showed his adaptability to changing conditions and mindsets, including his own. The early Union policy of trying not to offend secessionists in hopes of winning back their loyalties had extended to slave masters, but between June and July 1862, Grant's belief in that policy's efficacy waned. Although in June, while still in Corinth, he had written home decrying "negro-stealing" by his soldiers because it encouraged Confederate charges of Union abolitionism, a month later, with his family occupying the plantation house of a Confederate sympathizer at Corinth, Grant wrote Halleck to ask if he could "let . . . go" enslaved women and children whom the plantation master wanted to send to his relatives farther south—farther from chances to escape and closer to supporting Dixie's war effort.[195]

In the space of a month, Grant had obviously come to a conclusion well stated by his foremost congressional sponsor, Representative Elihu Washburne. In July, Washburne wrote Grant his opinion that "the idea that a man can be in the rebel army, leaving his negroes and property behind him to be protected by our troops, is to me shocking. . . . If [either] the [C]onstitution or slavery must perish," Washburne asserted, "let slavery go to the wall."[196]

This was in reply to a letter Grant had written the congressman outlining his designs on Vicksburg. Washburne had written back to advise his favorite general that the Lincoln administration was beginning to agree with the majority of Northern civilians that the formerly enslaved people must be used by the army to work or fight—and that the general who best instituted such a revolutionary policy would "be held in the highest estimation."[197] It is important to note, though, that Grant's request to Halleck for permission to release the enslaved Corinth plantation family before its members could be sent farther south occurred a few days *before* he received this advice from

Washburne. Obviously, his request to free the black women and children emanated from the same sensitivity that a few years earlier had freed the only enslaved person Grant himself ever owned.

As biographer Ron Chernow has noted, the antislavery stance Grant took was on middle ground between that of "renegade generals like George McClellan, a reactionary Democrat and an open racist who hated the thought of abolition," and "generals like John Frémont and David Hunter, who brazenly issued freelance emancipation proclamations in their departments."[198] Grant's military approach to politics was almost always measured and workmanlike, aimed specifically at aiding what he intended to accomplish as a soldier. And perhaps vice versa, too: what he intended to accomplish as a soldier reflected his evolving views of politics.

Grant soon appointed a prominent army chaplain to arrange work—*paid* work—for the freed people on plantations. This thus extended the idea that Washburne had advocated of making the freed people useful to the military effort that was freeing them while also benefiting those people themselves by giving most of them the first pay they had ever received for their labors. This concept soon became a corollary to Grant's all-out approach to subjugation. As author Russell F. Weigley has noted in *The American Way of War*, the philosophy of depleting Confederate nonhuman war resources, most famously exemplified by the smoking ruins in the wake of Sherman's march from Atlanta to Charleston, was intended to lessen the Union's *human* casualties in the long run.[199] Weigley defines Grant's strategy as "war of annihilation" and quotes the general's admission that after the fall of central and western Tennessee post-Shiloh and the subsequent Confederate countercampaigns, he saw no alternative to moving away from the lenient policies toward the South that the North practiced well into 1862.

"I gave up all idea of saving the Union except by complete conquest," Grant eventually wrote.

> After this [Confederate resurgence] . . . I regarded it as humane to both sides to protect the persons of those found at their homes but to consume everything that could be used to support or supply armies. Protection was still continued over such supplies as were within lines held by us which we expected to continue to hold; but such supplies within reach of Confederate armies I regarded as much contraband as arms or ordnance stores. Their destruction

> was accomplished without bloodshed and tended to the same result as the destruction of armies. I continued this policy to the close of the war.[200]

This policy followed systematically and logically from other decisions Grant previously made that had the same aim, although of narrower scope. The underlying principle was always the same: every tactic or strategy had to contribute to winning the war. When preserving the status quo appeared to aid that effort, that is what Grant ordered; his proclamation to the citizens of Paducah was an earlier example, as was his strenuous regulations against his soldiers molesting civilians or their property. When advancing Union war aims required upsetting the status quo, on the other hand, he did *that,* as when he banished the relatives of Confederate military and civilian officials southward from Memphis and demanded civilian restitution for Union losses to guerrilla incursions.

From July 1862 onward, as the physical distance between him and Halleck widened and—with his long and dogged conquest of Vicksburg and his all-but-miraculous delivery of Confederate-besieged Chattanooga—the barely tolerated underling increasingly became the North's most victorious soldier. In the process, Grant's difficulties with his commander decreased. Halleck no longer had time to be a nuisance. A year and a half before Lincoln brought Grant east to become general-in-chief and busted Halleck to chief of staff in early 1864, the president—who had with his own eyes seen Halleck break under pressure, "nerve and pluck all gone," while dealing simultaneously with the Second Bull Run battle and the Confederate invasion of Kentucky—was describing the once-vaunted "Old Brains" as "little more than a first-rate clerk."[201] During the months between Halleck's departure from the West and Grant's ascension to the East, Halleck was in the gradual process of almost becoming *Grant's* clerk, increasingly submitting to the nominal subordinate's bidding instead of demanding the reverse.

In the meantime, Grant had to face plots from jealous underlings. These he generally met with sphinxlike impassivity until he possessed unquestionable evidence of their incompetence (rather than their perfidy); then he swiftly removed them from his army. *Never* did he mention the substance of their most frequent whisper against him, drinking.

Grant's technique in these cases seems influenced—and aided—by his lower-class roots. With just a lone—albeit powerful—congressman (whom he barely knew) championing his cause in high government circles (where many if not most of his fellow generals had a number of personal friendships), he had to have been conscious that he was lucky just to be in such company. In the early months, as mentioned, he feared losing his army to one of them before he got a chance to fight. So he had to know that he could not afford to indulge in the fits of pique that they often shamed themselves with. Whereas they came from a class that was in the habit of being high-handed, he did not. He came from one that was perpetually conscious of needing to deal carefully with theirs.

His worst and most dangerous intra-army foe, other than Halleck, was McClernand, and Grant's mode of dealing with him exemplifies his way of managing intra-army conflict as a whole. He endured the ex-congressman's disrespect, treachery, and inadequacy for many months until he felt certain his own influence was stronger; then he used a public McClernand error to rid his command of the man.

McClernand, at first a powerful congressman as well as a fellow brigadier general, had been a scheming enemy ever since the Kountz episode at Cairo, where he praised and encouraged Kountz's meddling in Grant's command—and may well have fed the steamboat magnate the substance of many of the scandalous charges the man filed against Grant on the eve of the Fort Henry and Fort Donelson victories. Grant finally put Kountz under house arrest to get him out of the way of the war effort, but McClernand, the "damned, slinking Judas bastard" in Rawlins's words,[202] was a more challenging case.

McClernand, as the long-standing sometime-associate of President Lincoln as well as of important national legislators, was the kind of inimical fellow officer who could end a general's career if not handled with the kind of care Grant was in the habit of employing in the chain of command. That meant pulling superior rank only deftly. Grant tolerated some two years of insubordination as McClernand sought to one-up him in public and undermine him in private. But when Grant finally caught the ex-politico selfishly squandering soldiers' lives in a futile, glory-seeking charge at Vicksburg, he sent the former congressman home to Illinois for good. As the vehicle to accomplish it, though, he used a McClernand post-battle "order" commending his troops (and most particularly himself), which had been released to the press without Grant's required permission.[203]

Grant had other Union army enemies, though, and he dealt with them with the same low-key skill. An example is Major General Charles Hamilton, a West Point classmate. In February 1863 Hamilton unctuously proffered loyalty to his schoolmate in a letter in which, apparently referring to McClernand's attempt to take over the Vicksburg campaign, he asserted that taking Vicksburg "is your right . . . as the most successful general of the war." But two days later the same Hamilton, who had operated a flour-milling business in Wisconsin between the Mexican War and the Confederate firing on Fort Sumter, wrote a Wisconsin U.S. senator that "Grant is a drunkard" and added that he and another classmate, Brigadier General Isaac F. Quinby, had once had to stand guard over Grant to keep him away from whiskey while sending north for Julia because Grant got "beastly drunk" for days and was "utterly incapable of doing anything." Hamilton then proved the worthlessness of his professed affinity by cautioning the senator that the letter must be kept confidential because "Grant is a warm friend of mine."[204]

Hamilton soon found that the friendship got cooler when he tried to take the commands of two of Grant's other subordinates. Grant refused to sustain Hamilton's quarrel over rank with Major General Stephen A. Hurlbut; in response, he put the duplicitous ex-classmate under the duplicitous ex-politician McClernand. Hamilton then tried to argue that he outranked Major General James McPherson, the able subordinate as well as friend to whom Grant was strongly attached. Hamilton threatened to take his case all the way to Washington, at which point Grant swiftly countered by asking Halleck to transfer Hamilton out of the department and to send the question directly to Lincoln. Hamilton quickly resigned.

It should be noted that this Grant action, like the others, was in furtherance of the war effort. McPherson was a close friend, yes, and, unlike Hamilton, had proved himself to be so by showing his open-mindedness at a dangerous time in Grant's career—to say nothing of refusing to spy on Grant for Halleck during the Henry-Donelson campaign. Instead, he had become an unabashed Grant admirer. But he was also an excellent military engineer who had graduated first in his West Point class and had shown himself worthy of Grant's absolute trust. Grant, as well as Sherman, was deeply attached to him. In fact, Grant would soon write that McPherson and Sherman were the two soldiers to whom he owed his own prominence.

Grant was measured, careful, and understatedly considerate in his dealings with fellow Union generals.

CONCLUSION: THE GUTS OF GRANT'S GENERALSHIP

✯✯✯✯

Doggedly braving the post Shiloh calumny and innuendo and, thanks to Sherman's intervention, the subsequent shelving by Halleck, Grant was now ready to proceed to his greatest campaigns: Vicksburg, Chattanooga, and the titanic Virginia struggle with Lee.

In the process of prevailing in those epic battles, he became a model against whom his American military successors could be measured. Some of the best have been compared to him—rightly or wrongly. One of the latter is World War II Supreme Allied Commander in the European theater Dwight D. Eisenhower. Both Ike and Grant were former farm boys who graduated from West Point. But that and their auras of humility, dissimilar as they were, are about as far as the resemblance goes. Eisenhower never saw combat until he was a general, and only at long distance when he did. He also was very skilled at ingratiating himself with superiors who could and did aid his spectacular rises in rank; Grant shrank from even the appearance of such. In Europe, Eisenhower prolonged World War II by an estimated six months, and cost untold additional lives on both sides, by employing a so-called head-on attack policy taught at the Army War College. That policy led him to insist that the five Allied armies in Europe advance more or less abreast across the theater. He rejected requests by British general Bernard Montgomery and America's Omar Bradley to have elements under each of them race forward across many miles of all-but-undefended territory to reach vital industrial areas of Germany—the Ruhr in the case of Montgomery or, with Bradley, the Saar farther south. Eisenhower compromised with both men and chose both approaches but then melded them into the "head-on" model.

Historian Jean Edward Smith, who has written celebrated biographies of both Grant and Eisenhower, has noted that attributing a similar "head-on" strategy to Grant results from a "superficial reading" of the Civil War savior of the Union.[1] This "reading" may be rooted in an illegitimate construction of Grant's (and Abraham Lincoln's) favored policy of pressuring every major enemy army at once so that no commander of a large Confederate unit could feel able to break off any of its elements and send them to the aid of another. Grant would not have allowed a lightly defended sector of the enemy front to go unattacked. At Fort Donelson he charged where he only suspected there was such a sector, sending Brigadier General Charles Ferguson Smith forward on the battle's third day against what turned out to be an all-but-abandoned Confederate right. Again, at Vicksburg, as historian Smith notes, Grant intentionally avoided most of the Confederate cannon by bypassing the fortress on the Mississippi River and taking his army south, then swinging it eastward to approach the fortress from that less-defended side. He obviously had reflected on Winfield Scott's Mexico tactics, particularly the use of a surprise attack route around impregnable Cerro Gordo.

But the roots of Grant's readiness to become the Civil War's supreme victor stretched back not just to Mexico but to his very beginnings. His extraordinary leadership was based first on extraordinary character. This rumpled little man so roundly and wrongly dismissed in the higher circles of his era, and subsequent others, as a gutter-crawling sot—and still so regarded in some less-informed circles even today—proved to possess more decency, honesty, fairness, guts, and regard for fellow humanity (*all* of it) than his pretentious, pseudo-superior detractors could imagine, let alone display. Ulysses S. Grant turned out to be one of the few giants of American history who fully deserved the popularity and fame heaped upon him in his time. He not only saved the Union but also went on to try to make it a better one, when most of America wanted to just forget the inconvenient national assertion that all men had been created equal. Whereas Grant's supreme adversary, Robert E. Lee, has long been celebrated by many as a man-god, Grant has come to be seen as what he was: an ultimate military example of the best of the average American.

The building of character, good or bad, always starts at home. Grant's garrulous, acquisitive father did not contribute much that was helpful, but one trait that he did hand down stands out. While the pushiness of Jesse's abolitionism repelled his son, Ulysses absorbed the racial fairness aspect underlying the best of it, and it became a salient aspect of his nature. Whether in admiration and pity for poverty-plagued Mexicans during the Mexican War or identification with the enslaved people alongside whom he worked his fields as a peacetime farmer, his bent toward justice was a strong, albeit silent, part of his personality. Some of his dogged, indomitable drive on battlefields—*vocational* pushiness—may also have come from Jesse. Most of Jesse's other gifts, though, were negative. The patriarch's opinionated bluster and eye for the main financial chance seem to have produced opposite tendencies in Ulysses, although in California the son did display some of the lust, if not the talent, for the latter.

Hannah Grant's influence on her firstborn, in contrast, was plainly immense, but its actual extent is hard to gauge. Hannah was very religious, and although her son's religious views are difficult to track, evidences of her piety were discernible in him. Her laconic quietude was his most immediately noticeable public feature. His absolute avoidance of profanity, a profound departure from time-honored army tradition, is another example. Deep humility is implicit in his uncertainty in 1861, after having spent a decade as an officer in the old army, whether he would be able to lead a regiment. He obviously felt a heavy obligation to help others; witness his seeking out of wounded to aid in disregard of his own weariness after battles in Mexico. Like most soldiers of lengthy service, he knew army regulations by heart, abided by them himself, and tried to see that they were followed by the men under him—except when rigid adherence might hinder prosecution of the war. Although hardly unmindful of the need for money, he insisted on paying debts when doing so hurt him financially, and he disliked trying to collect debts he was owed.

Grant's restless personality combined just the right amounts of patience and *im*patience—a powerful impulse to see the next thing he had not yet seen—as when he was driving wagons for his father and refused to retrace his course when he missed a turn, if there was another potential route to his objective. He also possessed the patience to see that the wagons he drove were loaded and equipped sufficiently to take him where he wanted to go and satisfy the need awaiting them. Militarily, these traits made him not only an excellent quartermaster but also an excellent commander of a company, a regiment, or an army. But there is a less immediately obvious aspect of his early long-distance wagon driving and thirst for new roads: a lack of fear of the unknown. That lack of fear was a critical aspect of his style of war-making.

He did not like war and its blood and suffering, but he did not shrink from it. Its onset did not shatter him psychologically. In Mexico he often abandoned his quartermaster post to dash into battle. He was as careful under fire as any other prudent soldier, and he quickly developed a psychological antidote to fear of *commanding* under fire: realization that his enemy was at least as affrighted as he and that if he did his job correctly he had no time for fear. The dread of being under fire, he wrote home from Mexico, was worse than *being* under fire. These mental defenses, or some such, are indispensable to the psychological stability of a leader of men. During the Civil War, Grant saw fellow generals mentally shattered by the pressures of the battlefield and its ever-looming specter of defeat: William S. Rosecrans at Chickamauga, for example. Others, such as George B. McClellan and often Henry Halleck, appeared to fear the very *prospect* of battle.

Carl von Clausewitz ranked boldness as supreme among the attributes of a great military commander, and perseverance next behind it.[2] Grant and Lee possessed both of these traits in gigantic quantities but to differing ends. Lee employed them to all but decimate his own army; Grant used them to achieve utter victory with his. The difference lay not so much in the disparity in numbers of their two forces but rather, as historian Russell Weigley has noted, in Lee's relying too much on the promise of a Napoleonic "final battle" to bring ultimate victory. Grant innovated by ensuring that there could *be* no "final" battle until it was the one he would win.[3] Put another way, Lee mistakenly placed his faith in a climactic fight, campaign, or simple refusal to lose that he assumed would break the will of the Northern people, whereas Grant actually *did break* the will of the Confederacy by all but destroying its armies in battle, *whether he won the battles or lost them*, by simply refusing to retreat.

Grant's boldness is implicit in the urgency suggested in his great definition of the art of successfully waging war: "Find out where your enemy is. Get at him as soon as you can. Strike him as hard as you can and as often as you can and keep moving on."[4] The final three words imply the indispensability of the perseverance that destroyed Lee's army. The "on" obviously means "up" or "forward." And what Grant meant by that, as he clearly enunciated to Civil War subordinates, was this: be utterly relentless.

But in Grant's character, this relentlessness, this obsession to exploit an enemy weakness and to create one wherever possible, was balanced by a singularly civilian psyche. When it was over, he always wanted to go home. He hated war and its bloodletting and did not aspire to military glory. He would not have trained to become a soldier at tuition-free West Point had his dollar-wise father not insisted. And, had fate accommodated his heartfelt desire, he would not have *been* a soldier had the Civil War not come along and required further discharging of the obligation he felt he owed the nation for his education. This civilian psyche enhanced the practical, macrocosmic view he took of war.

To push past military obstacles that only persistence could render temporary—ones that would have been defeats had he not kept "moving on" to transform them into parts of an advance toward victory—Grant *needed* his civilian psyche, with its nineteenth-century lower-class understanding that an individual's, or an army's, very survival depended on pushing past reverses. Successful military tactics and strategy consist mostly, Clausewitz tells us, of common sense. And common sense is generally in best supply on society's lower—"common"—levels, where reverses are costliest. People from those levels are thus theoretically better fitted to deal psychologically and logically with the stresses, surprises, and savagery of war and its tyrannical necessity of winning. Those best able to power through, and thus prevail over, these stresses, surprises, and savagery are most likely to be those who believe they *can* do it—because, on some level, they have had to do it before.

Grant had little interest in textbook-taught military hypotheses of tactics and strategy. He retained just enough of these subjects to pass West Point exams. He did, however, display an inordinate interest in *concrete examples* of tactics and strategy that were *actually practiced* in the Mexican War as well as in other conflicts. Associates said he enjoyed discussing them and could do so with clarity and obvious insight into the turning points of each battle. Similarly, his memory could retain almost photographically the important features of maps, allowing him to view these features in tactical and strategic terms.

Few of Grant's written sentences more clearly indicate which side of the class divide he felt personal military allegiance to than his admiring description of General Zachary Taylor's written prose: "He knew how to express what he wanted to say in the fewest well-chosen words, but would not sacrifice meaning to the construction of *high-sounding* sentences."[5] Grant might as well have been describing himself. There was nothing "high-sounding" about him, from his letters home after his first battle to the final sentence of his memoirs. Everything was close to the ground, where he had always lived.

In Old Zack, Grant found a model for the role he wanted to play. There was no pretension in him, and it showed in his handling of officers and enlisted men. He made the officers share the lot of the men in their commands and held them responsible for the men's conduct. The reasons for doing so made sense—*common* sense. Officers had more training than their men and had presumably welcomed, if not indeed sought, the mantle of leadership. With its prospective glories, they had also contracted for its griefs.

Much of the character that made Grant what he has become in recent history's prevailing opinion appears rooted in the values and energies of that lower level of society from which he sprang. A few other Union generals rose from the same class, but not many—maybe none—had the benefit, if that is the word, of such a rigorous "refresher course" in against-the-wall psychology as Grant endured in the seven difficult years between his first army stint and his second. Any hardship that does not kill a man makes him stronger, popular wisdom has it. By the time of the Civil War, Ulysses S. Grant was very strong.

He never strutted like McClellan, bragged like John Pope, or quailed in battle like Rosecrans. Beneath his thick coat of humility lay a hard core of resolution. He did what he conceived to be his job, which was to rid the earth of his country's enemies, and he did it without complaining about any lack of resources needed to do it. Most soldiers who served under him ended up loving him with a special pride. Hard-bitten souls who had been with him under the fire of battle, they recognized him for what he was: the best of the very best of their own.

ACKNOWLEDGMENTS

NOTES

BIBLIOGRAPHY

INDEX

ACKNOWLEDGMENTS

I had much indispensable assistance in producing this book. Dr. Timothy Smith suggested that I write it and then encouraged me to take the tack I took. I first met Dr. Smith a good decade—and for him, several books—ago, and my admiration for him as a historian and a man has only grown. Without him, this book would not have been possible.

I also have to thank another author and benefactor, Dr. John F. Marszalek, who over several years has unfailingly responded to my appeals for aid with his abundant knowledge of the men and history of the period of which I have been writing. He has been of great assistance in keeping me headed in the proper direction and saving me from many embarrassing mistakes. I also want to thank a newer friend, Sylvia Frank Rodrigue, Southern Illinois University Press's adept and personable executive editor, who answered every question I had, often before I could ask it. And this book could never have been produced without the understanding and guidance of production manager Linda Jorgensen Buhman and project manager Khara Lukancic or without the adept and insightful line editing of copy editor Julie Bush.

The work of other authors, especially Grant biographers, supplied information and viewpoints without which my own book could not exist. Most notable among these are the late Lloyd Lewis and Hamlin Garland, as well as Jean Edward Smith and Ron Chernow—and the aforementioned Drs. Smith and Marszalek.

I am also thankful for the writing and memory of Grant himself. I have been privileged to write substantially about him in three books now, and my appreciation of him has multiplied with each. He was simply a supreme example of the kind of American we should all strive to be.

Finally, I most gratefully thank Donna, my wife of fifty years, for good-humoredly putting up with me and my projects while enduring daunting physical trials of her own.

NOTES

Introduction

1. Weigley, *American Way of War,* 82.
2. Schmelzer, "Strong Mind."
3. Quoted in Smith, *Grant,* 288.
4. Weigley, *American Way of War,* 127.
5. Quoted in Perret, *Ulysses S. Grant,* 157.
6. See, for example, Mosier, *Grant,* 7.
7. Clausewitz, *On War* (hereinafter referred to as "Clausewitz"), 97.
8. Weigley, *American Way of War,* 139.

1. Farm Boy

1. Quoted in Lewis, *Captain Sam Grant,* 22.
2. Chernow, *Grant,* 13.
3. Smith, *Grant,* 28.
4. Smith, 42.
5. Grant, *Personal Memoirs* (hereafter referred to simply as *Memoirs*), 7–12.
6. Smith, *Grant,* 629n.
7. Mosier, *Grant,* 7.
8. Lewis, *Captain Sam Grant,* 33.
9. Wilson, *Patriotic Gore,* 147.
10. Smith, *Grant,* 106–7.
11. Smith, 83.
12. Daniel, *Shiloh,* 306.
13. Wilson, *Patriotic Gore,* 148.
14. Chernow, *Grant,* 506.
15. Smith, *Grant,* 403.
16. Chernow, *Grant,* 507.
17. Porter, *Campaigning with Grant,* 475.
18. Wilson, *Patriotic Gore,* 148.
19. *Memoirs,* 722.

20. *Memoirs*, 724.
21. Wilson, *Patriotic Gore*, 151.
22. Clausewitz, 75.
23. Clausewitz, 184–85.
24. *Memoirs*, 16–17.
25. Smith, *Grant*, 25.
26. Smith, 11.
27. *Memoirs*, 22.
28. Wilson, *Patriotic Gore*, 160.
29. Lewis, *Captain Sam Grant*, 63.
30. Lewis, 66.
31. Smith, *Grant*, 26.
32. *Memoirs*, 48.
33. Quoted in Smith, *Grant*, 26.
34. Lewis, *Captain Sam Grant*, 24.
35. Quoted in Lewis, 75.
36. Clausewitz, 178.
37. Weigley, *American Way of War*, 83.
38. Weigley, 84. Halleck, Weigley says, was the "first American writer to attempt an exploration of the principles of strategy in the form of a book, his *Elements of Military Art and Science* of 1846." Halleck "owed his ideas on strategy mainly to Jomini."
39. Marszalek, *Commander*, 123–24.
40. Smith, *Grant*, 27.
41. Johnson and Buel, *Battles and Leaders of the Civil War*, 1:404–5.
42. Smith, *Grant*, 26, 630n.
43. Quoted in Wilson, *Patriotic Gore*, 143.
44. Wilson, 132.
45. Quoted in Smith, *Grant*, 15.
46. Smith, 93.
47. *Memoirs*, 23, 24.
48. *Memoirs*, 22.

2. *Mexico*

1. *Memoirs*, 27.
2. Smith, *Grant*, 31.
3. Chernow, *Grant*, 40.
4. Smith, *Grant*, 37.
5. Howe, *What Hath God Wrought*, 742.

6. Howe, 703. Italics mine.
7. Howe, 746.
8. *Memoirs*, 34.
9. Simon, *Papers of Ulysses S. Grant* (hereafter *PUSG*), 1:97.
10. *Memoirs*, 35.
11. Howe, *What Hath God Wrought*, 747.
12. *Encyclopedia Britannica*, vol. 21 (Chicago, 1970), s.v. "Zachary Taylor."
13. Weigley, *American Way of War*, 68.
14. Weigley, 72–73.
15. Smith, *Grant*, 39.
16. *Memoirs*, 65.
17. *Memoirs*, 65.
18. Quoted in Smith, *Grant*, 59.
19. Smith, 40.
20. Lewis, *Captain Sam Grant*, 128.
21. *Memoirs*, 45–46.
22. *Memoirs*, 43.
23. *Memoirs*, 45.
24. *Memoirs*, 55–56.
25. *Memoirs*, 56, 56n.
26. Lewis, *Captain Sam Grant*, 135–36; *Memoirs*, 56, 57.
27. The most notable exception, perhaps, is Dwight D. Eisenhower, who was a general before he faced combat.
28. Lewis, *Captain Sam Grant*, 136.
29. Lewis, 137.
30. Smith, *Grant*, 45.
31. Lewis, *Captain Sam Grant*, 137.
32. Smith, *Grant*, 44–45.
33. Smith, 45.
34. Lewis, *Captain Sam Grant*, 137–38.
35. Lewis, 149.
36. Lewis, 139.
37. Smith, *Grant*, 45.
38. Lewis, *Captain Sam Grant*, 140.
39. Lewis, 141.
40. Quoted in Smith, *Grant*, 45.
41. Smith, 45.
42. Lewis, *Captain Sam Grant*, 141.
43. *Memoirs*, 59, 59n.

44. *PUSG*, 1:95.
45. Lewis, *Captain Sam Grant*, 132.
46. *Memoirs*, 60.
47. *Memoirs*, 60–61.
48. *Memoirs*, 60.
49. Smith, *Grant*, 47.
50. *Memoirs*, 61.
51. *Memoirs*, 61.
52. Richardson, *Personal History of Ulysses S. Grant*, 45.
53. *Memoirs*, 62.
54. *PUSG*, 1:85.
55. Smith, *Grant*, 49.
56. *Memoirs*, 62.
57. *PUSG*, 1:85.
58. *Memoirs*, 62–63, 63n.
59. Porter, *Campaigning with Grant*, 85.
60. Porter, 85.
61. Quoted in McPherson, *Battle Cry of Freedom*, 726.
62. Smith, *Grant*, 338.
63. *PUSG*, 1:85.
64. *Memoirs*, 63.
65. *PUSG*, 1:96.
66. Smith, *Grant*, 50.
67. *Memoirs*, 64.
68. *PUSG*, 1:86.
69. *PUSG*, 1:96, 97, 95–96.
70. Quoted in Smith, *Grant*, 40.
71. *Memoirs*, 198.
72. Clausewitz, 103, quoted in Schmelzer, "Strong Mind," 2.
73. *Memoirs*, 198.
74. Quoted in Porter, *Campaigning with Grant*, 97.
75. Lewis, *Captain Sam Grant*, 159–66.
76. *PUSG*, 7:270–73.
77. *PUSG*, 1:106–7, 107n.
78. Lewis, *Captain Sam Grant*, 168.
79. *Memoirs*, 69.
80. Lewis, *Captain Sam Grant*, 171.
81. *PUSG*, 8:151, 153, 162, 164, 168, 172, 178–179n, 183, 266.
82. Smith, *Grant*, 53.

83. Lewis, *Captain Sam Grant*, 172–73; Smith, *Grant*, 53.
84. Lewis, *Captain Sam Grant*, 174–75; Smith, *Grant*, 54.
85. *Memoirs*, 73.
86. *Memoirs*, 73–74.
87. *Memoirs*, 73.
88. Lewis, *Captain Sam Grant*, 176–78.
89. *Memoirs*, 75–76.
90. Howe, *What Hath God Wrought*, 773.
91. Smith, *Grant*, 56–57; Howe, *What Hath God Wrought*, 773.
92. *Memoirs*, 387.
93. *Memoirs*, 77.
94. Quoted in Smith, *Grant*, 57.
95. Clausewitz, 185.
96. Quoted in Lewis, *Captain Sam Grant*, 153.
97. *Memoirs*, 79.
98. Smith, *Grant*, 59.
99. *Memoirs*, 81–82.
100. Smith, *Grant*, 59–60.
101. Porter, *Campaigning with Grant*, 193.
102. *Memoirs*, 23.
103. *Memoirs*, 93.
104. Warner, *Generals in Blue*, 429.
105. Weigley, *American Way of War*, 66, 72.
106. Lewis, *Captain Sam Grant*, 194.
107. Weigley, *American Way of War*, 76, 196.
108. Weigley, 200.
109. *Memoirs*, 84.
110. Smith, *Grant*, 61.
111. Smith, 62.
112. Smith, 62, 64.
113. Lewis, *Captain Sam Grant*, 205.
114. *Memoirs*, 88.
115. Clausewitz, 198.
116. Eisenhower, *So Far from God*, 276–78.
117. *Memoirs*, 89.
118. *PUSG*, 1:134. In this letter published by a third party, the *Midland Monthly*, Grant's usual careless spelling and grammar have obviously been edited and his customary low-key narrative seems to have been enhanced.
119. *PUSG*, 1:134–35, 135n; Lewis, *Captain Sam Grant*, 168–69.

120. *Memoirs*, 89; Lewis, *Captain Sam Grant*, 207–8; Smith, *Grant*, 62.
121. *PUSG*, 1:136.
122. Eisenhower, *So Far from God*, 296.
123. Eisenhower, 298–303, 305–7.
124. Lewis, *Captain Sam Grant*, 228.
125. Eisenhower, *So Far from God*, 309, 314.
126. *PUSG*, 1:145.
127. *PUSG*, 1:145.
128. Eisenhower, *So Far from God*, 319.
129. Eisenhower, 327.
130. Lewis, *Captain Sam Grant*, 236.
131. *Memoirs*, 111–12.
132. Eisenhower, *So Far from God*, 330.
133. Bauer, *Mexican War*, 307–8.
134. Lewis, *Captain Sam Grant*, 238–39.
135. *Memoirs*, 104–5.
136. Quoted in *Memoirs*, 241–42.
137. *Memoirs*, 54.
138. Cozzens, *Shipwreck of Their Hopes*, 246–73.
139. Chernow, *Grant*, 54.
140. Chernow, 54.
141. *Memoirs*, 111–12.
142. *PUSG*, 1:145.
143. Lewis, *Captain Sam Grant*, 249.
144. Eisenhower, *So Far from God*, 340–41; Bauer, *Mexican War*, 316–18; Lewis, *Captain Sam Grant*, 246–48; Smith, *Grant*, 66–67.
145. Bauer, *Mexican War*, 319.
146. Lewis, *Captain Sam Grant*, 250–51; *Memoirs*, 106–8.
147. *Memoirs*, 108.
148. *Memoirs*, 108–9.
149. Lewis, *Captain Sam Grant*, 253–54.
150. *Memoirs*, 111.
151. *Memoirs*, 109n.
152. *Memoirs*, 353.
153. *Memoirs*, 465.
154. Clausewitz, 152.
155. Lewis, *Captain Sam Grant*, 281.
156. *Memoirs*, 56.
157. *Memoirs*, 115.

158. *PUSG*, 1:97.
159. *Memoirs*, 81–82.
160. *Memoirs*, 108.
161. *Memoirs*, 69.
162. *Memoirs*, 132–33.
163. *PUSG*, 1:145.
164. *Memoirs*, 114.

3. *Peacetime: Limbo of Horrors*

1. Lewis, *Captain Sam Grant*, 186.
2. Lewis, 268.
3. Bauer, *Mexican War*, 327.
4. Bauer, 275.
5. *PUSG*, 1:149.
6. *Memoirs*, 128; PUSG, 1:157.
7. Lewis, *Captain Sam Grant*, 82, says Grant sometimes joined in drinking with fellow cadets at West Point.
8. Chernow, *Grant*, 5.
9. Chernow, 58, quoting a letter in the Ulysses S. Grant Presidential Library at Mississippi State University in Starkville.
10. Quoted in Chernow, 58.
11. *PUSG*, 1:122–23.
12. *PUSG*, 1:162, 162n–163n. Twice, Ohio congressmen petitioned the U.S. House of Representatives to release Grant from the obligation, but nothing came of either attempt. The second was in 1852.
13. *PUSG*, 1:137.
14. Lewis, *Captain Sam Grant*, 284.
15. See Noel Perrin's introduction to Henry Adams's *Democracy: An American Novel*, a roman à clef picturing Washington, D.C., during the Grant administration, viii, ix.
16. Chernow, *Grant*, 63.
17. Lewis, *Captain Sam Grant*, 285.
18. *PUSG*, 1:174, 174n, 175–77, 177n–178n.
19. Lewis, *Captain Sam Grant*, 296.
20. *PUSG*, 1:247.
21. Lewis, *Captain Sam Grant*, 295.
22. Lewis, 298.
23. Lewis, 299.
24. Garland, *Ulysses S. Grant*, 117.

25. Quoted in Chernow, *Grant*, 73.
26. *PUSG*, 1:248–49.
27. *Memoirs*, 135.
28. McCullough, *Path between the Seas*, 130.
29. *Memoirs*, 136.
30. *Memoirs*, 137.
31. *Memoirs*, 137n.
32. Garland, *Ulysses S. Grant*, 119.
33. *PUSG*, 1:251–52.
34. Garland, *Ulysses S. Grant*, 122.
35. Lewis, *Captain Sam Grant*, 309.
36. *Memoirs*, 141.
37. Lewis, *Captain Sam Grant*, 312, 316, 318, 319.
38. Lewis, 315.
39. *PUSG*, 1:302.
40. Lewis, *Captain Sam Grant*, 319–20.
41. Lewis, 320–21.
42. Garland, *Ulysses S. Grant*, 124.
43. Lewis, *Captain Sam Grant*, 108.
44. Lewis, 323.
45. Lewis, 101.
46. Lewis, 324.
47. Lewis, 312.
48. Lewis, 327.
49. Lewis, 330–31.
50. *PUSG*, 1:328–29.
51. Garland, *Ulysses S. Grant*, 128.
52. Lewis, *Captain Sam Grant*, 332.
53. *PUSG*, 1:332.
54. Garland, *Ulysses S. Grant*, 128–29.
55. Garland, 129.
56. *Memoirs*, 146.
57. Garland, *Ulysses S. Grant*, 131.
58. *PUSG*, 1:330–31n.
59. Garland, *Ulysses S. Grant*, 129. Garland, who interviewed people from Bethel who knew the Grants, said the male members of the family—although not his mother—regarded Ulysses after his resignation as "criminally improvident."
60. *PUSG*, 1:330.

61. Lewis, *Captain Sam Grant*, 340.
62. Lewis, 341.
63. Lewis, 340.
64. Lewis, 341.
65. Lewis, 317.
66. Garland, *Ulysses S. Grant*, 135.
67. "Hardscrabble: The House That Grant Built," National Park Service, https://www.nps.gov/places/hardscrabble-the-house-that-grant-built.htm (accessed November 9, 2019).
68. Lewis, *Captain Sam Grant*, 343.
69. *PUSG*, 1:334–35.
70. *PUSG*, 1:336–37.
71. Lewis, *Captain Sam Grant*, 347.
72. Lewis, 345–47.
73. Lewis, 346.
74. *PUSG*, 1:341.
75. Garland, *Ulysses S. Grant*, 140; Lewis, *Captain Sam Grant*, 31.
76. Chernow, *Grant*, 102.
77. Chernow, 355–56.
78. *PUSG*, 1:344.
79. *PUSG*, 1:344.
80. *PUSG*, 1:347n.
81. Chernow, *Grant*, 104.
82. Chernow, 105.
83. Chernow, 105.
84. Chernow, 105.
85. Brands, *Man Who Saved the Union*, 87, 650n.
86. *PUSG*, 1:347.
87. *PUSG*, 1:347.
88. J. Grant, *Memoirs*, 80.
89. *PUSG*, 1:348, 348–349n, 350.
90. *PUSG*, 1:355, 355n.
91. Chernow, *Grant*, 109.
92. Chernow, 109.
93. Lewis, *Captain Sam Grant*, 373.
94. Lewis, 377.
95. Lewis, 375.
96. *PUSG*, 1:359.
97. Chernow, *Grant*, 109.

98. *PUSG*, 1:359.
99. *PUSG*, 1:359.
100. *PUSG*, 2:35.
101. *Memoirs*, 152, 154.
102. Garland, *Ulysses S. Grant*, 156.
103. Garland, 157–58.
104. Garland, 159.
105. Garland, 158–60.
106. Garland, 162.
107. Lewis, *Captain Sam Grant*, 415–16; Chernow, *Grant*, 130.
108. Lewis, *Captain Sam Grant*, 417.
109. Lewis, 417.
110. Smith, *Grant*, 103.
111. Chernow, *Grant*, 133.
112. Chernow, 134.
113. Lewis, *Captain Sam Grant*, 421–22.
114. *Memoirs*, 166. Italics mine.
115. *Memoirs*, 167–69, 168n.
116. *PUSG*, 2:41.
117. *Memoirs*, 169, 169n.
118. Garland, *Ulysses S. Grant*, 168–69.

4. 1861–1863: Last Lessons

1. *PUSG*, 2:37.
2. *PUSG*, 2:43, xxx, 45.
3. *PUSG*, 2:43n–44n.
4. *PUSG*, 2:44n; Garland, *Ulysses S. Grant*, 165.
5. Lewis, *Captain Sam Grant*, 427–28.
6. *PUSG*, 2:45–46.
7. Lewis, *Captain Sam Grant*, 428.
8. *PUSG*, 2:46.
9. *PUSG*, 2:47.
10. *PUSG*, 2:46n–47n. The letter writer's spelling has been corrected.
11. *Memoirs*, 171–73.
12. Garland, *Ulysses S. Grant*, 172.
13. Garland, 172.
14. Clausewitz, 154.
15. Peter Paret in his essay "The Genesis of On War," in Clausewitz, 5.
16. *PUSG*, 2:13–14.

17. *Memoirs*, 45–46.
18. *Memoirs*, 155–56.
19. *Memoirs*, 155.
20. Lewis, *Captain Sam Grant*, 428.
21. Quoted in Chernow, *Grant*, 353.
22. For example, *PUSG*, 1:352.
23. *PUSG*, 2:7.
24. *PUSG*, 2:xxx.
25. *PUSG*, 2:45–46. Italics mine.
26. *PUSG*, 2:51n.
27. *PUSG*, 2:56n–57n.
28. Smith, *Grant*, 92.
29. Smith, 96, 97.
30. *PUSG*, 2:50.
31. *PUSG*, 2:60.
32. *PUSG*, 2:62.
33. *PUSG*, 2:67.
34. *PUSG*, 2:57n.
35. *PUSG*, 2:61, 61n.
36. *PUSG*, 2:66.
37. *Memoirs*, 174.
38. *PUSG*, 2:67.
39. *Memoirs*, 175.
40. *Memoirs*, 179n.
41. Lewis, *Captain Sam Grant*, 417.
42. *PUSG*, 2:86n.
43. *PUSG*, 2:94, 95n.
44. *PUSG*, 2:124n.
45. Chernow, *Grant*, 147.
46. Clausewitz, 446.
47. *PUSG*, 2:152n.
48. *Memoirs*, 150; Smith, *Grant*, 94–95.
49. Chernow, *Grant*, 145.
50. *PUSG*, 2:189.
51. *PUSG*, 2:190, 191n.
52. *PUSG*, 2:193.
53. *PUSG*, 2:191n.
54. *Memoirs*, 187.
55. *PUSG*, 2:196–97.

56. *PUSG*, 2:194–95.
57. *PUSG*, 2:197n.
58. *PUSG*, 2:195.
59. *PUSG*, 2:189n.
60. Smith, *Grant*, 122n.
61. *PUSG*, 1:343.
62. *Memoirs*, 150.
63. Quoted in Weigley, *American Way of War*, 133.
64. Quoted in Chernow, *Grant*, 155.
65. Weigley, *American Way of War*, 132.
66. *Memoirs*, 206n.
67. Clausewitz, 192. Italics mine.
68. *PUSG*, 2:225.
69. *PUSG*, 2:242.
70. *PUSG*, 2:301n.
71. Smith, *Grant*, 122–23, 123n.
72. *PUSG*, 2:300.
73. *PUSG*, 3:143–44.
74. *PUSG*, 3:108–9. Italics mine.
75. *PUSG*, 3:114–15.
76. *Memoirs*, 191.
77. Hurst, *Men of Fire*, 44.
78. *Memoirs*, 193.
79. *Memoirs*, 193.
80. *Memoirs*, 194.
81. Smith, *Grant*, 129–30.
82. Chernow, *Grant*, 158–60.
83. *Memoirs*, 196–97.
84. *PUSG*, 3:128. Italics mine.
85. *Memoirs*, 197.
86. Smith, *Grant*, 132.
87. Smith, 131.
88. Smith, 647n.
89. Clausewitz, 190.
90. Marszalek, *Commander*, 8.
91. Marszalek, 67–84.
92. Tucker, *Andrew Foote*, 122.
93. Tucker, 134.
94. *Memoirs*, 201–2.

95. Marszalek, *Commander*, 127.
96. Catton, *Grant Moves South*, 124, citing John W. Emerson, "Grant's Life in the West," *Midland Monthly*, May 1898.
97. *War of the Rebellion* (hereafter referred to as *O.R.*), series 1, vol. 7, 120, 121.
98. *O.R.* (1), 7, 121.
99. *PUSG* 3:278, 317n., 370.
100. Hurst, *Men of Fire*, 89–96, 158–59.
101. Cooling, *Forts Henry and Donelson*, 89–91.
102. Smith, *Grant*, 141, citing John W. Emerson, "Grant's Life in the West," *Midland Monthly*, June 1898.
103. *PUSG*, 4:79.
104. Quoted in Cooling, *Forts Henry and Donelson*, 100.
105. Johnson and Buel, *Battles and Leaders of the Civil War*, 1:371.
106. *O.R.* (1), 7, 131.
107. *PUSG*, 4:157.
108. Smith, *Grant*, 164, citing *New York Tribune*, February 18, 1862.
109. *O.R.* (1), 7, 583.
110. *O.R.* (1), 7, 595.
111. Wallace, *Autobiography*, 375–77.
112. *PUSG*, 4:177.
113. *PUSG*, 4:188.
114. Marszalek, *Sherman*, 39, 196.
115. *PUSG*, 4:189n.
116. Richardson, *Personal History of Ulysses S. Grant*, 217.
117. Wallace, *Autobiography*, 378.
118. *Memoirs*, 206n.
119. *O.R.* (1), 7, 609.
120. Kiner, *One Year's Soldiering*, 28.
121. *O.R.* (1), 7, 206, 209.
122. *O.R.* (1), 7, 398.
123. *PUSG*, 4:211.
124. *Memoirs*, 212.
125. *Memoirs*, 212.
126. *Memoirs*, 213.
127. *Memoirs*, 213.
128. *O.R.* (1), 7, 161.
129. *PUSG* 4:215n.
130. Quoted in Brinton, *Personal Memoirs*, 131.
131. *PUSG*, 4:222n.

132. *PUSG*, 7:275n.
133. Smith, *Grant*, 164, citing *New York Tribune*, February 18, 1862.
134. *O.R.* (1), 7, 628. Italics mine.
135. *O.R.* (1), 7, 632.
136. Marszalek, *Commander*, 121.
137. *PUSG*, 4:287.
138. *O.R.* (1), 7, 680.
139. *PUSG*, 4:320.
140. *PUSG*, 4:319.
141. *PUSG*, 4:331. Italics mine.
142. *O.R.* (1), 7, 683. Italics mine.
143. *O.R.* (1), 7, 684.
144. *O.R.* (1), 10, pt. 2, 32.
145. *PUSG*, 4:343.
146. Smith, *Grant*, 177.
147. Smith, 180–81.
148. *O.R.* (1), 10, pt. 1, 185; Daniel, *Shiloh*, 175.
149. Daniel, *Shiloh*, 175–76.
150. Daniel, 175–76.
151. Cunningham, *Shiloh and the Western Campaign*, 318, 318n, 319.
152. Cunningham, 201, quoting Sherman interview with the *Washington Post*, which in turn was quoted in *Army and Navy Journal*, December 30, 1893.
153. Smith, *Grant*, 200, quoting *Personal Memoirs of Gen. W. T. Sherman* (New York: D. Appleton, 1875), 1:266.
154. Quoted in Catton, *Grant Moves South*, 241.
155. Smith, *Grant*, 201, quoting Stacey D. Allen, "Shiloh! The Campaign and First Day's Battle," *Blue and Gray* 14 (1997).
156. *O.R.* (1), 10, pt. 1, 384. Italics mine.
157. Wyeth, *That Devil Forrest*, 77.
158. Daniel, *Shiloh*, 262.
159. Quoted in Smith, *Grant*, 200n.
160. Johnson and Buel, *Battles and Leaders of the Civil War*, 1:493n.
161. Johnson and Buel, 1:492.
162. Johnson and Buel, 1:494.
163. Johnson and Buel, 1:493.
164. *Memoirs*, 236.
165. *Memoirs*, 236.
166. *Memoirs*, 244.

167. Smith, *Grant*, 171, citing a December 10, 1862, letter from Buell to McClellan in the Buell Papers in the Huntington Library, San Marino, California.
168. *Memoirs*, 242.
169. Cunningham, *Shiloh and the Western Campaign*, 383.
170. *O.R.* (1), 10, pt. 1, 113–14.
171. Smith, *Grant*, 205, quoting Alexander K. McClure, *Abraham Lincoln and Men of War Times* (Philadelphia: Times Publishing, 1892).
172. *Memoirs*, 230.
173. *Memoirs*, 230.
174. *Memoirs*, 244.
175. *PUSG*, 5:48–49n.
176. Smith, *Grant*, 207.
177. *O.R.* (1), 10, pt. 2, 106.
178. Smith, *Grant*, 208.
179. Quoted in Marszalek, *Commander*, 122.
180. Warner, *Generals in Blue*, 231.
181. Daniel, *Shiloh*, 306.
182. *O.R.* (1), 10, pt. 2, 182–83.
183. *Memoirs*, 254.
184. *Memoirs*, 258.
185. *Memoirs*, 259.
186. Quoted in Nevins, *War for the Union*, 2:112.
187. Smith, *Grant*, 212, citing Sherman's *Personal Memoirs*, 1:275–76.
188. Chernow, *Grant*, 215.
189. Quoted in Smith, *Grant*, 212.
190. Smith, 212.
191. Chernow, *Grant*, 216, citing Major Thomas J. Newsham, "The Turning Point of the War," *New York Times*, September 1, 1889.
192. *PUSG*, 4:306.
193. *O.R.* (1), 11, 234.
194. Smith, *Grant*, 214, citing *O.R.* (1), 17, pt. 2, 30, with italics in original document.
195. *PUSG*, 5:218, 264.
196. *PUSG*, 5:226n.
197. *PUSG*, 5:226n.
198. Chernow, *Grant*, 223.
199. Weigley, *American Way of War*, 148–50.

200. Weigley, 147.
201. McPherson, *Tried by War,* 119, quoting Michael Burlingame and John R. Ettinger, eds., *Inside Lincoln's White House: The Complete Civil War Diary of John Hay* (Carbondale: Southern Illinois University Press, 1997), 191–92, entry of April 28, 1864.
202. Kiper, *Major General John Alexander McClernand,* 29–30.
203. *O.R.* (1), 24, pt. 1, 103.
204. *PUSG,* 7:307–308n.

Conclusion

1. Smith, *Eisenhower in War and Peace,* 394n.
2. Clausewitz, 190–93.
3. Weigley, *American Way of War,* 139.
4. Smith, *Grant,* 15, quoting T. Harry Williams, *McClellan, Sherman, and Grant* (New Brunswick, N.J.: Rutgers University Press, 1962), 105.
5. *Memoirs,* 93. Italics mine.

BIBLIOGRAPHY

✯✯✯✯

Bauer, K. Jack. *The Mexican War 1846–1848*. Reprint, Lincoln, Neb.: Bison Books, 1992.

Brands, H. W. *The Man Who Saved the Union*. New York: Doubleday, 2012.

Brinton, John H. *Personal Memoirs*. New York: Neale Publishing, 1914.

Catton, Bruce. *Grant Moves South*. Boston: Little, Brown, 1960.

Chernow, Ron. *Grant*. New York: Penguin Press, 2017.

Clausewitz, Carl von. *On War*. Translated by Michael Howard and Peter Paret. Indexed ed. Princeton, N.J.: Princeton University Press, 1984.

Cooling, Benjamin Franklin. *Forts Henry and Donelson: The Key to the Confederate Heartland*. Knoxville: University of Tennessee Press, 1987.

Cozzens, Peter. *Shipwreck of Their Hopes: The Battles for Chattanooga*. Urbana: University of Illinois Press, 1994.

Cunningham, O. Edward. *Shiloh and the Western Campaign of 1862*. Edited by Gary B. Joiner and Timothy B. Smith. New York: Savas Beatie, 2007.

Daniel, Larry J. *Shiloh: The Battle That Changed the Civil War*. New York: Simon and Schuster, 1997.

Eisenhower, John S. D. *So Far from God*. Reprint, Norman: University of Oklahoma Press, 2000.

Garland, Hamlin. *Ulysses S. Grant: His Life and Character*. New York: Macmillan, 1920.

Grant, Julia. *The Personal Memoirs of Julia Dent Grant*. Edited by John Y. Simon. Reprint, Carbondale: Southern Illinois University Press, 1975.

Grant, Ulysses S. *The Personal Memoirs of Ulysses S. Grant: The Complete Annotated Edition*. Edited by John F. Marszalek. Cambridge, Mass.: Belknap Press of Harvard University Press, 2017.

Greenberg, Amy S. *A Wicked War*. New York: Alfred A. Knopf, 2012.

Howe, Daniel Walker. *What Hath God Wrought: The Transformation of America, 1815–1848*. New York: Oxford University Press, 2007.

Hurst, Jack. *Men of Fire.* New York: Basic Books, 2007.
Johnson, Robert U., and Clarence C. Buel, eds. *Battles and Leaders of the Civil War.* 4 vols. 1887. Reprint, Secaucus, N.J.: Castle, 1988.
Kiner, F. F. *One Year's Soldiering, Embracing the Battles of Fort Donelson and Shiloh.* Lancaster, Pa.: E. H. Thomas, 1863.
Kiper, Richard L. *Major General John Alexander McClernand: Politician in Uniform.* Kent: Kent State University Press, 1999.
Lewis, Lloyd. *Captain Sam Grant.* Boston: Little Brown, 1950.
Marszalek, John F. *Commander of All Lincoln's Armies: A Life of General Henry W. Halleck.* Cambridge, Mass.: Belknap Press of Harvard University Press, 2004.
———. *Sherman: A Soldier's Passion for Order.* New York: Free Press, 1993.
McCullough, David. *The Path between the Seas: The Creation of the Panama Canal, 1871–1914.* New York: Simon and Schuster, 1977.
McPherson, James M. *Battle Cry of Freedom.* New York: Oxford University Press, 1988.
———. *Tried by War: Lincoln as Commander-in-Chief.* New York: Penguin Press, 2008.
Mosier, Don. *Grant: A Biography.* New York: Palgrave MacMillan, 2006.
Nevins, Allan. *The War for the Union.* 4 vols. New York: Charles Scribner's Sons, 1960.
Perret, Geoffrey. *Ulysses S. Grant: Soldier and President.* New York: Random House, 1987.
Perrin, Noel. Introduction to *Democracy: An American Novel,* by Henry Adams, v–xi. New York: Harmony Books, 1982.
Porter, Horace. *Campaigning with Grant.* 1897. Reprint, Secaucus, N. J.: Blue and Gray Press, 1984.
Richardson, Albert Deane. *A Personal History of Ulysses S. Grant.* Hartford, Conn.: American Publishing, 1868.
Schmelzer, Paul L. "A Strong Mind: A Clausewitzian Biography of U. S. Grant." Ph.D. diss., Texas Christian University, 2010.
Simon, John Y., ed. *The Papers of Ulysses S. Grant.* 30 vols. Carbondale: Southern Illinois University Press, 1967–2009.
Smith, Jean Edward. *Eisenhower in War and Peace.* New York: Random House, 2012.
———. *Grant.* New York: Simon and Schuster, 2001.
Tucker, Spencer C. *Andrew Foote: Civil War Admiral on Western Waters.* Annapolis, Md.: Naval Institute Press, 2000.
Wallace, Lew. *An Autobiography.* New York: Harper and Bros., 1906.

Warner, Ezra J. *Generals in Blue.* Baton Rouge: Louisiana State University Press, 1964.

War of the Rebellion: A Compilation of the Official Records of the Union and Confederate Armies. Edited by Robert N. Scott. 127 vols. Washington, D.C.: Government Printing Office, 1880–99.

Weigley, Russell F. *The American Way of War: A History of United States Military Strategy and Policy.* New York: Macmillan, 1973.

Wilson, Edmund. *Patriotic Gore: Studies in the Literature of the Civil War.* New York: W. W. Norton Paperback, 1994.

Wyeth, John Allan. *That Devil Forrest: Life of Lieutenant-General Nathan Bedford Forrest.* Reprint, Dayton: Morningside Bookshop, 1975.

INDEX

✵✵✵✵

JACK HURST is a historian and former journalist who has written for newspapers including the *Chicago Tribune*, the *Philadelphia Inquirer*, and the *Nashville Tennessean*. His books include *Nathan Bedford Forrest: A Biography*; *Men of Fire: Grant, Forrest, and the Campaign That Decided the Civil War*; and *Born to Battle: Grant and Forrest—Shiloh, Vicksburg, and Chattanooga*. He is the creator of the blog *Civil War & Civil Rights*.

THE WORLD OF ULYSSES S. GRANT

Edited by John F. Marszalek & Timothy B. Smith

After the assassination of Abraham Lincoln, Ulysses S. Grant became the most popular American alive. He symbolized the Federal victory, the destruction of slavery, and the preservation of the Union. Grant remained a popular topic among historians who have written about those years, but over time scholars and the public removed Grant from his place in the pantheon of leading Americans. As the decades passed and attitudes toward the Civil War and war itself changed, the public's perception of Grant devolved: no longer a national idol, Grant was instead written off as a heartless general and corrupt president. In the early twenty-first century, however, Grant's place in history is being reinterpreted. Now he is increasingly seen as a success on the battlefield, a leading proponent of African American civil rights, and the first of the modern American presidents.

To further an understanding of Ulysses S. Grant through a close analysis of his life and work, this innovative book series provides a thorough examination of particular events and periods of Grant's life in order to present important insights into his generalship, presidency, influence, and reputation. Books in the series explore Grant's character as well as his role in American history. By delving into the deeper detail and context of what Grant did and saw, this series aims to break new ground and provide the historical profession and the general reading public with accurate, readable perspectives showing Grant's significant contributions to the world he lived in and to the years that followed.